TV GUIDE

book of lists

By the editors of *TV GUIDE* Magazine

RUNNING PRESS
PHILADELPHIA · LONDON

Library of Congress Control Number: 2007928093

ISBN-13: 978-0-7624-3007-9
ISBN-10: 0-7624-3007-9

Cover and interior design by Jason Kayser
Edited by Jennifer Kasius
TV GUIDE Editing by Sue Tuttle with Karina Reeves
Typography: ITC Officina Serif and Trade Gothic

This book may be ordered by mail from the publisher.
Please include $2.50 for postage and handling.
But try your bookstore first!

Running Press Book Publishers
2300 Chestnut Street
Philadelphia, PA 19103-4371

Visit us on the web!
www.runningpress.com

TV GUIDE Acknowledgements:
Erin Daly • Christopher Franklin • Beth Gehman • Tim Holland
Jennifer Meininger • Tom LeSage • Sonya Oliver • Stephanie Rowcotsky
Ray Stackhouse • Todd Thatcher • Todd Wakai • Paul Wolfe

How do I love TV?

Let me count the ways.

Better yet, let's make it a group effort.

When Karina Reeves and Sue Tuttle, the spitfire geniuses behind this handy little tome you're holding, honored me with the chance to write the forward, the first thing I thought was, "Ooh, I'll make a list of why TV is better than chocolate or sex or shopping. It'll be a hoot." Then it dawned on me that a) the idea was so embarrassingly obvious, it deserved its own list of reasons *not* to do it, and b) there wasn't enough room to run down everything that makes television such a cause for celebration.

Think about it. Every couch potato, news junkie, reality-show freak, soap addict, sports devotee, TiVo codependent and closet *Baywatch* fan could spend a day or 50 ranking their favorite things about their favorite shows. Hell, listing each of the *Law & Orders* could eat up a few hours. Here at TV GUIDE, we have more than 50 years of lists under our belt and, based on the mountains of alternately hostile and hilarious letters sent in by readers, our varied efforts have bounced between spot-on, dead wrong and not even close to being complete. Whether it's been our take on TV's sexiest guys, Lucille Ball's 50 funniest bits or the Top 10 moments from *The O.C.*, fans across the planet have willingly— and vocally—weighed in on what we got right and what we missed completely. When it comes to television, like us, you guys have a fierce passion, loyalty and expertise.

And that is the #1 reason to love TV: it has the power to unite, regardless of race, creed, religion, sexual preference, socio-economic station and all that other stuff that tries so hard to separate us. You love *Ugly*

Betty? Me too! Who cares what God you pray to! Did *90210*'s Brenda Years change your life? Let's hug it out, even though we differ on, say, stem-cell research or the relative success of Rory Gilmore's bangs. TV is a shared connection in a world filled with myriad disconnects.

It's also a medium that demands the keeping of lists. Having been around far longer than most people who are actually on TV these days, that electronic candy dispenser in the living room has fed us more information and images since Philo T. Farnsworth did his thing back in 1927 than you can shake a universal remote at. Lists may be our best hope of keeping the truly important things in this world straight.

I mean, sure it's easy to remember *South Park*'s seasonal bowel-movement Mr. Hankey and *Seinfeld*'s Festivus, but how do *The Honeymooners* rate when it comes to our most beloved holiday episodes? How many TV brats can you name who aren't Bart Simpson, Danny Partridge or *Little House on the Prairie*'s Nellie Oleson? And let's not even deal with who tops the seemingly endless roster of great moms and dads. (Personally, that would be Helen and Gene Holbrook, who gifted their sons with a respect for all things small-screen through childhoods punctuated by *The Young and the Restless, M*A*S*H, Charlie's Angels, Saturday Night Live* and *The Rockford Files*.)

So as you page through this book, remember that these lists are meant not just to entertain but also to inspire those memories so many of us share. We've updated some of our previously published collections to accompany an impressive array of originals. It is our sincere hope that you'll find among them many of *your* reasons for loving TV as much as we do.

Happy reading,
Damian Holbrook
Senior Writer
TV GUIDE Magazine

ALGORITHMS

CTU's been assaulted by various algorithms, including the Bainbridge and the Blowfish algorithms, which wreaked havoc on their computers. So what's an algorithm? "I have no idea what an algorithm is," says coexec producer Stephen Kronish. "It sounds kind of neat, though."

BANK GOTHIC

The font used for the intro to each episode: "The following takes place between..."

CUBS

Carlos Bernard, who played Tony Almeida, loves the Chicago Cubs. Each season, he was shown with a Cubs mug.

DILLON, KEVIN

The *Entourage* star played the paranoid hermit who held Kim Bauer hostage in Season 2.

EBOLA

One of many viruses considered for Season 3's threat. All were dismissed because their symptoms weren't quick enough. Instead, they invented the hemorrhage-inducing Cordilla virus.

FREDALBA

The rap-rock band fronted by Eric Balfour, who plays CTU curmudgeon Milo Pressman.

GO-BETWEENS, THE

The pop group that inspired the name McLennan/Forster, Season 4's corrupt corporation. It turns out that one of the show's executive producers is a big fan of the band's two founders, Grant McLennan and Robert Forster.

HENDERSON, CHRISTOPHER

The Season 5 bad guy played by Peter Weller, best known for his role as RoboCop.

I "I'LL EXPLAIN AS SOON AS I GET THERE"

Jack Bauer says this—or a variation of it ("I'll explain as soon as I can") constantly.

J JIN

Daniel Dae Kim, best known as the Korean-speaking Jin on *Lost*, played one of Jack's very-English-speaking right-hand men, Tom Baker, in Seasons 2 and 3.

KING, STEPHEN

The best-selling author is a fan of the show, especially of Mary Lynn Rasjkub's character, Chloe O'Brian. "The more Chloe pouts, the better," King once said.

LA FEMME NIKITA

The four-year USA Network series was a trial run for many of the *24* crew. Creators Joel Surnow and Robert Cochran were behind the similarly edge-of-your-seat thrills of *Nikita*. Both shows feature the music of composer Sean Callery.

McCAIN, JOHN

The senator had a blink-and-you'll-miss-it cameo in Season 5's seventh episode. Look closely at the top left corner of the screen as the clock counts "1:32:22" and you'll see McCain hand Audrey Raines a file at CTU headquarters.

"NICK OF TIME"

A 1995 movie in which Johnny Depp must kill a governor or risk losing his kidnapped daughter. Like *24*, the movie takes place in real time.

OTSUKA PHARMACEUTICAL

This Japanese company hired Kiefer Sutherland for a series of surreal ads plugging snack bar Calorie Mate. Check it out at ifilm.com.

PRODUCT PLACEMENT

You think it's happenstance that Jack drove a Toyota and uses a Treo cell phone? As far as computers go, CTU doesn't play favorites: Dell and Apple products appear on the show.

QUALITY

Viewers aren't the only ones who love the show: as of early 2007, *24* has won 16 Emmys (including Outstanding Drama Series) and two Golden Globes.

REINCARNATION

No, not Jack. We're talking about production designer Joseph Hodges' skill at reincarnating old sets. In Season 4, the house that the Araz family lived in became the presidential bunker.

SENTOX NERVE GAS

The fictional biological agent that killed Edgar Stiles (Louis Lombardi) and Lynn McGill (Sean Astin) in Season 5. Symptoms include foaming at the mouth, paralysis and, needless to say, death.

TELEPHONES

Fans have re-created the CTU rings as a downloadable cell-phone ring.

UNDER EIGHT MINUTES

The amount of time in a typical episode that's without music, according to composer Callery.

VETO POWER

One of several books in the *24 Declassified* series, which chronicles Jack's off-show exploits. *Veto Power* has Jack infiltrating a militia.

WEB SITE

When fans rushed to a Web site (sylvaniaimports.com) mentioned during a Season 3 episode, they found this message: "A Big Thank-you from the crew of *24*. Thanks for watching, we love making it for you, and yes, we did get picked up for Season 4."

XANDER BERKELEY

His Seasons 1 and 2 character, CTU director George Mason, sacrificed himself to die in a nuclear bomb blast while Jack parachuted to safety.

YELENA

When Nina Meyers (Sarah Clarke), *24*'s ultimate villain, calls her terrorist bosses at the end of Season 1, she identifies herself as Yelena.

ZIGLER, TRACY

The former script supervisor is one of many *24* staffers who've had their names mentioned on the show. Zigler was name-checked during Season 1 by a David Palmer staffer. More recently, the shipping port suspected of housing Season 5's nerve gas was raided by an agent named Atkins, a nod to the show's former assistant editor, Nate Atkins.

AUTHORIZED PERSONNEL ONLY (APO)
The code name for the CIA's top-secret black-ops team, formerly headed by Arvin Sloane and then Jack Bristow.

BLUEBIRD
Sydney's field name during her SD-6 years; it later changed to Phoenix.

CHOSEN ONE
Milo Rambaldi (see M) predicted the coming of a woman with great powers, and all the signs—including a sketch in his manuscript—point to Syd.

DYSFUNCTIONAL FAMILY
Aka the Bristow clan. Syd's spy daddy Jack is emotionally distant and manipulative, while spy mom Irina Derevko was a traitor who staged her own death—and announced she was alive by shooting her daughter in the shoulder. And you thought *your* family reunions were a nightmare.

ERIC WEISS
Syd's good friend and fellow agent (and her half sister's beau) who left APO for Washington after receiving a promotion.

FORTY-SEVEN
Way before *Lost*, *Alias* had a thing for numbers—or at least this one, which has popped up repeatedly throughout the drama's five-year run. (It's the page number of Rambaldi's manuscript that features Syd's picture, and the number on the classified document Sydney discovered authorizing Irina's execution at Jack's hands.)

GRAD SCHOOL STUDENT
Sydney's real-world alias when she wasn't working for SD-6 and the CIA. During Season 2, she graduated with a Master's in English lit.

HECHT, DANNY
Syd's first fiancé was killed by SD-6 way back in the first episode after she told him that she was a spy. She's blamed herself (and Sloane) for his death ever since.

"IN DREAMS..."
Title of the fourth-season episode that star Jennifer Garner directed. It focused on wearing down an evil "Sloane Clone" played by Tony winner Joel Grey and marked the reappearance of Amy Irving as Sloane's deceased wife, Emily.

JULIAN SARK
A pretty-boy villain whose ever-shifting allegiances made him a thorn in the CIA's side for years.

KELLY PEYTON
Prophet Five operative and Rachel's personal nemesis. We bet that she could also give Syd a run for her money in the martial-arts department.

LANGUAGES
Syd speaks 13, including French, Taiwanese, Russian and German.

MILO RAMBALDI
A 15th-century genius with a gift for prophesying the future and hiding important secrets (like a formula for zero-point energy) in works of art. His primary area of interest was immortality, a subject of particular interest to Sloane.

NADIA SANTOS
Syd's half sister, Nadia, was transformed into a mindless killing machine then spent much of the next season in a coma.

OUTRIGGER
Field name for Marcus Dixon, Syd's most trusted ally in the spy game.

PROPHET FIVE
A top-secret project that gathered some of the finest minds in mathematics and linguistics to crack a code contained in a 500-year-old document about advanced genetics. Once the code was broken, each member of the group was successively picked off, except for those wise enough to change their identity, like Vaughn's father.

QUENTIN TARANTINO
The "Pulp Fiction" director and *Alias* junkie has appeared on the show as former SD-6 agent-turned-international criminal McKenas Cole.

Alias
Jenna Fischer (*The Office*) auditioned for the role of Sydney Bristow but was never called back.

RENÉE RIENNE

A notorious criminal who was helping Vaughn learn the truth about his past, and worked with Sydney to uncover the truth about Prophet Five and what happened to her father.

SD-6

One of the 12 criminal cells established and controlled by the Alliance. SD stands for Section Disparu, aka "the section that does not exist." Syd, Dixon and Marshall were all recruited to join the group's ranks believing it to be part of the CIA.

TOM GRACE

Tom was personally recruited by Jack Bristow to take Vaughn's place on the team. Naturally, he didn't hit it off with Syd at first, but he repeatedly proved himself a good person to have on one's side in the field.

UZBEKISTAN

One of the dozens of countries that Syd's adventures have taken her to. She's also visited Algeria, India, Switzerland and England.

VAUGHN, MICHAEL

Before he "died," Syd's second fiancé and the father of her child revealed his real name wasn't Michael Vaughn, but Andre Michaux.

WILL TIPPIN

Syd's best guy friend is one of the few people who learned her secret and didn't die. He was buried deep in the Witness Protection Program for a time.

XENON

A decryption program that is illegal for CIA agents to download. Syd was once asked to poke around Vaughn's computer in search of the program when the agency suspected him of collaborating with the enemy.

"YOU ALL EVERYBODY"

Apparently Syd is a big fan of Charlie's band Drive Shaft on *Lost*. She was spinning their hit single during one episode. Maybe they should send her to find those castaways?

ZAMBONI

Syd's second favorite part of going to a hockey game was watching this ice-cleaning vehicle doing its thing. Coming home with Vaughn, she said, was No. 1. All together now: Awww.

A ABATTOIR

Aka slaughterhouse, meat-packing plant...and the place where a gutsy young Nebraskan named Mary Margaret Helgenberger worked to earn some extra cash.

B "BLOOD DROPS"

Seven episodes into the series' premiere season came this, *CSI*'s first masterpiece. The harrowing story of a suburban family massacre was based on a real-life case culled from the files of Los Angeles County criminalist Elizabeth Devine (who went on to become the show's technical adviser and, later, a co-executive producer of *CSI: Miami*).

C CAST-OFF

This bloody bit of nomenclature refers to the crimson spray emitted from the motion of a weapon, as with a blunt object. It's a form of blood spatter, which is *all* the red stuff that splashes off the victim's body.

D DOUBLE-UPS

Ever find yourself puzzled (or elated) when a particular *CSI* episode features, say, only Grissom (William Petersen) and Nick (George Eads), and is followed the next week by one about only Sara (Jorja Fox) and Catherine (Helgenberger)? Such character divisions occasionally happen because of a production double-up—when the show's scheduling demands require the series to shoot two episodes simultaneously.

E ECKLIE, CONRAD

A former CSI Level 3, current assistant director of the Las Vegas crime lab and a perpetual thorn in Grissom's side. As played by Marc Vann, Ecklie is the anti-Grissom: motivated by politics, ego and spite. As Grissom—the embodiment of pure scientific passion—once remarked of his colleague's ambitions: "That's what's so sad, Conrad. You think of this as a career."

F FURRIES

The fetishist conventioneers profiled in Season 4's hilarious episode "Fur and Loathing." Their particular brand of zoomorphism entails donning full-body suits resembling various mammals. They refer to their playful grooming of one another as scritching, while an appropriately adorable partyer might be fortunate enough to get him- or herself yiffed (don't ask).

G GC-MS

Gas chromatograph-mass spectrometer, i.e., the amazing contraption used by lab guy Hodges (Wallace Langham) to determine the chemical makeup of an evidence sample.

The gas chromatograph separates a sample into its component parts, then the mass spectrometer bombards them with electrons, producing a distinctive mass spectrum that precisely identifies a chemical. Got that? Good.

HEATHER, LADY

The dominatrix-for-hire and could-be Grissom lover who figured prominently in several *CSI* episodes (including "Slaves of Las Vegas" and "Lady Heather's Box"). Lady Heather was played by Melinda Clarke, who also doled out punishment as a money-hungry Julie Cooper on *The O.C.*

INSECTS

The passionate hobby of entomologist Grissom, and the unsung heroes of *CSI*. If it's creepy and crawly, the show has featured it: beetles, moths, chiggers, flies, maggots and, in Nick's terrifying trial-by-entombment from Season 5 ("Grave Danger"), fire ants.

JIM BRASS

Or maybe the *J* should be for *Job*, 'cause it seems like life's got it in for the good captain (Paul Guilfoyle). As if his estrangement from his down-and-out hoochie of a daughter weren't enough ("Hollywood Brass"), he was also responsible for the accidental shooting death of an LVPD officer ("A Bullet Runs Through It").

"KEYS TO HER PAST"

In an uncanny foreshadowing, this little-seen 1994 TV-movie features Helgenberger as a pathologist named Maureen "Kick" Kickasola. Her costar? Gary Dourdan, as a neighbor who helps her solve crimes.

LEE, DR. HENRY C.

Legendary forensic scientist who established the theory of four-way linkage, which maintains that the goal of forensic analysis is to find connections among the physical evidence, victim, suspect and crime scene.

"MURDER CENTRAL"

A hotel room or apartment located at the end of a hallway, with no room facing it (ergo, probably no witness) and an adjacent exit door.

NBC, ABC AND FOX

The networks that passed on the *CSI* pilot when creator Anthony E. Zuiker and executive producer Jerry Bruckheimer came knocking. That's the evidence—now, book 'em on three counts of extreme stupidity.

OTOSCLEROSIS

The hearing malady (in which an abnormal bone growth interferes with proper functioning of the ear) that afflicted Grissom through Seasons 2 and 3, only to be summarily nipped in the bud by an outpatient procedure...and never spoken of again. Say what?

PRADER-WILLI SYNDROME

A rare genetic disorder that causes manic, insatiable hunger and, in the case of one Jerry Gable, death by $1.99 casino buffet—as depicted in the dark-humored Thanksgiving episode "Dog Eat Dog."

QUENTIN TARANTINO

CSI fan and maverick director of "Pulp Fiction" and the "Kill Bill" films who took the helm on Season 5's emotionally riveting finale, in which Nick got buried alive by an irate dad with an explosive temper. Did we mention the fire ants?

RAMPART

One of the fictional casinos—along with the Tangiers and the Monaco—where the sinning of *CSI*'s Sin City often takes place.

STAHL, JERRY

The ace screenwriter behind nearly all of *CSI*'s most out-there plotlines. From transgenderism to cannibalism to mutilation, if you're looking for a walk on the wild side, he's your man. His own dissolute days were the inspiration for the 1998 biopic "Permanent Midnight," starring Ben Stiller. Fun fact: Stahl found his way to *CSI* after a chance meeting with Petersen in the Hollywood YMCA's sauna.

22 CALIBER

The hit man's ammo of choice, according to *CSI* medical examiner Dr. Albert Robbins (Robert David Hall). The bullet's low weight allows slugs to ricochet around inside the skull, thereby inflicting maximum tissue damage.

UNAVAILABLE

That would be the newly married Warrick (Dourdan). When Catherine was unable to hide her shock and dismay at the revelation, she finally admitted what fans have long suspected: She's been carrying a torch all this time.

CSI

All of *CSI*'s lab equipment is authentic, according to coproducer and technical consultant Elizabeth Devine, who often tests prototypes sent by manufacturers.

VICAP

When Google won't do the trick, there's the Violent Criminal Apprehension Program's database, created by the FBI and used to investigate homicides and missing-persons cases in which foul play is suspected.

WLVU

A young mind is a terrible thing to waste, yet *CSI*'s Western Las Vegas University seems to specialize in turning out six-feet-undergrads. So far, one suffered a fatal fall into a trash chute ("Chaos Theory"), and the "blue railing" serial killer and his copycat have offed three women in "The Execution of Catherine Willows" and another trio of students in "What's Eating Gilbert Grissom?" One guy even got himself involved, fatally, with a doomsday cult ("Shooting Stars").

X-FILES, THE

How was the groundbreaking paranormal series *CSI*'s most kindred stylistic spirit? It was a science-oriented procedural drama with high production values, a mordant sense of humor and a painfully repressed romance (Mulder and Scully, meet Grissom and Sara). Also remarkable is the number of actors who've guest-starred on both. To wit: Nicholas Lea, Doug Hutchinson, Nick Chinlund, Xander Berkeley, Krista Allen, Jeremy Roberts, Timothy Carhart and Michael Silver, to name a few.

Y INCISION

For a coroner, this first cut is the deepest, longest and most telling. Beginning at the shoulders, it converges at the center of the rib cage and heads down south, exposing the deceased's lungs, heart and sweetbreads.

ZAMBONI

The gliding, boxlike machines that clean and smooth ice-skating rinks. In Season 2's "Primum Non Nocere," one Zamboni holds a key piece of evidence in the death of a hockey player. Ever the hopeless romantic, Grissom opines in an intimate moment with Sara: "There are three things people love to stare at: a rippling stream, a sunset and a Zamboni going around and around." Sigh...

Desperate Housewives A to Z

ANAGRAM FUN
Desperate Housewives' shady detective Mr. Shaw is played by Richard Roundtree, best know as the legendary '70s crimefighter Shaft. Susan locates Shaw in the yellow pages under the "Hafts" Detective Agency.

BODY COUNT
In Season 1 we learned of the deaths of seven people: Mary Alice, Deidre, Mama Solis, Mrs. McCluskey's son, Bree's mother, Martha Huber and Rex Van de Kamp.

COSTELLO, ELVIS
Mike's favorite band...or, as he puts it, "guy with a band." Perhaps not coincidental: *DH* creator Marc Cherry has a poster of the four-eyed pop barb in the writer's room. Girls talk, indeed.

DEAD WOMEN TALKING
In the original, unaired pilot, Mary Alice was played by Sheryl Lee, aka Laura Palmer, the corpse who set the plot in motion in David Lynch's masterwork *Twin Peaks*. Not spooky enough for ya? Brenda Strong, the current Mary Alice, also played a spouse who died in the first episode of WB's *Everwood*.

EAGLE STATE
The fictional location of *DH*'s Fairview. Its seal and motto ("Confidence, Justice, Union") are shown in the season finale's courtroom scene. Also: Fairview's ZIP code is 29102 (which in real life would put it in South Carolina), while Wisteria Lane is located in the 456 area code (in real life, an "international inbound" modem line).

FYI
As in, "How devastating for you—FYI," Edie's mercilessly catty comeback to Susan when the latter finds her hot date with Mike ixnayed by Kendra's arrival. Nicollette Sheridan ad-libbed that part, BTW.

GOLDEN GIRLS, THE
Maybe G should stand for genius. Both Cherry and Mitchell Hurwitz, creator of *Arrested Development*, are writing-room alums of the NBC sitcom.

HENNESSEY, CAMP
The Van de Kamps send pot-smoking, hit-and-run son Andrew to this center that emphasizes "discipline and responsibility—two things that you're sorely in need of," says Rex. At the camp, Andrew tells his parents he thinks he might be gay.

IMITATION

The sincerest form of flattery, and a sign that you've infiltrated the zeitgeist. Thus, there's MAD magazine's *DH* satire; *Sesame Street*'s spoof "Desperate Houseplants" and the *Charmed* episode "Desperate Housewitches."

JOHN

Fans of Gabrielle's studly gardener can get a closer look at his famed "naked" scene courtesy of the *DH* DVD set. The "Easter egg" can be found on the bonus features menu of Disc 4. Simply click your arrow to gain access to a couple of more revealing takes that didn't pass standards-and-practices muster.

KANSAS

Susan and Paul take the floor at the high-school dance to the strains of the band's 1977 cheese-ball ballad "Dust in the Wind"—thus evoking Martha Huber's ashes, which were tossed in Susan's face in the previous episode.

LLOYD, SAM

Sure, Brenda Strong guest-starred on *Seinfeld* as "braless wonder" Sue Ellen Mischke, Teri Hatcher as Jerry's squeeze with the "spectacular" breasts and Marcia Cross as a life-saving dermatologist, but our favorite appearance was by Lloyd, *DH*'s own Dr. Goldfine, who played the geeky TV GUIDE fan who becomes infatuated with Elaine.

MULTITASKING

It's Lynette's specialty—witness her frantic attempt to land a new job while changing Penny's nappy—and an ongoing challenge as she tries to work and keep an eye on things at home.

NATIONAL INFORMER, THE

Ersatz scandal sheet shown on a coffee table featuring a (highly unlikely) cover story on Mary Alice's death: "Inside the Suburban Suicide Mom!"

$100,000 PYRAMID, THE

The $15,000 he won in the '80s on the game show helped keep Cherry afloat while he tried to break into the screenwriting biz.

PEYTON PLACE

Tom Scavo's parents are named Rodney and Allison, which were the names of characters in the salacious 1956 novel, the grandmommy of suburban soap. And...oh, yeah: Ryan O'Neal (Rodney Scavo) played Rodney in the TV adaptation.

QUESTIONS

What are the odds that Martha Huber would end up living on the same block as Mary Alice, her sister's former colleague in Utah? How could Carlos not have gotten wise to Gabrielle and John sooner? Consider this a warning: Asking too many of these logic-based queries will ruin your *DH* experience. Just go with it!

RIBEYE STEAK
Susan's favorite dish…though probably a little less so after Edie horned in on her dinner with Mike, and his dog, Bongo, munched an earring off her gravy-basted lobe.

SCROTUM
The only thing Bree doesn't like about sex. "I mean, obviously, it has its practical applications," she admits, "but I'm just not a fan."

"THERE WON'T BE TRUMPETS"
The title of the 17th *DH* episode. Like all the others, it's named after a song; like most of them, it's a Stephen Sondheim composition.

UNFAIR BUSINESS PRACTICES
What Carlos is arrested for, seeing as his company imported goods manufactured by slave labor.

VAN EYCK, JAN
The Flemish painter's famed 1434 work "The Arnolfini Portrait" is featured at the beginning of *DH*'s ingenious opening-credits sequence.

WISTERIA
A flowering vine native to the southeastern U.S., China and Japan. Pretty and aromatic, yes, but its sprawling tentacles are often dense, tangled and troublesome. Sound familiar?

XOA581
Trivia alert: Delight—and possibly disturb—your friends when you identify the license plate number of Mrs. Greenberg's hatchback (which Susan borrows to follow Paul Young).

YATES, ANDREA
The deranged Texas woman who made news in 2001 when she drowned all five of her children. It was after his mother admitted relating to Yates' desperation that a stunned Marc Cherry got the idea for the show.

ZEMAN, NED
The journalist's cover story in the May 2005 issue of *Vanity Fair* portrayed a *DH* set rife with egomania, jealousy and backbiting. Cherry has since assured the press that Zeman was way, way off base and that all is copacetic on Wisteria Lane. Uh-huh…

AFTERMATH

This is what producers will call the conclusion of a *Law & Order* opening, aka teaser, showing the detectives' arrival at the crime scene and previously concluded with a world-weary Lennie Briscoe (Jerry Orbach) wisecrack.

BALDWIN, ALEC

The ubiquitous actor took his loathing of the paparazzi public when he cowrote the May 1998 episode "Tabloid," in which a journalist chases a celebrated professor into the path of an oncoming car.

"CHING-CHING"

The term for the series' trademark sound effect, according to *L&O* creator Dick Wolf and its composer, Mike Post (who was aiming, he says, to evoke the sound of a slamming jail door). The Associated Press offers "Bee-Bong." Sounds to us like cha-ching!

DESATURATION

The process, achieved in postproduction, in which color is removed from *L&O*'s raw film, creating a "cooler" look. All the better, Wolf believes, to give the show a subtle, documentary-like feel.

EMMY NOMINATIONS

L&O netted an astounding 11 in a row (1992-2002) for Outstanding Drama Series, a record.

FARINA, DENNIS

In 2005, Farina took on the part of Det. Joe Fontana and the unenviable job of replacing 13-year veteran Jerry Orbach (who played Lennie Briscoe) following the character's retirement and the actor's passing.

GUARDIAN AD LITEM

A court-appointed representative for a child or incompetent adult involved in a legal proceeding. A sadly familiar concept in *SVU*'s dark world.

"HUB"

Need to shoot scenes in a preschool, a strip club and a synagogue? All in one day? No problem. The shows' location managers will search out an area of a few city blocks—i.e., the hub—to accommodate that varied slate while minimizing everyone's travel time and production costs.

INTERNET SPYING

Jack McCoy, punk rocker? When ADA Serena Southerlyn hacks into McCoy's online history, she discovers that he uses his grandmother's name as a password, listens to a lot of Beatles and has, she says, "what I can only describe as a very weird obsession with the Clash."

"JORGE, SUNDAY IN THE PARK WITH"

One of the only *L&O* episodes never to be re-aired on NBC. The network made the decision in response to allegations that the story line portrayed the Puerto Rican community negatively.

KUNSTLER, WILLIAM

Sure, the famed civil-rights attorney was a wacky choice for an *L&O* guest star. But not nearly as odd as some of the shows' fish-out-of-water appearances, which include baseball player Keith Hernandez, writer and social critic Fran Lebowitz, and New York mayors Rudolph Giuliani and Michael Bloomberg.

"LIFE CHOICE"

A favorite of Wolf's, this *L&O* episode centers on the bombing of an abortion clinic. The controversial Season 1 hour provoked $800,000 in advertiser pullouts, and wasn't re-aired for 11 years.

MUNCH, JOHN

Richard Belzer's wry conspiracy maven made TV history when he became the first character to appear on six different shows on three different networks! He originated on *Homicide: Life on the Street* before showing up on *L&O*, Fox's *The X-Files*, *SVU*, *Trial by Jury* and UPN's *The Beat*.

NEW YORK LEDGER

All the news that's fit to fake: Not only is the ersatz tabloid the *L&O* franchise's stand-in for the *New York Post*, it was also the newspaper of record in Wolf's 2000 NBC drama *Deadline*.

OZ

Before charming fans as *Criminal Intent*'s Det. Alexandra Eames, Kathryn Erbe was chilling in HBO's brutal prison drama as a death-row seductress convicted of slaying her own daughter. Also doing time were *SVU*'s Christopher Meloni as fatally attractive (and bisexual) inmate Chris Keller and B.D. Wong as the clink's even-tempered chaplain.

PIQUERISM

A fetish diagnosed by *SVU*'s Dr. Huang in which a male perp is compelled to assault his victims with sharp objects. The perp in this case (the standout episode "Pique") was guest star Chad Lowe. His weapon of choice? Hat pins.

QUESTION OF FACT

In a courtroom, a contested fact whose truth is usually decided by a jury. Conversely, only a judge can resolve a "question of law."

REBA, THE MAIL LADY

Once a civil servant, always a civil servant: Way back in the '80s, *L&O*'s Lt. Van Buren (S. Epatha Merkerson) went happily postal as a recurring character on *Pee-wee's Playhouse*.

SUPPRESS, MOTION TO

That telltale clutch of papers with the blue cover sheet wielded by defense attorneys hoping to get evidence excluded. Good thing, too, or viewers would find a lot of *L&O* episodes wrapped up in a half hour.

THOMPSON, FRED

The former Tennessee senator left the Capitol rotunda for the halls of justice when he joined *L&O* as conservative district attorney Arthur Branch.

"UNBLINKING EYE, THE"

This *Criminal Intent* episode might also be called "The Uncredited Cameo," featuring as it does an off-camera, voice-only appearance by Will Hunting himself, Matt Damon.

VOIR DIRE

The pretrial procedure during which the presiding judge and opposing attorneys question prospective jurors in order to determine their suitability to sit on a given case.

"WRONG IS RIGHT"

SVU's second-season opener, and beginning of the series as most fans know it. "Wrong" marked the addition to the cast of Ice-T's "Fin" Tutola and Stephanie March's ADA Alexandra Cabot.

X IS FOR "EXILED"

Sure, the success of the 1998 TV-movie was a boon for Chris Noth fans, but Wolf claims it also convinced him of the possibility of expanding the *L&O* "brand." Come '99, enter *SVU*.

THE YEAR 2010

The point at which *L&O* will surpass *Gunsmoke* as the longest-running television drama ever.

ZIMKILTON, STEVE

The man behind the velvety baritone that opens every *L&O*, *SVU* and *CI* episode with "in the criminal justice system…"

Smallville A to Z

ACTION COMICS NO. 1
The first appearance of Superman, published in June 1938. The Man of Steel was created by writer Jerry Siegel and artist Joe Shuster.

BLY, NELLIE
Pioneering female investigative journalist, popular in the late 19th century and hero of Clark's pal Chloe, former editor of Smallville High's student newspaper, *The Torch*.

CROSBY, BRIDGETTE
Colleague of scientist Virgil Swann (Christopher Reeve, see *V*), played by Margot Kidder. Crosby tells Martha Kent she had a relationship with Swann "in a different lifetime," a nod to the Superman movies, in which Kidder played Lois Lane to Reeve's Superman.

DOOMED DOCTORS
Medical and research professionals haven't fared terribly well on *Smallville*. Drs. Hamilton, Foster, Walden, Garner and Teng were either killed or put into vegetative states.

EINSTEIN
The original name of the Kent family dog, who temporarily had superstrength as a result of a LuthorCorp experiment. Clark wanted to rename him Krypto but they settled on Shelby, after Martha's childhood dog.

"FLAMING CROWS FEET"
The Torch comic strip drawn by Justin Gaines (guest star Adam Brody, before he moved to *The O.C.*).

GUEST STARS
The Who's Who of young guest stars on *Smallville* has included *Desperate Housewives*' Jesse Metcalfe, *The O.C.*'s Adam Brody and *Lost*'s Evangeline Lilly and Ian Somerhalder (see *I*).

HELEN BRYCE
Smallville Medical center doctor who married Lex Luthor at the end of Season 2—with nefarious motives. She unsuccessfully tried to kill Lex—only to have him turn around and send her to her (presumed) death in Season 3.

IAN SOMERHALDER
Before boarding Oceanic Air Flight 815, Somerhalder did a six-episode arc on *Smallville* as Adam Knight, a mysterious newcomer sent by Lionel Luthor to keep tabs on Clark.

There was much Internet speculation that his name was a nod to Batman (Adam West played the Dark Knight on TV in the 1960s). "That was people's imaginations running wild," says executive producer Al Gough. "But we didn't go out of our way to dispel that!"

JUSTICE LEAGUE ALLUSIONS

Two superfriends hinted at a future Justice League of America when they showed up in Smallville. In Season 4, Bart Allen, aka the Flash, suggested that he and Clark find other superpowered types and "start, like, a club or league or something." This season, Aquaman-in-training Arthur Curry proposed he and Clark start a Junior Lifeguard Association, to which Clark responded, "I'm not sure I'm ready for the JLA just yet."

KRYPTONITE

The meteor rocks that crashed into Smallville with Clark's spaceship have varying effects on him. Green kryptonite, the most common, makes him sick and weak. Red lowers his inhibitions, black can separate Clark from Kal-El (his Kryptonian alter-ego), and silver makes him paranoid.

LEX LUTHOR, LANA LANG AND LOIS LANE

What's up with all those *L*s? Legend has it that the initials most prevalent in Superman's world were a tribute to a girlfriend of unrequited love of one of the character's creators. *Smallville* producers put their own spin on it with Chloe Sullivan—the only main character created for the series—who has the double L embedded in her last name.

"MUFFIN-PEDDLING COLLEGE DROPOUT"

Insult Lex hurled at Lois after she was kicked out of Metropolis University, moved to Smallville and got a job at the town coffeehouse, the Talon.

"NO TIGHTS, NO FLIGHTS"

The producers' edict when the series launched: Clark would never fly, nor be seen in the Superman costume. They cheated on the flying part in the fourth-season premiere when he took to the air. But since he was Kal-El at the time, and not technically Clark, Gough says "we found a loophole." He hints that flying may reappear in later seasons.

OSCAR NOMINATION

Annette O'Toole, who plays Clark's mom, Martha Kent, was nominated for an Academy Award in 2004 for cowriting the song "A Kiss at the End of the Rainbow" from the film "A Mighty Wind." O'Toole wrote the song with her husband, Michael McKean, who guest-starred on *Smallville* as tabloid journalist (and future *Daily Planet* editor) Perry White.

PETE ROSS

Clark's best friend in Seasons 1-3. At the end of Season 3, Pete (Sam Jones III) moved to Wichita. "Knowing Clark's secret was a huge burden for him," Gough says. "It ultimately cost them their friendship."

QUIGLEY

The coach of the Smallville High School football team. Clark joined the team in his senior year, vowing not to use his superpowers during games.

RICHARD DONNER
Director of "Superman." "The first Superman movie was hugely influential for us," says Gough, who, with producing partner Miles Millar, worked with Donner on 1998's "Lethal Weapon 4." Donner "was always trying to ground the character," Gough reveals. "He wanted Clark Kent and Superman to feel real, like they could exist in the world."

"SAVE ME"
The *Smallville* theme song, performed by alternative rock band Remy Zero. Gough says it was chosen to give the show a contemporary feel and, of course, because "it's about looking for a hero." Five for Fighting's "Superman (It's Not Easy)" was a contender, "but ultimately we felt it was a little slow for a theme song," Gough says.

TERENCE STAMP
British actor who provides the voice of Jor-El, Clark's biological father. Stamp's connection to Superman mythology runs deep: He played General Zod (see *Z*) in the first two Superman movies.

UNCLE FESTER
Pete's nickname for the bald Lex.

VIRGIL SWANN
Reclusive billionaire who taught Clark about the fate of planet Krypton. Swann was played by the ultimate Superman, the late Christopher Reeve.

WALL OF WEIRD
Chloe's extensive collection of news reports of the freakish mutations caused by the meteor shower.

X-RAY VISION
Clark's ability to see though anything—except lead.

"YOU WILL BE A GOD AMONG MEN"
The ominous inscription inside the spaceship that brought Clark to Earth. The message also said humans "are a flawed race" and instructed Clark to "rule them with strength." Clark has struggled to understand this destiny, and it remains unclear how literally the message was meant to be interpreted.

ZOD
Rebel Kryptonian general and adversary of Jor-El's. In the "Solitude" episode, Brainiac (James Marsters) tricks Clark into nearly setting Zod free from his extradimensional prison.

The Office

A to Z

AMY ADAMS
The Oscar-nominated actress ("Junebug") played Katy, aka the Hot Girl, who dated Jim Halpert (John Krasinski). But he unceremoniously dumped her during the...

BOOZE CRUISE
It became the night that Jim made the ill-advised decision to tell Michael Scott (Steve Carell) about his feelings for Pam (Jenna Fischer). Executive producer Greg Daniels calls the episode "our Scranton version of Jim Cameron's 'Titanic.'"

CRYSTAL CLUB COLA
The soft drink that you see Dunder-Mifflin employees occasionally sip in the employee lunchroom is a real regional soda brand from eastern Pennsylvania.

DIVERSITY DAY
The hilarious episode about sensitivity training was partly inspired by a sexual-harassment seminar the cast and production staff was required to go through once NBC hired them for the show.

EDGAR
Steve Carell has played unctuous and annoying before as Edgar, Ellie's ex-boyfriend on Julia Louis-Dreyfus' short-lived sitcom *Watching Ellie.*

FUNDLE BUNDLE
The clip of this fictional Scranton kiddie TV show with little Michael Scott gave us an early glimpse of his lonely misfit side.

GRASS ROOTS
Remember the 1960s hit "Midnight Confessions" by the Grass Roots? Cast member Creed Bratton played guitar in that band.

HALLOWEEN
Only Michael would wear a Halloween costume with a papier-mâché likeness of himself on his shoulder on the same day he attempted to terminate an employee.

"ISLANDS IN THE STREAM"
One of the most annoying songs of the '80s made a great karaoke moment for Jim and Michael.

JAY FERGUSON

The composer of *The Office* theme, Ferguson was lead singer in the rock bands Spirit and Jo Jo Gunne, and had a solo Top 40 hit in 1977 with "Thunder Island."

KISS

The big cliff-hanger moment in Season 2's finale was when Jim finally planted one on Pam, even though she was engaged to shipping-department lug Roy (David Denman). Think she got back the deposit on the reception hall?

LAMPSHADES

The singing duo that includes Kate Flannery, who plays tipsy customer-service rep Meredith. They play regularly at an improv club in Hollywood.

MEN'S ROOM

Assistant to the regional manager Dwight Schrute (Rainn Wilson) once found his desk in there courtesy of his torturer, Jim.

NANCY WALLS

She plays Carol, Michael's realtor and potential love interest, and is Steve Carell's real-life wife. They met while both were players in the Second City comedy troupe.

OLYMPICS

Not to be outdone by NBC's coverage of the Winter Games in Torino, Dunder-Mifflin's office Olympics offered Flonkerton, the highly specialized sport that uses paper boxes as snowshoes.

PHYLLIS SMITH

She was the show's casting associate until she got the role of Phyllis—based on her reading parts with other auditioning actors.

QUINCY, M.E.

Melora Hardin, who plays Michael's boss, Jan Levinson, appeared on the medical examiner drama twice when she was a teen actress.

REALITY TV

Camera crews that have worked on *Survivor* are often used to give *The Office* its documentary-style look.

SCRANTONICITY

The Police cover band with Kevin (Brian Baumgartner) from accounting on drums. Pam's fiancé, Roy, wanted the group to play at their wedding, but instead they got to perform at Phyllis's nuptials.

TOBY

Paul Lieberstein, the show's coexecutive producer, who has never acted before, plays the morose human-resources guy. NBC execs cast him in the show when they saw his brief appearance in the second episode. He's not the only cast member who works on both sides of the camera—B.J. Novak (Ryan Howard) is a coproducer and Mindy Kaling (Kelly Kapoor) is story editor.

URINE

Dwight provided some to Michael to help him pass a drug test. But his guilt over it forced him to resign as a Lackawanna sheriff's deputy—a tragic loss for the law enforcement community.

VALENTINE'S DAY

Dwight got his own personal bobblehead. Angela (Angela Kinsey) got his key. Michael got a big kiss from Jan. Phyllis got flowers and a giant bear from Bob Vance of Vance Refrigeration. And Pam got a promise from Roy that she would get the best sex of her life. Uh-oh.

WEBISODES

In the summer of 2006, a series of Web-only episodes featured accountants Kevin, Angela and Oscar (Oscar Nunez) and a story about $3,000 in missing Dunder-Mifflin funds.

XMAS PARTY

The most popular gift in the episode was a video iPod, which in real life boosted *The Office*'s popularity. It's been one of the most downloaded shows on Apple's iTunes store.

YOUTUBE

Fans have made their own music videos about Pam and Jim's relationship and posted them on this Web site.

ZBORNAK, KENT

When *The Office* producer worked for *The Golden Girls*, the writers borrowed his last name for Bea Arthur's character, Dorothy.

Great Sportscasters

1 Howard Cosell	**2** Bob Costas	**3** Mel Allen	**4** Jim McKay
5 Curt Gowdy	**6** Al Michaels	**7** Vin Scully	**8** Tim McCarver
9 Pat Summerall	**10** Chris Berman	**11** Brent Musberger	**12** Joe Buck
13 Marv Albert	**14** Jim Nantz	**15** Keith Jackson	**16** John Madden

5 **Biggest** Off-the-Field

Super Bowl Moments

Though watching the season's two best NFL teams meet on the gridiron is ostensibly the reason millions tune in to the Super Bowl every year, sometimes it's what happens outside of the game that really gets people talking...

 During a 2004 halftime performance at Super Bowl XXXVIII, ex-boy bander Justin Timberlake rips off a piece of singer Janet Jackson's costume, exposing one of her breasts and igniting a firestorm of controversy that lasts for years.

 An anxious nation at war in the Persian Gulf gets an emotional boost from Whitney Houston's stirring rendition of the national anthem before Super Bowl XXV in 1991.

 Songbird Diana Ross departs Sun Devil Stadium in a helicopter at the climax of her over-the-top halftime performance at Super Bowl XXX in 1996.

4 The Dallas Cowboys Cheerleaders make their Super Bowl debut in 1971 at Super Bowl V; by 1976, they reach icon status.

5 Super Bowl XIV in 1980 includes a commercial that still resides in the heart. When a tentative young fan in the stadium tunnel offers Pittsburgh Steeler Mean Joe Greene a Coke, the ferocious lineman flips his game jersey to the lad in gratitude. Gulp.

The 10 Greatest Cinderella Teams

The wondrous thing about the fairy tale that is the NCAA men's basketball tournament is that every spring brings another unexpected hero, another team beating an unbeatable foe. Here's a look at our choices for the Top 10 Cinderella teams ever. Once upon a time...

(1) **North Carolina State** (1983):

It's probably the most replayed highlight in tournament history—the 30-foot shot by Dereck Whittenburg that fell agonizingly short of the basket, only to be retrieved and stuffed by forward Lorenzo Charles at the buzzer. The basket gave NC State a 54-52 upset over the Phi Slama Jama superstars of Houston, sending Coach Jim Valvano careening around the court looking for someone to hug. What the highlights don't show is that practically every NC State tournament game that year ended as dramatically. The team beat Pepperdine in double OT and Nevada-Las Vegas on a last-second shot, and made it to the Final Four with a comeback win over Virginia. They weren't called the Cardiac Pack for nothing.

(2) **Villanova** (1985):

With a killer instinct—and Patrick Ewing, the best player in the country—Georgetown had already beaten Villanova twice that year, and the only way Villanova could turn the tide in the tournament was to play a near-perfect game. Which is exactly what the Wildcats did. They made 13 of their first 18 shots and led by a point at the half. They missed only one shot in the second half, limited Ewing to 14 points and held on to win it all, 66-64. "You can't play tentative, you can't play scared," Coach Rollie Massimino told his team before the game. "You can't play not to lose."

(3) **Texas Western** (1966):

Despite the fact that Texas Western was ranked third in the nation with only one loss, no one thought a team of five African-American starters—none of them superstars—could take on all-white powerhouses Kentucky and Duke. But Texas Western (which later became Texas-El Paso) shattered those illusions, winning the championship 72-65 and changing college basketball forever.

(4) **Valparaiso** (1998):

This tiny Indiana school, seeded 13th in its region, was trailing Mississippi 69-67 with 2.5 seconds left in the game. Valpo coach Homer Drew called for a play that began with a full-court baseball pass that went to Bill Jenkins, and, with a touch, to Bryce Drew, the coach's son, who'd missed a three-point attempt just seven seconds before. The ball left Drew's hand with one second showing on the clock and swished through the basket.

5 — Gonzaga (1999):

Now they're a fixture in the Top 25, but in 1999, the Zags were struggling to make a reputation, seeded 10th in their region. Then, led by long-range shooter Matt Santangelo, they defeated Minnesota, seventh-ranked Stanford and Florida, and came within five points of knocking off eventual champion Connecticut. They've been in the tournament every year since.

6 — Loyola Marymount (1990):

Hank Gathers and Bo Kimble were childhood friends from Philadelphia who went to play for Loyola Marymount University in Los Angeles, the highest-scoring team in the country. Tragedy struck when Gathers collapsed on the court during the West Coast Conference tournament and never regained consciousness. Kimble and the rest of the Lions voted to continue their season, mounting a 149-115 victory over defending champion Michigan to set an NCAA tournament record. In honor of Gathers, the right-handed Kimble shot his first free throw of every tournament game with his left hand.

7 — Kansas (1988):

Kansas was one of the top-ranked teams in the country before injuries and suspensions took their toll. The Jayhawks limped into the tournament as a sixth seed, with 11 regular-season losses. But senior star Danny Manning made one of the most impressive individual runs in tournament history, scoring 31 points and grabbing 18 rebounds to lead Kansas past Oklahoma, earning the Jayhawks a new nickname: Danny and the Miracles.

8 — Princeton (1996):

Every year, the undersize, outmanned Tigers would run rings around a highly ranked opponent before losing in the end. Coach Pete Carril's teams always looked a bit slow of foot, but patient beyond belief. Then, in 1996, against defending national champion UCLA, Princeton freshman forward Gabe Lewullis made a layup with 3.9 seconds left. Princeton won, 43-41.

9 — Hampton (2001):

After Hampton, a No. 15 seed, defeated Iowa State in a first-round upset, Coach Steve Merfeld, a pudgy man in a dark suit, was lifted off the floor by forward David Johnson, kicking his feet in the air like a toddler. "All I remember," Merfeld said, "is David saying in my ear, 'I gotcha, Coach, I gotcha.'"

10 — UNC-Charlotte (1977):

UNCC had been playing Division I basketball for only seven seasons when it went to the Final Four, defeating top-ranked Michigan along the way and losing a last-second heartbreaker to Marquette.

Since this list was compiled, the NCAA tournament has continued to offer great stories of small schools pulling off big upsets—Vermont's win over Syracuse and Bucknell's victory over Kansas (both in 2005) are prime examples. But midnight always came early for these basketball Cinderellas—they may win a few, but the Final Four was exclusively the playground for the big teams from the power conferences. Since the tourney expanded to 64 teams in 1985, no school from the so-called "mid-major" conferences had advanced to the Final Four (few ever made it to the Elite Eight). That all changed in 2006...

George Mason (2006):

The Patriots didn't win their conference tournament (and the automatic NCAA bid that goes with it). But their league, the Colonial Athletic Association, was one of the strongest mid-major conferences in the country. When Mason received the CAA's first at-large invite in 20 years, their selection was immediately questioned on-air by CBS announcers Billy Packer and Jim Nantz, who felt more schools from the major conferences should have been included. But powered by three experienced seniors and two talented sophomores, and led by veteran coach Jim Larranaga, George Mason went on an unprecedented run. The Patriots upset 2000 champ Michigan State in the first round, defending champ North Carolina in the second round, and a strong Wichita State squad in the Sweet Sixteen. But they didn't make history until their overtime victory over No. 1 seed (and 2004 champ) UConn. A Final Four loss to eventual champ Florida did not diminish the fact that George Mason had become the NCAA tourney's greatest Cinderella ever.

15 Movies About Odd Sports

1 — **"Over the Top"**
A trucker (Sylvester Stallone) enters an arm-wrestling contest to win the affection of his son in this 1987 drama.

2 — **"Kingpin"**
A 1996 comedy about a one-handed former bowling prodigy (Woody Harrelson).

3 — **"Cool Runnings"**
A 1993 John Candy comedy following Jamaica's bobsled team en route to the 1988 Olympics.

4 — **"Men With Brooms"**
Paul Gross and Leslie Nielsen star in this 2002 comedy about curling teammates who reunite to win a prestigious tournament.

5 — **"The Big Lebowski"**
The offbeat and visually striking 1998 farce about a shiftless bowling enthusiast (Jeff Bridges) who's drawn into a kidnapping plot.

6 — **"BASEketball"**
In 1998, *South Park* creators Trey Parker and Matt Stone made this comedy about a game that combines baseball and basketball.

7 — **"Lords of Dogtown"**
A fact-based 2005 drama story about the famed Zephyr skateboarding team of the 1970s.

8 — **"Kansas City Bomber"**
Raquel Welch fends off lecherous males and envious females as a roller-derby queen in this 1972 drama.

9 — **"Breaking Away"**
A 1979 Oscar-winning comedy-drama about a young man's passion for bicycle racing.

"Blood and Sand"
This drama, which follows the rise of Spain's most celebrated matador, was made three different times: 1922's silent classic with Rudolph Valentino; 1941's colorful version with Tyrone Power; and 1989's less-than-stellar account with Christopher Rydell and Sharon Stone.

"The Boy in Blue"
The 1989 drama starring Nicolas Cage as a 19th-century Canadian rowing champ who started out as a bootlegger.

"Nacho Libre"
In this 2006 romp, a monk (Jack Black) becomes a wrestler to raise money for his orphanage.

"Ready to Rumble"
Two sewer workers flush out a plan to get their banished pro-wrestling hero back into the ring in this manic 2000 comedy.

"Cloud 9"
Burt Reynolds stars in this flat 2006 romp about a con man who recruits strippers to form a beach-volleyball team.

"The Karate Kid" series
A bullied high-school student learns to defend himself by studying martial arts in an inspirational 1984 crowd-pleaser that kicked up three sequels, including one starring Hilary Swank.

Strangest Moments in TV Sports

1 Fan Man

A propeller-powered parachute flew into the ring ropes during the fight between Evander Holyfield and Riddick Bowe. (November 6, 1993)

2 Down Goes Frazier

During ABC's *Superstars* competition, boxer Joe Frazier belly flopped into the 50-yard freestyle swim and nearly drowned. (February 25, 1973)

3 The Heidi Bowl

When the NFL game between the Oakland Raiders and the New York Jets ran long, NBC cut to other programming; Oakland proceeded to score two touchdowns in nine seconds. (November 17, 1968)

4 Road Rage

Donnie Allison and Cale Yarborough, running one-two at the Daytona 500, crashed on the final lap, then got out of their cars and began throwing punches. (February 18, 1979)

5 The Fog Bowl

During the second half of the NFC divisional playoff game between the Philadelphia Eagles and the Chicago Bears, heavy fog rolled onto Soldier Field and neither the CBS announcers nor the viewers could see anything. (December 31, 1988)

6 Playing Footsie

At the opening bell of the World Martial Arts Championship between Japanese wrestler Antonio Inoki and Muhammad Ali, Inoki dropped to his backside and spent the next 15 rounds crab-walking and kicking Ali in the legs. (June 26, 1976)

7 The Snake River Canyon Jump

Evel Knievel was strapped atop a one-man rocket to "leap" across the canyon; he didn't clear the near side of the canyon because his parachute popped out before he was 15 feet in the air. (September 8, 1974)

8 The Great Pretender

During the Olympic marathon in Munich, a German prankster ran into the stadium just ahead of the front-runner, Frank Shooter. (September 10, 1972)

9 The Cacophonous Kickoff

Stanford was leading Cal 20-19; the horn sounded and the Stanford marching band ran onto the field before the play was finished, allowing Cal to win the game when they returned the kickoff for a touchdown. (November 20, 1982)

10 Time Goes So Slowly

The Soviet basketball team got an assist from the officials in their gold-medal game against the U.S. in Munich; with three seconds on the clock, the Soviets were given three separate opportunities to make a last shot until they finally made one, stealing an upset victory. (September 19, 1972)

This list was originally published in the mid-'90s. Since then, a few other odd sports moments have ensued...

11 Tyson Bites Holyfield's Ear

When Evander Holyfield started to dominate this heavyweight showdown, the self-proclaimed "baddest man on the planet" showed how bad he can really be. Only Hannibal Lecter would have been proud. (June 28, 1997)

12 Pistons/Pacers Brawl

Ron Artest's hard foul on Ben Wallace (and Wallace's retaliatory shove) ignited a Pacers revolt at the Palace of Auburn Hills. With Artest and Stephen Jackson going after fans in the seats, and fans going after Pacers on the floor, this really doesn't classify as "strange." "Scary" is more like it. And perhaps the ugliest scene in NBA history. (November 19, 2004)

13 World-Class Head Butt

During the finals of the 2006 World Cup, France's Zinedine Zidane headbutted Italy's Marco Materazzi in the chest, having taken offense to a comment Materazzi had made about his sister. Since Zidane had previously announced his retirement following the 2006 Cup, and this incident resulted in his expulsion, this would be the final act of his career. (July 9, 2006)

14 Sky Fan

It's a strange moment indeed when a made extra point becomes one of *Monday Night Football*'s most memorable plays. Former Bears kicker Kevin Butler booted 413 extra points during his NFL career, including one right through the uprights during a 1995 *MNF* game against the Packers. No big deal. Seen it hundreds of times, right? Well, this time Bears fan Mike Pantazis perfectly timed a jump out of his seat, caught the ball in mid-air and fell 20 feet into the tunnel behind the end zone of Soldier Field. When sideline reporter Lynn Swann found Pantazis, he was unharmed and still clutching the ball. Months later he was clutching an ESPY for "Most Outrageous Play of the Year." (September 11, 1995)

15 Joe Namath Tries to Get Jiggy with Suzy Kolber

During a sideline interview at a 2003 Jets-Patriots game, Kolber asks Namath how he feels about the Jets lackluster season; Namath instead responds with, "I want to kiss you" and that he "couldn't care less about the team struggling." Yeah, thanks for the support there, Broadway Joe. (December 20, 2003)

Favorite Feuds

WrestleMania's Five Best Bouts

Andre the Giant vs. Hulk Hogan
(WrestleMania III, March 29, 1987)
The Lowdown: A record crowd of 93,173 witnessed Andre the Giant, undefeated for 15 years, versus Hulk Hogan, wrestling's golden boy.
The Payoff: Hogan body-slammed the 500-pound Giant, becoming the sport's biggest star and jump-starting wrestling's first big boom.

The Rock vs. "Stone Cold" Steve Austin
(WrestleMania X-7, April 1, 2001)
The Lowdown: The two biggest stars of wrestling's modern era went toe-to-toe in the culmination of a two-year-long feud.
The Payoff: Good-guy Austin aligned with "evil" WWE owner Vince McMahon and decimated the Rock to win the title in front of a shocked crowd.

Hulk Hogan vs. The Ultimate Warrior
(WrestleMania VI, April 1, 1990)
The Lowdown: The most divisive feud ever—fan favorite Hulk Hogan defended his title against up-and-coming phenom the Ultimate Warrior.
The Payoff: Half the crowd went into cardiac arrest (the other half were in tears) when Hogan missed his patented leg drop and the Warrior won.

Bret Hart vs. Shawn Michaels
(WrestleMania XII, March 31, 1996)
The Lowdown: Two men who didn't like each other outside the ring locked up in a 60-minute Iron Man match for the title.
The Payoff: After an hour, neither man had scored a pinfall. Finally, Michaels, aka the Heartbreak Kid, pinned Hart in overtime to win the belt.

Kurt Angle vs. Brock Lesnar
(WrestleMania XIX, March 30, 2003)
The Lowdown: Olympic medalist Angle squared off against former NCAA wrestling champ Lesnar in a punishing bout.
The Payoff: The 295-pound Lesnar landed on his head after attempting a high-flying attack, but he recovered to pin Angle and capture the championship.

Tiger's Top TV Moments

From the day he first appeared on *The Mike Douglas Show* to hit balls with Bob Hope at age 2, Tiger Woods has been made for TV. Since then, there have been a slew of TV moments in Tiger's evolution into the world's most telegenic competitor. In each case, Woods displayed a sense for the moment, an undeniable joie de vivre and an uncanny ability to deliver. Here are five faves.

The 1994 U.S. Amateur, 17th green, Tournament Players Club at Sawgrass
Tiger hits a wedge over the pin to the island green and sinks the putt to punctuate a dramatic comeback and win his first of three U.S. Amateur titles. This was his first televised fist pump. The celebratory gesture becomes a trademark.

The 1997 Phoenix Open; 16th green, Tournament Players Club at Scottsdale
This par-3 hole was designed to be a grass amphitheater that can hold an estimated 25,000. Rick Reilly in *Sports Illustrated* described it as a "Woods-stock." When Woods two-hopped a 9-iron into the hole, it created a highlight for all time. The gallery's eruption was called the loudest in golf history.

The 1997 Masters, 18th green, Augusta National Golf Club
Woods had not three-putted all week, and needed to make a four-footer on the 72nd hole to establish a tournament record of 18 under par. Tiger buried the putt, gave the air one right-handed uppercut, and stepped into history as both the youngest person and the first African-American to win the Masters.

The 1999 Nike commercial
Totally spontaneous, it brought into focus Tiger's virtuosity and his ability to play to the camera. Killing time between takes of a commercial shoot, Woods started tapping a golf ball off the face of his wedge. On the fourth take, Woods tap-danced his ball 49 times off his club, going between his legs and behind his back before popping it in the air and sending it out into the driving range with a baseball swing.

The 2000 PGA Championship, 16th green, Valhalla Golf Club
On the first of a three-hole playoff against Bob May, Woods stroked a 25-foot birdie putt and then started chasing it across the green, pointing at it with his right index finger and grabbing the ball almost before it hit the bottom of the cup.

Since this list first published, Tiger has continued to captivate TV audiences. Here are a few more dazzling moments.

The 2005 Masters, second cut of rough off the 16th green, Augusta National Golf Club

Chris DiMarco had pulled to within one shot of Woods and then stuck his tee shot just 15 feet from the hole at this picturesque par 3. Tiger, meanwhile, flew his tee shot over the green and into the second cut of rough. Momentum clearly was in DiMarco's favor. Looking at a green sloping severely from left to right, Tiger took his wedge and knocked his ball a good 25 feet to the left of the hole. It caught the slope and began tracking toward the hole. The ball stopped momentarily at the edge of the cup with its Nike logo clearly in view. And then, with one more rotation, it fell in for a birdie. A short while later Woods put on his fourth green jacket—and Nike had perfect footage for yet another classic Tiger commercial.

The 2006 British Open, 18th green, Royal Liverpool

After tapping in the final putt to win his third Claret Jug, Tiger embraced caddie Steve Williams and burst into tears. The victory was Woods' first since the recent death of his father, Earl, and Tiger finally let his emotions show, sobbing on Williams' shoulder for several seconds. Woods wasn't the only golfer with a heavy heart at the awards ceremony on the 18th green—second-place finisher Chris DiMarco had lost his mother, Norma, a month earlier.

The 2000 Canadian Open, bunker on the 18th hole, Glen Abbey Golf Club

His tee shot's in a bunker off the right side of the fairway. He has 218 yards to a narrow green that's protected by a lake in the front and thick rough in the back. The safe (and, perhaps, smart) play is to hit out of the bunker and yet keep the ball short of the water. But that would give Grant Waite a shot to tie him. So Tiger hits a six-iron out of the sand, over the water and on to the green. As they walk up the 18th fairway, Waite turned to Tiger and said, "You're not supposed to do that!"

Winners of the Inaugural

TV GUIDE Awards

Christina Applegate and French Stewart hosted the magazine's first ceremony on February 1, 1999. The awards honored performers and shows voted on by 1.2 million fans, via magazine ballots and the Internet.

Editors' Award
Drew Carey, *The Drew Carey Show* (ABC)

The Best Show You're Not Watching
7th Heaven (WB)

Favorite Star of a New Series
Christina Applegate, *Jesse* (NBC)

Favorite Actor in a Comedy
Tim Allen, *Home Improvement* (ABC)

Favorite Actress in a Comedy
Jenna Elfman, *Dharma & Greg* (ABC)

Favorite Actor in a Drama
David Duchovny, *The X-Files* (Fox)

Favorite Actress in a Drama
Roma Downey, *Touched by an Angel* (CBS)

Favorite New Series
Martial Law (CBS)

Favorite Comedy Series
Frasier (NBC)

Favorite Drama Series
ER (NBC)

Favorite Soap Opera
Days of Our Lives (NBC)

Favorite Sportscaster
Terry Bradshaw (Fox)

Favorite Daytime Talk Show
The Rosie O'Donnell Show (Syndicated)

Favorite Late-Night Show
The Tonight Show With Jay Leno (NBC)

Favorite Sci-Fi/Fantasy Show
Buffy the Vampire Slayer (WB)

Favorite TV Pet
Joey's duck, *Friends* (NBC)

Favorite News Program
Dateline NBC (NBC)

Favorite Children's Show
Sesame Street (PBS)

Favorite Teen Chracter
Buffy, *Buffy the Vampire Slayer* (WB)

Favorite Prime-time Animated Show
The Simpsons (Fox)

Scariest Villain
Spike, *Buffy the Vampire Slayer* (WB)

Sexiest Male
David Duchovny, *The X-Files* (Fox)

Sexiest Female
Sarah Michelle Gellar,
Buffy the Vampire Slayer (WB)

Best Kiss
Richard and Caroline,
Caroline in the City (NBC)

Best-Dressed Male
David Duchovny, *The X-Files* (Fox)

Best-Dressed Female
Sarah Michelle Gellar,
Buffy the Vampire Slayer (WB)

Favorite Women's Hair-do
Sarah Michelle Gellar,
Buffy the Vampire Slayer (WB)

Favorite Men's Hair-do
David Boreanaz,
Buffy the Vampire Slayer (WB)

Favorite TV Theme Song
Dawson's Creek (WB)

Favorite Commercial
Taco Bell

Winners of the Second Annual

TV GUIDE Awards

On March 6, 2000, TV GUIDE presented awards to the following honorees, chosen as the favorites by 1.6 million TV fans, who voted online and via magazine ballots.

Editors' Award
Cast of *Friends* (NBC)

The Best Show You're Not Watching
Sports Night (ABC)

Favorite Actor in a New Series
Martin Sheen, *The West Wing* (NBC)

Favorite Actress in a New Series
Amy Brenneman, *Judging Amy* (CBS)

Favorite Actor in a Comedy
David Hyde Pierce, *Frasier* (NBC)

Favorite Actress in a Comedy
Jenna Elfman, *Dharma & Greg* (ABC)

Favorite Actor in a Drama
David James Elliott, *JAG* (CBS)

Favorite Actress in a Drama
Melina Kanakaredes, *Providence* (NBC)

Favorite New Series
Judging Amy (CBS)

Favorite Comedy Series
Everybody Loves Raymond (CBS)

Favorite Drama Series
ER (NBC)

Favorite Soap Opera
Days of Our Lives (NBC)

Favorite Sportscaster
Bob Costas (NBC)

Favorite Daytime Talk Show
The Rosie O'Donnell Show (Syndicated)

Favorite Game Show
Who Wants to Be a Millionaire (ABC)

Favorite News Personality
Peter Jennings (ABC)

Favorite Late-Night Show
The Tonight Show With Jay Leno (NBC)

Favorite Sci-Fi/Fantasy Show
Buffy the Vampire Slayer (WB)

Favorite Reality TV
The Real World (MTV)

Favorite TV Pet
Eddie, *Frasier* (NBC)

Favorite TV Movie or Miniseries
"Annie" (ABC)

Favorite News Program
Entertainment Tonight (Syndicated)

Favorite Music Show
Total Request Live (MTV)

Favorite Children's Show
Rugrats (Nickelodeon)

Favorite Teen Show
Buffy the Vampire Slayer (WB)

Winners of the **Third Annual**

TV GUIDE Awards

More than 1.5 million fans voted for their most-loved celebrities and programs, with Craig Kilborn hosting the festivities on February 24, 2001.

Actor of the Year in a New Series
Tom Cavanagh, *Ed* (NBC)

Actress of the Year in a New Series
Bette Midler, *Bette* (CBS)

Actor of the Year in a Comedy Series
Ray Romano,
Everybody Loves Raymond (CBS)

Actress of the Year in a Comedy Series
Debra Messing, *Will & Grace* (NBC)

Actor of the Year in a Drama Series
Martin Sheen, *The West Wing* (NBC)

Actress of the Year in a Drama Series
Amy Brenneman, *Judging Amy* (CBS)

Supporting Actor of the Year in a Comedy Series
Sean Hayes, *Will & Grace* (NBC)

Supporting Actress of the Year in a Comedy Series
Doris Roberts,
Everybody Loves Raymond (CBS)

Supporting Actor of the Year in a Drama Series
Noah Wyle, *ER* (NBC)

Supporting Actress of the Year in a Drama Series
Tyne Daly, *Judging Amy* (CBS)

New Series of the Year
CSI: Crime Scene Investigation (CBS)

Comedy Series of the Year
Everybody Loves Raymond (CBS)

Drama Series of the Year
The West Wing (NBC)

News Person of the Year
Katie Couric (NBC)

Reality Series of the Year
Biography (A&E)

Music Series of the Year
Behind the Music (VH1)

Music Special of the Year
Elton John: Greatest Hits Live (CBS)

Comedy Special of the Year
Saturday Night Live: Presidential Bash 2000 (NBC)

Personality of the Year
Regis Philbin

Talk-Variety Star of the Year
Rosie O'Donnell

Breakout Star of the Year
Jessica Alba, *Dark Angel* (Fox)

The Brandon Tartikoff Award
David E. Kelley

Actors

Who Have Never Won Emmys

As of 2007, some of TV's most respected actors have never won the most coveted of television honors, the Emmy. Among them...

Jason Alexander

Gracie Allen

Charles Durning

Buddy Ebsen

Judy Garland

Dave Garroway

Jackie Gleason

John Goodman

Andy Griffith

David Janssen

Martin Landau

Angela Lansbury

Jack Paar

Courteny Cox

Elizabeth Montgomery

Phylicia Rashad

Micheal Landon

Jerry Orbach

Larry Hagman

12 Great Shows

That Never Won an Emmy

Dallas

Friends

Kojak

Maude

Marcus Welby, M.D.

The Odd Couple

Perry Mason

Roseanne

St. Elsewhere

Star Trek

Twilight Zone

Twin Peaks

TV GUIDE

Soap Stars

Who Have Gone Home Empty-Handed
From the Daytime Emmys

Jeanne Cooper (*The Young and the Restless*)
*Received a Lifetime Achievement Award

Doug Davidson (*The Young and the Restless*)

Genie Francis (*General Hospital*)

Deidre Hall (*Days of Our Lives*)

Bill Hayes (*Days of Our Lives*)

Jon Hensley (*As the World Turns*)

Joseph Mascolo (*Days of Our Lives, The Bold and the Beautiful*)

Robin Mattson (*General Hospital, All My Children*)

Brad Maule (*General Hospital, Port Charles*)

Beverlee McKinsey (*General Hospital, Guiding Light, Texas, Another World*)

Robert Newman (*Guiding Light*)

Stephen Nichols (*Days of Our Lives, Santa Barbara, General Hospital*)

Frances Reid (*Days of Our Lives*)
*Received a Lifetime Achievement Award

Stephen Schnetzer (*Another World*)

Kin Shriner (*General Hospital, Port Charles*)

Melody Scott Thomas (*The Young and the Restless*)

Helen Wagner (*As the World Turns*)

Jack Wagner (*General Hospital, Santa Barbara, The Bold and the Beautiful*)

Ruth Warrick (*Peyton Place, All My Children*)
*Received a Lifetime Achievement Award

People Who Have Won Multiple Awards

Winning just one of the major awards in the entertainment industry (Oscar, Emmy, Tony and Grammy) is a stroke of good fortune. These talented artists have walked away with three...and sometimes all four.

People Who Have Won
AN EMMY, A GRAMMY, AN OSCAR AND A TONY

Mel Brooks

John Gielgud

Marvin Hamlisch

Helen Hayes

Audrey Hepburn

Rita Moreno

Mike Nichols

Richard Rogers

Jonathan Tunick
(composer, arranger and musical director)

Barbra Streisand
(honorary Tony)

Liza Minnelli
(honorary Grammy)

Whoopi Goldberg
(Daytime Emmy)

People Who Have Won
AN OSCAR, AN EMMY AND A TONY

Jack Albertson

Anne Bancroft

Ingrid Bergman

Shirley Booth

Ralph Burns
(composer and arranger)

Melvyn Douglas

Bob Fosse

Jeremy Irons

Thomas Mitchell (actor)

Al Pacino

Vanessa Redgrave

Jason Robards

Paul Scofield (actor)

Maggie Smith

Maureen Stapleton

Jessica Tandy

People Who Have Won
AN OSCAR, A TONY AND A GRAMMY

Henry Fonda

Oscar Hammerstein

Elton John

Alan Jay Lerner
(playwright/lyricist)

Frank Loesser (composer)

Tim Rice

Stephen Sondheim

Jule Styne

Andrew Lloyd Webber

People Who Have Won
AN OSCAR, AN EMMY AND A GRAMMY

John Addison (composer)

Julie Andrews

Burt Bacharach

Alan Bergman (composer)

Marilyn Bergman
(composer)

George Burns

Cher

Randy Newman

Peter Ustinov

John Williams

Robin Williams

People Who Have Won
AN EMMY, A TONY AND A GRAMMY

Harry Belafonte

Leonard Bernstein

Martin Charmin
(composer and producer)

Cy Coleman
(producer and writer)

Fred Ebb

Julie Harris

James Earl Jones

John Kander

Marc Shaiman
(producer and writer)

Charles Strouse (composer)

Lily Tomlin

Dick Van Dyke

James Whitmore

Best Award Show Moments

Award shows are rampant in Hollywood. Some actors use the opportunity to spout about their political leanings or pet philanthropies. However, the moments listed below are those rare ones that keep us coming back to see who will make us cry, who will bring the laughter, who will shock us and who will make the biggest fool of themselves (…perhaps the streaker from 1973?).

- **Barbra Streisand** and **Katharine Hepburn** tying for Best Actress in 1968, for "Funny Girl" and "The Lion in Winter," respectively, the only time a tie has occurred in a major category.
- **George C. Scott** refusing his 1970 Best Actor award for "Patton"; two years later, **Marlon Brando** would follow suit for his win for "The Godfather," albeit in a flashier way, sending Native American Sacheen Littlefeather on stage to accept for him.
- **Charlie Chaplin** returns to Hollywood in 1971 to accept an honorary Oscar
- **A streaker** bolts behind David Niven at the 1973 award show; Niven responded with the classic comeback: "Well, ladies and gentleman, that was bound to happen. But isn't it fascinating to think that the only laugh that man will probably ever get in his life was when he stripped off to show his shortcomings."
- In 1984, **Sally Field** makes her "You like me" acceptance speech for Best Actress for "Places in the Heart" (which, contrary to legend, is actually, "I can't deny the fact that you like me, right now, you like me!").
- **Laurence Olivier** forgets to read the nominees when presenting Best Picture at the 1985 awards ceremony. He walked on stage, opened the envelope and announced "Amadeus."
- In 1991, **Jack Palance** drops to the ground for some one-handed push-ups during his acceptance of the Best Supporting Actor award for "City Slickers."
- **Tom Hanks** outs his drama teacher during his win for Best Actor for "Philadelphia" in 1993, thus inspiring the plot for the Kevin Kline film "In & Out."
- **Cuba Gooding Jr.** gives an exuberant acceptance speech when awarded the Best Supporting Actor trophy for "Jerry Maguire" in 1996.
- **Roberto Benigni** climbs over the seats (and Steven Spielberg's head) to accept his 1998 award for Best Foreign Language film for "Life Is Beautiful."
- **Woody Allen** finally makes an appearance at the Academy Awards, to honor New York following the attacks of September 11.
- **Halle Berry** gives an emotional speech following her historic 2001 win for Best Actress for "Monster's Ball."
- **Adrien Brody** plants a kiss on Halle Berry the following year when he won his Best Actor award for "The Pianist."

- **Lucille Ball** realizes she can't read the winner for Best Comedy Series of 1975 because she forgot her reading glasses. **Milton Berle** got her a pair of specs, after which she declared *The Mary Tyler Moore Show* the winner.
- **Alan Alda** cartwheels down the aisle after his *M*A*S*H* win in 1979.
- **Ted Danson** finally wins his first Emmy in 1990, after 8 nominations.
- **Kirstie Alley** thanks then-husband Parker Stevenson for giving her "the big one for the last eight years" during her Best Comedy Actress win for *Cheers* in 1991.
- **Camryn Manheim** declares that her 1998 win for Outstanding Supporting Actress in a Drama Series for *The Practice* is for "all the fat girls."
- **Susan Lucci's** long-overdue win at the 1999 Daytime Emmys, after coming home empty-handed 18 times before for her legendary role of Erica Kane on *All My Children*.

- (Apparently) Bored and slightly drunk, **Frank Sinatra, Sammy Davis Jr.** and **Dean Martin** storm the stage of the 1957 award show and usher in the tradition of the stars handing out the Golden Globes, as opposed to the journalists.
- **The producers of "Z"** refuse their award for Best Foreign Language Film in 1970 because they wanted the film to be included in the Best Motion Picture category.
- Just before he refused his Best Actor Oscar, **Marlon Brando** similarly refused his Best Actor Golden Globe for "The Godfather."
- **Sigourney Weaver** wins twice in 1989: Best Actress for "Gorillas in the Mist" and Best Supporting Actress for "Working Girl."
- A three-way tie occurs in 1989 for Best Actress among **Jodie Foster** ("The Accused"), **Shirley MacLaine** ("Madame Sousatzka") and **Sigourney Weaver** ("Gorillas in the Mist").
- **Joan Plowright** wins twice in 1993: Best Supporting Actress (Motion Picture) for "Enchanted April" and Best Supporting Actress (TV) for *Stalin*.
- **Jack Nicholson** mooning the audience when accepting his award for Best Actor—Drama for "As Good as It Gets" in 1998.
- In 1998, **Ving Rhames** gives his trophy (for Best Actor in a Miniseries/TV Movie for *Don King: Only in America*) to Jack Lemmon.
- **Christine Lahti** rushes from the bathroom in 1998 to accept her Best Actress in a TV Drama award for *Chicago Hope*.
- **Renée Zellweger** pulling a Christine Lahti a couple of years later, when she almost missed accepting her award for "Nurse Betty."
- **Helen Mirren** wins twice in 2007: Best Actress (Motion Picture) for "The Queen" and Best Actress (Miniseries/TV Movie) for "Elizabeth I."

The Ecstasy,

Soon Followed by the Agony

Great TV Shows that were canceled after receiving an Emmy nomination.

Lucky (2003)

Outstanding Writing for a Comedy Series (nominated)

Freaks and Geeks (2001)

Outstanding Writing for a Comedy Series (nominated)

Sports Night (2000)

Outstanding Cinematography for a Multi-Camera Series (won)

Outstanding Casting for a Comedy Series (nominated)

Outstanding Directing for a Comedy Series (nominated)

Outstanding Multi-Camera Picture Editing for a Series (nominated)

Outstanding Guest Actor in a Comedy Series (for William H. Macy) (nominated)

My So-Called Life (1995)

Outstanding Writing for a Drama Series (nominated)

Outstanding Lead Actress in a Drama Series (for Claire Danes) (nominated)

Outstanding Directing in a Drama (nominated)

The Ben Stiller Show (1993)

Outstanding Writing in a Variety or Music Program (won)

Taxi (1983)

Outstanding Comedy Series (nominated)

Outstanding Writing in a Comedy Series (nominated)

Outstanding Lead Actor in a Comedy Series (for Judd Hirsch) (won)

Outstanding Supporting Actor in a Comedy, Variety or Music Series
(for Christopher Lloyd) (won)

Outstanding Supporting Actor in a Comedy, Variety or Music Series
(for Danny DeVito) (nominated)

Outstanding Supporting Actress in a Comedy, Variety or Music Series
(for Carol Kane) (won)

Barney Miller (1982)

Outstanding Comedy Series (won)

Outstanding Writing in a Comedy Series (nominated)

Outstanding Lead Actor in a Comedy Series (for Hal Linden) (nominated)

Outstanding Supporting Actor in a Comedy, Variety or Music Series
(for Ron Glass) (nominated)

Outstanding Supporting Actor in a Comedy, Variety or Music Series
(for Steve Landesberg) (nominated)

My World and Welcome to It (1970)

Outstanding Comedy Series (won)

Outstanding Continued Performance by an Actor in a Comedy Series
(for William Windom) (won)

The Bob Newhart Show (1962)

Outstanding Comedy Series (won)

Actors Who Never Won Oscars

Some of the industry's most talented actors have been snubbed by the Academy...

Peter O'Toole
(8 nominations, received an honorary award)

Richard Burton
(7 nominations)

Deborah Kerr
(6 nominations, received an honorary award)

Glenn Close
(5 nominations)

Albert Finney
(5 nominations)

Montgomery Clift
(4 nominations)

Tom Cruise
(3 nominations)

Kirk Douglas
(3 nominations, received an honorary award)

Greta Garbo
(3 nominations, received an honorary award)

James Mason
(3 nominations)

Michelle Pfeiffer
(3 nominations)

Gloria Swanson
(3 nominations)

James Dean
(2 nominations)

Judy Garland
(2 nominations, received a special award)

Cary Grant
(2 nominations, received an honorary award)

Richard Harris
(2 nominations)

Gena Rowlands
(2 nominations)

Lauren Bacall
(1 nomination)

Harrison Ford
(1 nomination)

Ava Gardner
(1 nomination)

Steve McQueen
(1 nomination)

Kathleen Turner
(1 nomination)

Donald Sutherland
(0 nominations)

Liv Ullman
(0 nominations)

Marilyn Monroe
(0 nominations)

the BEST TV Movies of the 1970s

"Jane Eyre" (1970): This adaptation of Charlotte Bronte's classic, which stars Susannah York and George C. Scott, is beautifully filmed in the Yorkshire countryside.

"Duel" (1971): A young Steven Spielberg directed this pulse-pounding tale of a deadly game between a motorist (Dennis Weaver) and a truck driver on a deserted highway.

"Brian's Song" (1971): Five Emmys went to this tear-jerker, which examines the real-life friendship between Chicago Bears teammates Gale Sayers and Brian Piccolo (Billy Dee Williams and James Caan), and Piccolo's battle with cancer.

"The Glass Menagerie" (1973): Katharine Hepburn stars in this Emmy-winning adaptation of Tennessee Williams' classic play about the hopes and frustrations of a 1930s St. Louis family.

"The Execution of Private Slovik" (1974): Martin Sheen portrays Pvt. Eddie D. Slovik, the only U.S. serviceman put to death for desertion during World War II.

"Helter Skelter" (1976): The chilling story of Charles Manson and the Tate-LaBianca murders of 1969. Based on the bestseller coauthored by prosecutor Vincent Bugliosi.

"Sybil" (1976): Sally Field won an Emmy for her unforgettable portrayal of a tormented woman with multiple personalities.

"The Miracle Worker" (1979): An affecting adaptation of William Gibson's play about Helen Keller (Melissa Gilbert) and her teacher Annie Sullivan (Emmy-winner Patty Duke Astin).

the BEST TV Movies of the 1980s

"Bill" (1981): This film is distinguished by the Emmy-winning performance of Mickey Rooney as Bill, a mentally disabled man who learns to live in society after spending most of his life in institutions.

"The Bunker" (1981): Anthony Hopkins portrays Adolf Hitler during his last days in his underground headquarters.

"The Executioner's Song" (1982): This adaptation of Norman Mailer's Pulitzer Prize-winning chronicle of the Gary Gilmore case stars Tommy Lee Jones and Rosanna Arquette.

"Adam" (1983): The deeply affecting story of John and Reve Walsh's agonizing days following the abduction and murder of their 6-year-old son, and their efforts to raise the nation's awareness of missing children.

"The Day After" (1983): A ratings blockbuster that offered a chilling view of the aftermath of a nuclear war, as it affects a small Kansas town.

"The Burning Bed" (1984): Farrah Fawcett stars in this chronicle of a woman who ends 13 years of abuse by incinerating her ex-husband while he sleeps.

"A Christmas Carol" (1984): George C. Scott stars as Ebenezer Scrooge, Charles Dickens' humbug who gets a large helping of Yuletide spirit.

"Something About Amelia" (1984): A sensitive, intelligent treatment of incest in a middle-class household, with Ted Danson in a powerful dramatic turn as the abusive father.

"Death of a Salesman" (1985): Dustin Hoffman won an Emmy for his portrayal of Willy Loman in Arthur Miller's tragedy of the common man.

"An Early Frost" (1985): A film dramatizing the plight of a homosexual man (Aidan Quinn) stricken with AIDS, focusing on the reactions of his parents, who didn't know he was gay, and on his own psychological trauma.

"Nobody's Child" (1986): This case study stars Marlo Thomas as a woman who wages a courageous struggle to overcome mental illness.

"The Betty Ford Story" (1987): Gena Rowlands won an Emmy for her portrayal of the former First Lady throughout her trying White House years and subsequent treatment for alcohol and prescription-drug addiction.

"Roe vs. Wade" (1989): Account of the drifter (Holly Hunter) whose unwanted pregnancy led to the 1973 Supreme Court abortion ruling.

the BEST TV Movies of the 1990s

"It" (1990): Harry Anderson and John Ritter star as childhood friends forced to face their long-forgotten fears in this winning Stephen King adaptation.

"Sarah, Plain and Tall" (1991): Glenn Close gives an Emmy-nominated performance in this period piece about a prospective mail-order bride in the early 20th century.

"Stalin" (1992): Robert Duvall portrays the Soviet Union's man of steel in this Emmy-winning biopic.

"Gypsy" (1993): Bette Midler's turn as an irrepressible stage mother dominates this version of the 1959 Broadway musical.

"Barbarians at the Gate" (1993): James Garner and Jonathan Pryce star in this seriocomic chronicle of the 1988 RJR Nabisco buyout.

"And the Band Played On" (1993): Matthew Modine stars in this Emmy-winning dramatization of Randy Shilts' chronicle of the early years of the AIDS epidemic.

"Serving in Silence: The Margarethe Cammermeyer Story" (1995): Thoughtful docudrama about a respected and decorated Army colonel and nurse (played by Emmy-winner Glenn Close), whose coming out as a lesbian jeopardizes her military career.

"The Tuskegee Airmen" (1995): Laurence Fishburne is commanding as the top gun of the first unit of black U.S. fighter pilots, who battled bigotry and the Nazis during World War II.

"Gulliver's Travels" (1996): Ted Danson portrays the titular character in this technically accomplished take on Jonathan Swift's novel about the adventures of a shipwrecked 18th-century physician.

"Rasputin" (1996): Alan Rickman portrays the "mad monk of Russia," who gains entry to the court of Nicholas and Alexandra (Ian McKellen, Greta Scacchi) when he is summoned to treat the ailing Prince Alexei.

"12 Angry Men" (1997): Jack Lemmon and George C. Scott head a stellar cast in this remake of the classic legal drama, which eavesdrops on a dozen jurors deliberating a verdict in a murder trial.

"Miss Evers' Boys" (1997): Alfre Woodard and Laurence Fishburne star in this wrenching chronicle of a 40-year government study in which blacks with syphilis were monitored—but not treated.

"Gia" (1998): Angelina Jolie gives an Emmy-nominated performance as the drug-addled supermodel who rose to the top of the fashion industry in the early '80s, only to die of AIDS at age 26.

"Tuesdays With Morrie" (1999): Hank Azaria and Jack Lemmon star in this affecting tale of a writer who receives life lessons when visiting an old university professor suffering from a terminal disease.

the BEST TV Movies of the 2000s

"Conspiracy" (2001): In 1942, 15 high-ranking members of the Nazi party meet near Berlin to draw up the blueprint for Hitler's "Final Solution."

"Life With Judy Garland: Me and My Shadows" (2001): Judy Davis won an Emmy for her portrayal of the troubled singer-actress' later years.

"Wit" (2001): Mike Nichols directed this adaptation of Margaret Edson's Pulitzer Prize-winning play about an English professor (Emma Thompson) stricken with ovarian cancer.

"Door to Door" (2002): William H. Macy won an Emmy for his portrayal of a salesman with cerebral palsy who inspires people along his route in this fact-based drama.

"The Gathering Storm" (2002): On the eve of World War II, Winston Churchill (Albert Finney) tries to warn England of the Nazi menace, and leans on his wife, Clementine (Vanessa Redgrave), for support.

"The Life and Death of Peter Sellers" (2004): Geoffrey Rush won an Emmy for his performance as the complex, flawed comic genius in this stylish biopic that ricochets back and forth between the highs and lows of his personal and professional lives.

"Something the Lord Made" (2004): Alan Rickman is magnificent as a pioneering cardiac surgeon and Mos Def is a revelation as his black research assistant in this poignant, fact-based drama about their professional relationship and groundbreaking work.

"Lackawanna Blues" (2004): Ruben Santiago-Hudson wrote the script for the adaptation of his play about the eclectic residents of a New York boardinghouse in the '50s and '60s. S. Epatha Merkerson and Jimmy Smits costar.

"Elizabeth I" (2005): Helen Mirren gives an award-winning performance as the 16th-century English monarch in the later years of her tumultuous reign.

Most Memorable Daytime TV Moments

We do! We do! (1981)
The marriage of *General Hospital*'s Luke and Laura (Anthony Geary and Genie Francis)

Hurricane Erica (1970)
All My Children introduces Susan Lucci as Erica Kane

Tuck Me In (1984)
The facelift of Kay Chancellor (Jeanne Cooper) on *The Young and the Restless*

Goodbye Mr. Hooper (1983)
Will Lee dies and so does his character, Mr. Hooper, on *Sesame Street*

Heart to Heart (1994)
B.J. Jones dies and her heart is transplanted into her cousin Maxie on *General Hospital*

That Girl! (1988)
Phil Donahue wears a skirt during a show about cross-dressing

Marlena Is Alive (1982)
Days of Our Lives' Marlena (Deidre Hall) is thought to be dead but the audience is proved wrong

Wanton Woman (1984)
Guiding Light's Reva (Kim Zimmer) strips and calls herself "the slut of Springfield"

Wagons, Ho! (1988)
Oprah Winfrey rolls out a wagon with 67 lbs. of fat to show her weight loss

Boob Tube (1977)
The Price Is Right contestant Yolanda Bowsley comes out of her top

Let's not forget three of the wackiest daytime moments ever.

He's in Love! (2005)
Tom Cruise proclaims his love for Katie Holmes by jumping on Oprah Winfrey's couch

The Devil Made Her Do It (1994)
A possessed Marlena levitates over her bed on *Days of Our Lives*

Three's a Crowd (1998)
Guiding Light's Josh (Robert Newman), believing wife Reva was murdered, clones his beloved

The Oprah Winfrey Show

Oprah was encouraged to go into syndication by film critic Roger Ebert.

40 Movie Stars
Who Worked in Soaps

1 **Kevin Bacon**
Search for Tomorrow; Guiding Light

2 **Alec Baldwin**
The Doctors

3 **Warren Beatty**
Love of Life

4 **Tom Berenger**
One Life to Live

5 **Hayden Christensen**
Family Passions

6 **Robert De Niro**
Search for Tomorrow

7 **Taye Diggs**
Guiding Light

8 **Olympia Dukakis**
Search for Tomorrow

9 **Laurence Fishburne**
One Life to Live

10 **Vivica A. Fox**
Days of Our Lives; Generations

11 **Morgan Freeman**
Another World

12 **Mark Hamill**
General Hospital

13 **Anne Heche**
Another World

14 **Dustin Hoffman**
Search for Tomorrow

15 **James Earl Jones**
As the World Turns; Guiding Light

16 **Tommy Lee Jones**
One Life to Live

17 **Kevin Kline**
Search for Tomorrow

18 **Jack Lemmon**
The Brighter Day; The Road of Life

19 **Ray Liotta**
Another World

20 **William H. Macy**
Another World

21 **Demi Moore**
General Hospital

22 **Julianne Moore**
As the World Turns

23 **Brad Pitt**
Another World

24 **Parker Posey**
As the World Turns

25 **Christopher Reeve**
Love of Life

26 **Ving Rhames**
Another World

27 **Eric Roberts**
Another World

28 **Gena Rowlands**
Peyton Place; The Way of the World

29 **Meg Ryan**
As the World Turns

30 **Susan Sarandon**
A World Apart; Search for Tomorrow

31 Roy Scheider
    Love of Life; The Secret Storm

32 Tom Selleck
    The Young and the Restless

33 Martin Sheen
    The Edge of Night;
    As the World Turns

34 Mira Sorvino
    Guiding Light

35 David Strathairn
    Another World

36 Marisa Tomei
    As the World Turns

37 Kathleen Turner
    The Doctors

38 Christopher Walken
    Guiding Light

39 Sigourney Weaver
    Somerset

40 Billy Dee Williams
    Another World;
    Guiding Light

9 Actors Who Returned

to Their Soaps as Different Characters

Matthew Ashford
Originally as Drew Ralston, later as Dr. Stephen Haver on *One Life to Live*

Bradley Cole
Originally as Prince Richard Winslow, later as DA Jeffrey O'Neill on *Guiding Light*

Judi Evans
Originally as Adrienne Johnson, later as Bonnie Lockhart on *Days of Our Lives*

Andrea Hall
Originally as Samantha Evans, later as waitress Hattie Adams on *Days of Our Lives*

Vincent Irizarry
Originally as Brandon "LuJack" Spaulding Luvonaczek, later as Nick McHenry Spaulding Luvonaczek on *Guiding Light*

Robert Kelker-Kelly
Originally as Sam Fowler, later as Bobby Reno (who turned out to be Shane Roberts) on *Another World*

Joie Lenz
Originally as the clone of Reva Shane Lewis, later as Michelle Bauer Santos on *Guiding Light*

Quinn Redeker
Originally as Nick Reed, then as Joseph Tomas, later as Rex Sterling on *The Young and the Restless*

Josh Taylor
Originally as Chris Kositchek, later as Roman Brady on *Days of Our Lives*

Actors

Who Played Dual Roles on Soaps

The evil twin, the long-lost sibling and the doppelganger have become soap staples. Here, a few of the suds stars who have done double duty.

All My Children

David Canary as Adam and Stuart Chandler

Kate Collins as Natalie Dillon and Janet

Finola Hughes as Alexandra Devane and Anna Devane

Another World

Stephen Schnetzer as Cass Winthrop and Rex Allingham

Victoria Wyndham as Rachel Cory and Justine Duvalier

Ellen Wheeler, **Anne Heche** and **Jensen Buchanan** as Vicky and Marley Hudson

As the World Turns

Martha Byrne as Lily Walsh Snyder and Rose D'Angelo

Julianne Moore as Frannie Hughes and Sabrina Fullerton

Jennifer Landon as Gwen Norbeck and Cleo

Capitol

Catherine Hickland as Julie Clegg and Jenny Diamond

Days of Our Lives

Thaao Penghlis as Andre and Tony DiMera

Eileen Davidson played FIVE different characters: Kristen Blake, Susan Banks, Sister Mary Moira Banks, Thomas Banks and Penelope Kent

General Hospital

Tyler Christopher as Nikolas Cassidine and Connor

Anthony Geary as Luke Spencer and Bill Eckert

Kelly Monaco as Samantha McCall and Alicia Montenegro on *General Hospital* AND as Livvie Locke and Tess Ramsay on *Port Charles*

Guiding Light

Michelle Forbes as Sonni and Solita Carrera

Kim Zimmer as Reva Shayne Lewis and Clone Reva/Dolly

One Life to Live

Thom Christopher as Carlo Hesser and Mortimer Bern

Port Charles

Michael Easton as Caleb and Michael Morley

Santa Barbara

Roscoe Born as Robert Barr and Quinn Armitage

Sunset Beach

Clive Robertson as Ben and Derek Evans

The Young and the Restless

Jeanne Cooper as Katherine Chancellor and Marge Cotroke

Michelle Stafford as Phyllis Newman and Sheila Carter

Soap Characters Who Were "Dead,"

But Returned From Beyond

Once a soap character passes on, there's no guarantee that they'll stay dead (which always gives the die-hard fan hope when their favorite character bites the dust). Here are some fan faves who kept coming back like a bad penny...

All My Children

Dr. Maria Santos Grey (played by Eva LaRue)

Tad Martin (played by Michael E. Knight)

As the World Turns

James Stenbeck (played by Anthony Herrera)

The Bold and the Beautiful

Macy Alexander Forrester Chambers Sharpe (played by Bobbie Eakes)

Taylor Hayes Forrester (played by Hunter Tylo)

Days of Our Lives

Roman Brady (played by Wayne Northrop, then Josh Taylor)

Stefano DiMera (played by Joseph Mascolo)

Steve "Patch" Johnson (played by Stephen Nichols)

Hope Brady Williams (played by Kristian Alfonso)

General Hospital

Brenda Barrett (played by Vanessa Marcil)

Robert Scorpio (played by Tristan Rogers)

Guiding Light

Annie Dutton (played by Cynthia Watros, then Signy Coleman)

Beth Raines Spaulding (played by Beth Chamberlin)

Reva Shayne Lewis (played by Kim Zimmer)

Roger Thorpe (played by Michael Zaslow)

One Life to Live

Todd Manning (played by Roger Howarth, then Trevor St. John)

Passions

Julian Crane (played by Ben Masters)

Sheridan Crane (played by McKenzie Westmore)

The Young and the Restless

Sheila Carter (played by Kimberlin Brown, then Michelle Stafford)—also on *The Bold and the Beautiful*

Victor Newman (played by Eric Braeden)

Malcolm Winters (played by Shemar Moore)

General Hospital

General Hospital is credited for starting several trends in the soap-opera genre in the 1980s, most notably that of the supercouple, because of the popularity of Luke and Laura (Anthony Geary, Genie Francis).

Soap Deaths

That Shocked Viewers

Soap characters are often on the chopping block, but these characters were so beloved—or so young—that the audience never saw it coming.

All My Children

Dixie Martin (played by Cady McClain)

Edmund Grey (played by John Callahan)

Another World

Frankie Frame Winthrop (played by Alice Barrett)

Ryan Harrison (played by Paul Michael Valley)

As the World Turns

Vicky Hudson (played by Jensen Buchanan) Her character was killed off after it was moved over from the defunct *Another World*

Jennifer Munson (played by Jennifer Ferrin)

The Bold and the Beautiful

Macy Alexander (played by Bobbie Eakes)

Darla Forrester (played by Schae Harrison)

Days of Our Lives

Zack Brady (played by Spencer and Garrett Gray)

General Hospital

Dr. Tony Jones (played by Brad Maule)

B.J. Jones (played by Brighton Hertford)

Guiding Light

Nadine Cooper (played by Jean Cooper)

Brandon "Lujack" Spaulding Luvonaczek (played by Vincent Irizzary)

Ross Marler (played by Jerry ver Dorn)

Maureen Reardon (played by Ellen Parker)

One Life to Live

Jennifer Buchanan (played by Jessica Morris)

Ben Davidson (played by Mark Derwin)

Passions

Grace Bennett (played by Dana Sparks)

Timmy (played by Josh Ryan Evans)

The Young and the Restless

Phillip Chancellor (played by Thom Bierdz)

Cassie Newman (played by Camryn Grimes)

Soap Stars

Who Have Been Married in Real Life

1. Kristina Wagner and Jack Wagner

2. Melissa Reeves and Scott Reeves

3. Kassie (Wesley) DePaiva and James DePaiva

4. Crystal Chappell and Michael Sabatino

5. Susan Seaforth Hayes and Bill Hayes

6. Margaret Colin and Justin Deas

7. Colleen Zenk Pinter and Mark Pinter

8. Arianne Zuker and Kyle Lowder

9. Lesli Kay and Keith Coulouris

10. Britt Helfer and Robert Newman

11. Leslie Denniston and Don Hastings

12. Kelley Menighan Hensley and Jon Hensley

13   Maura West and Scott DeFreitas

14   Robin Christopher and Matt Crane

15   Kelly Ripa and Mark Consuelos

16   Lindsay Korman and Justin Hartley

17   Hunter Tylo and Michael Tylo separated

18   Amelia Heinle and Michael Weatherly divorced

19   Rena Sofer and Wally Kurth divorced

20   Signy Coleman and Vincent Irizarry divorced

21   Ellen Wheeler and Tom Eplin divorced

22   Shari Shattuck and Ronn Moss divorced

23   Eileen Davidson and Jon Lindstrom divorced

24   Eva La Rue and John Callahan separated

25   Eva La Rue and John O'Hurley divorced

People Who Have Hosted

Saturday Night Live the Most

Apparently, we just can't get enough of these *SNL* hosts. Steve Martin's streak began when he first helmed the show back in Season 2 (October 23, 1976, to be exact) but his 30-year streak is in danger of being surpassed by Alec Baldwin and John Goodman. Not if Steve has anything to say about it...

Steve Martin (14 times)

Alec Baldwin (13 times)

John Goodman (12 times)

Buck Henry (10 times)

Chevy Chase (9 times)

Tom Hanks (8 times)

Danny DeVito (7 times)

Elliott Gould (6 times)

Christopher Walken (6 times)

Drew Barrymore (5 times)

Candice Bergen (5 times)

Eric Idle (5 times)

Bill Murray (5 times)

Michael Palin (5 times)

Past *SNL* Cast Members

Who Have Hosted the Show

With so many *SNL* alums making it big in their own movies and TV series, many have been asked back (some several times) to host the show. As of April 2007, here's who's returned to the show that, for many, launched their careers.

Dan Aykroyd

Dana Carvey
(hosted three times)

Chevy Chase
(he's returned the most—7 times —including once with his "Three Amigos!" costars Steve Martin and Martin Short)

Billy Crystal
(hosted twice before joining the cast)

Robert Downey Jr.

Chris Farley

Will Ferrell

Phil Hartman
(hosted twice)

Julia Louis-Dreyfus

Jon Lovitz

Norm Macdonald

Michael McKean
(joined the cast after hosting)

Eddie Murphy
(hosted twice, once while still a cast member)

Bill Murray
(hosted five times)

Mike Myers

Don Novello

Chris Rock

Paul Shaffer

Molly Shannon

Martin Short
(hosted twice, including once with his "Three Amigos!" costars Chevy Chase and Steve Martin)

David Spade
(hosted twice)

Ben Stiller

Damon Wayans

Saturday Night Live's

Funniest "Commercials"

Commercial parodies are the backbone of every *SNL* episode. Below are some of the best.

Bad Idea Jeans: A parody of Levi's Dockers ads featuring the company's logo interspersed between scenes of people discussing "bad ideas," such as "Now that I have kids, I feel a lot better having a gun in the house."

Bathroom Monkey: Janeane Garofalo endorses a disposable primate that will keep your bathroom "monkey clean" and "monkey fresh."

Buh-Weet Sings: Eddie Murphy, playing an adult version of the Buckwheat character from *Our Gang*, sells a compilation of his renditions of "Fee Tines a Mady," "Una Panoonah Banka" and "Wookin' Pa Nub."

Canis—Cologne for Dogs: A send-up of a Calvin Klein fragrance commercial that features a golden retriever leaping into the arms of a shirtless, muscled man and seductively licking his face.

Cheapkids.net: Chris Parnell advertises a Web site that sells discounted items like "semi-flame retardant pajamas" and "pre-owned pacifiers" to parents who would rather spend their money on themselves. Its slogan: "When it comes to your children, why pay more?"

Cluckin' Chicken: Phil Hartman asks a KFC-like restaurant's animated mascot why Cluckin' Chicken is "so chick-alicious." Clucky then cheerfully describes how he's decapitated, plucked and gutted, chopped up and flame-broiled, before declaring that "being dead never tasted so good!"

Colon Blow: A take-off on the Total ads, Phil Hartman is told he would need 30,000 bowls of his favorite cereal to equal the fiber in just one bowl of Colon Blow. (Warning: May cause abdominal distention.)

Compulsion: A send-up of the Obsession cologne ads finds Jan Hooks as a compulsive housewife who was "Consumed. Obsessed. Never able to enjoy her own party." "The world's most indulgent disinfectant" was manufactured by Calvin Kleen.

Cracklin' Oat Flakes (Now with Ecstasy): When Will Ferrell discovers he's out of his normal cereal, his wife offers him Cracklin' Oat Flakes (Now with Ecstasy). What follows is a montage set to techno music of Ferrell at work making out with a board member at a meeting, then running half-naked down the street and finally curled up in bed with a pacifier in his mouth.

Dillon/Edwards Investments: A conservative financial company announces they have decided that the Internet is here to stay and finally registered for a Web site—however, the only address left unclaimed was "clownpenis.fart."

Excedrin RT: Queen Latifah plays a businesswoman who takes this medicine, which is specially designed to relieve headaches caused by questions about the stereotypical behavior of black people. "Excedrin for racial tension headaches. Fast relief for hundreds of years of nagging pain."

First Citiwide Change Bank: In a parody of late-'80s talking-head style bank commercials, a bank advertises that it specializes in making change—and delineates every possible combination of coins you could get for a dollar.

Gaystrogen: A parody of commercials for the Estroven hormone drug that warns potential customers, "If you're over 45 and a gay man, you could be suffering from queer loss."

Handi-Off: Victoria Principal, plagued by excess fingers, tries a topical treatment that contains "leprosin" and promises that "in just three days, unsightly fingers disappear—for good!" (Also available: "Toe-riffic!")

Happy Fun Ball: This commercial for a seemingly innocuous toy features a number of dire warnings, including: "Caution: Happy Fun Ball may suddenly accelerate to dangerous speeds" and "Do not taunt Happy Fun Ball."

Homocil: Will Ferrell is the parent of a flamboyantly gay boy who tries a new drug to help him deal with "parental anxiety." "Because it's your problem, not theirs."

Huggies Thong: A dig at parents who are overly concerned with their toddlers' fashions, in the shape of useless, leaky diapers shaped like thongs.

Jewess Jeans: In a parody of Jordache jeans commercials, Gilda Radner models new pants that you don't have to be Jewish to wear, "but it wouldn't hurt."

Jogger Motel: As a runner enters a tunnel, he realizes he's stuck in a gooey trap, which contains the remains of others who had been ensnared. "Joggers jog in, but they don't jog out."

K-Put Price-Is-Rite Stamp Gun: The price of groceries have you down? Order one of these pricing guns, and voila! A watermelon for 3 cents! A 12-pound turkey for 4 cents! You decide which food and goods you buy at rock-bottom prices. (Void where prohibited by law.)

Little Chocolate Donuts: In a parody of Wheaties' late-'70s Bruce Jenner commercials, John Belushi plays an Olympian who attributes his success to "the donuts of champions," proclaiming, "They taste good, and they've got the sugar I need to get me going in the morning. That's why Little Chocolate Donuts have been on my training table since I was a kid."

The Love Toilet: Victoria Jackson and Kevin Nealon "share the most intimate moment of all" in a commercial for a toilet with two seats placed side-by-side that's "imported from France, the nation of love." "Because when you're in love, even five minutes apart can seem like an eternity."

Mom Jeans: This fake JC Penney commercial proclaims that your mom will "love the 9-inch zipper and casual front pleats" on these pants, and suggests that this Mother's Day, you "give her something that says, 'I'm not a woman anymore—I'm a mom.'"

New Shimmer: Gilda Radner and Dan Aykroyd play a couple arguing over whether New Shimmer is a floor wax or a dessert topping, before announcer Chevy Chase steps in and tells them, "New Shimmer is both a floor wax *and* a dessert topping!"

Only Bangkok: A three-part parody of Las Vegas's "What Happens in Vegas Stays in Vegas" campaign. First, a businessman (Seth Meyers) needs help removing a dead Thai hooker from his room. Then, Ben Affleck sells his wife (Amy Poehler) to burly mob members after losing a bet during a Russian Roulette match. Finally, that same businessman needs to remove another dead prostitute—this time a male.

Oops! I Crapped My Pants: In this spoof of adult diapers Depends, which features repeated uses of the title phrase, a woman asks an elderly man, "Now how do you know so much about Oops I Crapped My Pants?" to which he replies with a smirk, "I'm wearing them, and I just did."

Puppy Uppers/Doggie Downers: When Gilda Radner complains to Laraine Newman that her dog Sparky has no energy, her friend recommends Puppy Uppers. Then, when Radner worries that "Sparky's perked up a little too much," Newman suggests she try giving him Doggie Downers.

Quarry: A spoof of ads for healthful breakfast cereals finds Jane Curtin serving Dan Aykroyd this cereal made of rocks that claims to be "Better tastin', 'cause it's mined."

Royal Deluxe II: In this '70s car-commercial parody, Dan Aykroyd demonstrates the smoothness of the car's ride by having a rabbi perform a circumcision in the backseat, while driving 40 mph on a bumpy road.

Rubik's Grenade: A Rubik's Cube takeoff featuring the tag line, "May be the last puzzle you'll never solve...Just in time for Christmas!"

Schmitt's Gay: In this parody of beer commercials and their bevvies of beautiful women, Chris Farley and Adam Sandler play gay house sitters whose pool is suddenly filled with muscled men in Speedos. As Farley notes while he and Sandler oil up the pool guys: "I think I'm gonna like house sitting." Sandler: "Uh, yeah!"

Speed: Cleveland housewife and mother Ellen Sherman is a nuclear physicist, commissioner of consumer affairs, crafter, reader, sculptor, equestrian, volunteer, baker and legal aide. How does she do it all? She's smart. She takes Speed! Why not ask your family doctor for a prescription today? And when that runs out, you can ask your neighbor's doctor. And your mother's doctor. And your college roommate's doctor...

Super Bass-O-Matic '76: In this take-off of '70s commercials by kitchen device-maker Ronco, spokesman Dan Aykroyd proclaims that "the days of troublesome scaling, cutting and gutting are over." He proceeds to puree a bass whole, which is then drunk by a smiling Laraine Newman.

Swiffer Sleepers: Amy Poehler suits her kids up in sleepers attached to the end of dust sticks, then proceeds to let them clean her house in this parody of Swiffer mops. However, the announcer sternly reminds us that Swiffer Sleepers are "not recommended for children with allergies.".

Swill: Bill Murray plays a traveling salesman hocking putrid mineral water dredged from the bottom of Lake Erie, which the announcer proclaims has "everything you've always wanted in a mineral water. And more."

Taco Town: A play on Taco Bell's over–stuffed burritos advertises a new taco wrapped in several layers of shells, a crepe, a Chicago-style deep-dish pizza and a blueberry pancake—before being battered and then deep-fried. "It's 15 great tastes, all rolled into one."

That's Not Yogurt: A parody of "I Can't Believe It's Not Butter" commercials, featuring Victoria Jackson and Kevin Nealon as a couple who wonder what the mysterious product they've just eaten is. The coy announcer refuses to tell them anything more, except that it's "from the makers of Those Aren't Olives."

Tressant Suprème: In a parody of her own hair-coloring commercials—and her peppy personality—Kelly Ripa deadpans that she prefers Tressant Suprème because it contains "just a little bit of crack cocaine."

Turlington's Lower Back Tattoo Removal: A roll-on remover for middle-aged women who want to remove the tattoo that they thought was so cool when they were younger. During a time-lapse expansion of a woman's mid-section, her "Pretty Lady" tattoo changes to read "Pretty Sad."

Woomba: A spoof of the Roomba vacuum system that features a self-operating, robotic feminine hygiene device that knows when women should use it...whether they want to or not.

Best Adam Sandler Moments

Over the last two decades, Sandler has slowly transitioned from comically moronic clown to goofily charming leading man, creating a number of memorable and hilarious characters along the way. Here's a look back at some of the *Saturday Night Live* veteran's career highlights:

Television Debut

A 21-year-old Sandler makes his first TV appearance in a 1987 episode of *The Cosby Show*, playing Theo Huxtable's dopey friend Smitty, a role he reprised in several subsequent episodes.

Saturday Night Live

On comedian Dennis Miller's recommendation, in 1990, Lorne Michaels hires Sandler as a writer for *Saturday Night Live*, beginning his association with the show that would help make him a star. After one season, Sandler is made a featured player and, in 1993, becomes a full-fledged cast member.

Opera Man and Cajun Man

Sandler creates two popular characters who become recurring "guests" on *SNL*'s "Weekend Update" segment: Opera Man, who wears a cape while singing about current events in a bad Italian accent, and Cajun Man, a Louisiana "country boy" whose one-to-three-word statements always rhyme.

Canteen Boy

Sandler creates the recurring character of Canteen Boy, a 27-year-old assistant Scout Master who always appears in uniform and with a canteen around his neck. The character was at the center of controversy when host Alec Baldwin, playing a Scout Master, attempted to seduce Canteen Boy with lines like, "My beard is scratchy, Canteen Boy, but it gives good back rubs."

"The Denise Show"

Sandler debuts the character of Brian, who hosts a cable-access series called "The Denise Show," where he reminisces about the ex-girlfriend who dumped him, and frequently bursts into tears while singing about her. Every episode features "the part of the show where I call Denise and lose my courage to speak, and then I talk to the dial tone."

"The Chanukah Song"

In 1994, Sandler releases his double-platinum debut album, *What the Hell Happened to Me?* It features "The Chanukah Song," which becomes a perennial holiday favorite on rock radio stations thanks to lines like "Paul Newman's half-Jewish, Goldie Hawn is, too. Put them together, what a fine lookin' Jew!" and even spawns two "sequel" songs.

The Bob Barker Battle

Sandler is beat up by *Price Is Right* host Bob Barker in the 1996 golf-as-hockey comedy "Happy Gilmore," in a hilarious scene that features the comedian's oft-quoted taunt of "The price is wrong, b*tch!"

"The Wedding Singer"

Sandler reveals a soft side in the title role of this 1998 romantic comedy, sweetly wooing waitress Drew Barrymore to an '80s-pop soundtrack and winning many new fans outside of his frat-boy base.

$100 Million Club

Playing a mentally challenged Louisiana man asked to join a football team in 1998's "The Waterboy," Sandler notches the first of several films to gross more than $100 million at the U.S. box office.

Golden Globe Nomination

In 2002, Sandler makes his dramatic debut opposite Emily Watson in Paul Thomas Anderson's twisted romantic comedy *Punch-Drunk Love*. Revealing surprising depth, he earns critical respect and a Golden Globe nomination for Best Actor for his performance as love-struck plunger salesman Barry Egan.

TEN THINGS

The Amazing Race

1 **There are *four* people per team, not two.** Each pair is trailed by its own cameraman and sound technician—and the teams have to stay within 20 feet of their crew at all times. "The simple rule I give the team is, 'Act like the crew are your kids,'" says creator Bertram van Munster. "You can't run away from the children." Not even when you go to the bathroom.

2 **Teams are given credit cards to book their flights.** There's no price limit, but teams must fly economy class. (And they have to make sure there are seats for their crew, too.) They're not allowed to buy out the whole plane or buy tickets on multiple flights. "We're trying to avoid people buying $250,000 worth of tickets [as teams did one day in Season 2] because they want to cover their butts in every direction known to mankind," Van Munster explains.

3 **Extra clothing is occasionally provided.** Teams generally must be prepared for all climates; however, in extreme conditions, the producers will provide such items as snowshoes and parkas. (Contestants' measurements are taken before the race begins.) "We don't want them to have to carry that extreme gear all around the world," says host Phil Keoghan.

4 **Cash for each leg of the race is always provided in U.S. dollars.** Whether in Italy or Mumbai, Keoghan says, "everybody takes greenbacks." Still, if teams ever run out of cash, they can tap their crew for a $200 emergency fund. "But it's like a Fast Forward," warns Van Munster. "You can only use it one time."

5 **The challenges are a lot safer than they look.** The security of each challenge, from bungee jumping to rappelling, is double- and triple-checked by experts. "[Safety] has to be 100 percent nailed down," Keoghan says. "We've got to know that when [the teams] leap off the bridge—and even when they eat the cheese—they're not going to choke."

6   **Medical help is always around the corner.** If someone gets hurt, there are doctors on call. "In every hick town, we know exactly where the doctor lives and how quickly he can get to us," van Munster says.

7   **Certain countries are off the map in a post-September 11 world.** "We tell teams, 'You cannot connect through Baghdad when you go from A to B,'" Keoghan says. "Because if they had a choice, who knows if they wouldn't?" Afghanistan and Sierra Leone are also off-limits. Counterterrorism expert Bob Parr, a 25-year veteran of Britain's Special Air Service regimen (the U.K. version of Delta Force), is in charge of security. He's the one who decides if teams can sleep safely outside or if they need bodyguards in more dangerous areas.

8   **Teams get exclusive access to some of those tourist attractions.** Past locations that *Amazing Race* producers have rented out include the northeast leg of the Eiffel Tower and the garden surrounding the Taj Mahal. "One reason," Van Munster recalls, "we made arrangements at the Christ the Redeemer statue in Rio de Janeiro was so we could put a cameraman inside the head of Christ!"

9   **Phil Keoghan wears MAC cosmetics.** The 36-year-old host applies his own makeup—including face powder and bronzer—to get himself camera-ready. "I have my own little kit, and I'm not always that great at putting it on," he says. "If I look really bad, it's because I'm doing it myself."

10   **Strangers on the street order Keoghan to eliminate them...**or, as the show's enthusiasts like to say, *Philiminate*. From New York City to Singapore, fans ask him to announce: "You're the last team to arrive. I'm sorry to tell you, you've been eliminated from the race." And he'd better get it right. "If I don't do it with a serious face," Keoghan says, "they direct me to do it again." Even stranger: "None of them has asked me to say they've won. Not one person."

TEN THINGS

NCIS

1 **Flash Power:** *NCIS*'s signature visual element is a black-and-white video image that brackets each act, accompanied by a noise that sounds like flashbulbs exploding. "It's called the phoof," explains Pauley Perrette (Abby Sciuto). "The *P* is silent."

2 **Good Girl Gone Goth:** Perrette herself buys the jewelry and clothes for the black-clad Abby, who sports chains, tattoos and skirts hoisted perilously high. "People always say to me, 'I love Abby'," Perrette says. "And I go, 'So do I. I'm with ya.' "

3 **A Cote Above:** Cote de Pablo (Ziva David) has a slit on her left earlobe, a scar from a childhood injury caused by an earring getting caught on a pillowcase. "People always used to cover it up," she says, "but I figured, why not incorporate it into Ziva's character?"

4 **Michael the Mimic:** Michael Weatherly does a fall-on-the-floor-funny impersonation of what he describes as *CSI: Miami* star David Caruso's Kabuki-like delivery. "He puts his hands on his hips and won't look at you until the last line. He'll say, 'There's a crime and a victim, but,' then he pauses to look up, 'there's never a victimless crime.' "

5 **Fans Gone Wild:** Married man Sean Murray (Timothy McGee) once Googled himself and discovered "McGee Gone Wild," a Yahoo! group for gays and bisexuals devoted to his *NCIS* character.

6 **The Real Gibbs:** Mark Harmon based aspects of Leroy Jethro Gibbs on David Lytle, a real-life NCIS agent. This will come as news to many other NCIS agents who are convinced they were the inspiration. Lytle was a former partner of on-set tech adviser Leon Carroll Jr.

7 **Train Man:** David McCallum (Dr. "Ducky" Mallard) has hung framed photographs of a power steam locomotive called The Mallard over his character's autopsy room desk. "I've always been a huge railway buff," McCallum says. He found the vintage photos of the train, which once held the land speed record, on eBay.

8 **Video Star:** Lauren Holly's young sons refer to her home collection of *NCIS* tapes as "Mommy's work videos."

9 **Gag Reflex:** Weatherly says he bases Anthony DiNozzo on "a lot of people I know from my generation. He can't help this Tourette's thing he has with jokes and pop culture."

10 **U.N.C.L.E. Bucks:** McCallum, who starred in *The Man From U.N.C.L.E.*, owns a lunchbox of the classic show and once paid $110 for an Illya Kuryakin doll for his wife, Katherine. "She's the only woman I know who has the action-figure version of her husband."

TEN THINGS
YOU DIDN'T KNOW ABOUT
The Sopranos

1 **The guns are rubber.** Objects used for beatings—handguns, golf clubs, xylophones—have one thing in common: They're all rubber. The second and third most popular substances on *The* - set are spaghetti sauce and stage blood. "I have three or four varieties," says prop master Diana Burton. "For oozing, coagulating or dried."

2 **The analyst gets analyzed.** Dr. Melfi's couch-side manner has been critiqued by many of her real-life counterparts. Her authenticity has been both praised ("She does a good job and is an excellent role model"—the *British Medical Journal*) and trashed ("Melfi's aggressively non-judgmental treatment of Tony has been an utter failure"—online libertarian magazine *Brainwash*). Although her brutally honest rejection of Tony's advances seemed harsh, Glen O. Gabbard, M.D., author of *The Psychology of the Sopranos*, gives it two thumbs up. "Tony's a potential stalker," Gabbard says. "You have to set limits."

3 **Does this stuff happen in real life?** Many of the show's plotlines are based on true events. Creator David Chase got the "Class of 2004" concept when he read a report about five New York crime bosses who were all simultaneously serving time. And Uncle Junior's faked senility during his trial for racketeering was inspired by crime boss Vincent "The Chin" Gigante, who tried the stunt (unsuccessfully) in the 1990s.

4 **Clothes make the character.** As boss, Tony has to remain a cut above the rest. He'll wear a loud shirt when he wants to be one of the guys. But when respect is needed, he reverts to a look that costume designer Julie Polcsa calls "dressed-up casual." He'd never wear a running suit outside the house, like Paulie, or a tacky suit to the Bada Bing, like Silvio. And Tony in the designer jeans favored by Christopher? Not a chance. Tony's not about showing off. "People have preconceived notions about gangsters," Polcsa says. "The reality isn't as flashy."

5 **Frank Sinatra's mug shot is real.** When producer Terence Winter found the poster in the fall of 2003, he knew it belonged in the Bada Bing. Sinatra was arrested in 1938 and charged with seduction, reportedly for bedding a woman "under the promise of marriage." The charge was later dropped.

6 **Carmela went soft.** In 2004, facing a life without Tony, Carmela finally sacrificed that stuck-in-the-'80s mob-wife hair "so she [could] feel sexier," said hairstylist Anthony Veader. "There's still fullness, but she's got a softer look." Her clothes loosened up, too—more jeans, fewer suits—and her makeup went more natural.

7 **Lookin' out the back door.** The view from the kitchen is actually a photograph: The real backyard was shot with a high-resolution camera and the image was blown up into a giant transparency. Although the exterior is a real home in North Caldwell, New Jersey, most indoor scenes are shot on a set in Long Island City. The interiors mirror those in the actual home, right down to the furniture and lack of clutter. "There wasn't a lot of junk around," says coexecutive producer Ilene Landress. "We had a directive from David to copy that."

8 **In real life, Steve Buscemi is one of the good guys.** A firefighter in Manhattan's Little Italy neighborhood from 1980 to 1984, he returned to the work temporarily as a volunteer at Ground Zero in the days following September 11 and has been involved as an advocate and fund-raiser ever since.

9 **New Jersey really has wandering bears.** Since bear hunting was banned from 1971 to 2003, the Garden State bear population skyrocketed from about 100 to 1400, says Bradley J. Campbell of the New Jersey Department of Environmental Protection. Tony's vigilante approach to controlling the problem is not advised, but Carmela's strategy—waving her arms and banging frying pans—is the correct one.

10 **The Sopranos drive American iron.** Tony drives a Cadillac Escalade. "It benefits his stature as boss," says prop master Burton. Paulie Walnuts is old school with a Cadillac Eldorado ETC, and Christopher tries for cool with a Hummer. But in a show of superiority over his New Jersey colleagues, New York boss Johnny Sack goes with a Mercedes.

FIVE THINGS

YOU DIDN'T KNOW ABOUT

Homicide: Life on the Street

1 **Julianna Margulies and Gloria Reuben** appeared on *Homicide* before they joined *ER*: Margulies as a waitress/cellist/girlfriend of former regular Ned Beatty, Reuben as a sex-crimes detective. "We have an agreement with *ER*: We discover them, they use them," said *Homicide* executive producer Henry Bromell.

2 **During their lunch break,** Andre Braugher and Richard Belzer often played chess together.

3 **At the time, *Homicide* was the only prime-time drama** shot entirely with handheld cameras, which created its distinctive look.

4 **The bar/restaurant owned on the show** by three detectives was actually the Waterfront Hotel Restaurant, which had seen business increase 20% since being on *Homicide*.

5 **Gary D'Addario,** who's appeared on several episodes as QRT Lieutenant Jasper, was an active Baltimore police captain who served as the show's technical consultant.

FIVE THINGS

Law & Order

1 **That really was Jerry Orbach** shooting pool in one episode. Orbach bragged about his talent, so producers had it written into the scene.

2 **Once, the location manager was scouting a river** for a scene where a body was supposed to wash up and found police standing over a real body that had done just that.

3 **Prominent people** who have asked to appear on the show include New York City Police Commissioner William Bratton, New York State Attorney General Dennis Vacco, lawyer Melvin Belli and talk-show host Sally Jessy Raphael.

4 **When Russian judges** wanted to learn about the U.S. judicial system, the State Department showed them half a dozen episodes of *Law & Order*.

5 **During the 1995-96 season,** more than a dozen real police officers played cops on the show.

SEVEN THINGS

YOU DIDN'T KNOW ABOUT

Batman

From comic books to cartoon series to an acclaimed big-screen franchise, Batman is big than ever. To celebrate the Dark Knight's omnipresence, we've uncovered a belfryful of secrets from his long, colorful history.

1 **2000+ covers:** The Dark Knight first appeared in "Detective Comics" No. 27 in 1939 (current value: $350,000). Since then, Batman has appeared on well over 2000 comic covers. His first TV GUIDE cover: March 26, 1966, with TV's original Batman, Adam West.

2 **"Gotham City is New York on steroids!":** That's how "Batman Begins" production designer Nathan Crowley imagined Batman's hometown. The franchise reboot's Gotham is four times bigger than New York and also includes elements of Tokyo and the Kowloon City slums of Hong Kong. But the location of Wayne Manor and the Batcave was inspired by the suburban Palisades of New Jersey, right across the river from Manhattan.

3 **Batman's link to reality TV:** *The Real World: San Francisco*'s Judd Winick has become a star in comicdom, thanks to a well-received run writing the "Batman" title, as well as his acclaimed work on DC Comics' "Green Arrow" and "Green Lantern." He even stuck a bat-reference into the first episode of the Cartoon Network series *The Life & Times of Juniper Lee*.

4 **The Caped Crusader gets frisky:** Bruce Wayne maintains a public image as a playboy primarily as a façade to protect his secret identity. But he is a man, after all, and he has his needs. In recent years, the comic book's story lines have found Batman flirting with his Justice League teammate Wonder Woman and getting up close and very personal with Catwoman.

5 **Famous voices revealed:** Among the actors who've lent their voices to Warner Bros. Animation's various Batman series are Mark Hamill, who went from Jedi to Joker on *Batman: The Animated Series* in the 1990s, and Tom Kenny, the voice of

Sponge-Bob Square Pants, who has quacked wise as the Penguin on the recent TV incarnation, *The Batman*. Also on *The Batman* was Frank Gorshin, the Riddler in the '60s live-action series, playing Arkham Asylum chief of psychiatry Hugo Strange in three episodes created prior to his May 2005 death. And Batman veteran West has been known to lend his voice to the mayor of Gotham City. "It gives me a certain political stature," jokes the erstwhile Caped Crusader.

6 **Batman pimps his ride:** The latest Batmobile, a 340-horsepower cross between a Humvee and a Lamborghini, was created by "Batman Begins" production designer Nathan Crowley and his team. "Batman has to drive a car that's tough enough for Gotham," Crowley says. The 2.5-ton vehicle can hit speeds of 100 miles per hour and jump from four to six feet off the ground for a distance of up to 60 feet. (Eight models were built for various sequences.) The vehicle is initially painted in Desert Storm camouflage in the film, which gives Christian Bale's Bruce Wayne a rare opportunity to crack wise, asking Lucius Fox (Morgan Freeman): "Does it come in black?"

7 **Batman's *Lost* connection found:** *Lost* writer and story editor Paul Dini—one of the architects of *Batman: The Animated Series* and *Batman Beyond*—hasn't snuck any bat-references into the ABC hit yet, but a comic book featuring the Caped Crusader's Super Friends, Green Lantern and the Flash, appeared in one episode in the hands of Walt: "It was a weird moment of DC Comics synergy," Dini says. But, "Batman is very special to me, so I kind of leave him alone. If it's a goof on Batman, I'd rather not do it."

EIGHT THINGS

Big Brother

1 **It takes a lot of big brothers (and sisters) to produce the show.** More than 200 production crew members, to be exact. Because much of the juicy stuff (strategizing, bedroom romps) takes place in the wee hours, they have on-site showers and beds, plus 24-hour food service.

2 **Even when nature calls, the camera is rolling.** But shy houseguests can rest assured: The monitor for the toilet room is in a discreet area of the control room. "We use it for safety and also for when people have discussions in there," says executive producer Allison Grodner. "We have no interest in watching people use the facilities."

3 **The houseguests get paid.** Though the winner earns $500,000 and the runner-up $50,000, all evictees get about $750 for each week spent in the house and for any sequestered time.

4 **The truth about the "X-Factor" is out there.** How did producers track down those ex-boyfriends and ex-girlfriends? Applicants were required to supply contact information for former mates under the pretense that producers would call them to verify information. What we don't know is how producers kept them from blabbing that they were approached to be on the show, too.

5 **Outside contact is strictly policed.** The house is protected by two layers of security—one at the entrance to the studio and another outside the Big Brother compound. Somehow, producers even monitor the airspace: When privately hired airplanes dragging strategy-revealing banners head for the house, contestants are promptly sent into lockdown.

6 **All applicants must undergo psychiatric and medical evaluations, plus tests for STDs.** Still, a few folks slip through the net, like Season 2's knife-wielding Justin and Season 3's Scott, who had a meltdown after being reunited with his disinterested ex-girlfriend Amanda, and later confessed to having genital warts. "The houseguests are in there for up to three months," Grodner says. "It takes a lot of psychological, physical and emotional stamina. Absolutely everyone has their bad days. You never know what's about to happen."

7 **The Internet feeds really are uncensored.** To preserve the action for TV, the live Web coverage is blocked during competitions and nomination ceremonies. But nudity? You'll see it—and then some. When David and Amanda hooked up—American *Big Brother*'s first couple to go all the way—online fans saw the whole dance. The feeds never go into the diary room or the loo however, and Grodner insists, "We don't look for people undressing." Yeah, right.

8 **Those weeklong PB&J diets aren't totally monotonous.** Three kinds of peanut butter are available: creamy, chunky and reduced-fat. Unfortunately, there's only one kind of jelly—grape.

FIVE THINGS

NYPD Blue

 1 **Detective Simone's badge number,** 3118, is the same one worn by the show's coproducer and technical adviser, Bill Clark, a former Queens homicide detective. Detective Russell's badge number, 4136, is that of Clark's former partner, Karen, now his wife.

 2 **The photos of police brass** on the squad-room walls were those of present-day New York City personnel. They were changed about a half-dozen times to keep them current.

 3 **Kim Delaney and Jimmy Smits met** while working on the 1992 TV-movie "The Broken Cord." She also had a 1987 stint as an associate on *L.A. Law*, but most of her scenes were with Corbin Bernsen.

4 **Set designers recently whipped up** a replica of the New York City precinct house that's used for exterior shots on the Twentieth Century Fox lot in L.A.

5 **Kim Delaney kept her private chocolate stash** in the top right-hand drawer of Detective Russell's desk.

American Idol:

From No-Name to Fame

To all of the *American Idol* hopefuls showcased during each season's tryouts, take heart: Even future studs and starlets get the thumbs-down now and then.

Both Season 1 champ **Kelly Clarkson** and second runner-up **Nikki McKibbin** failed to make the cut previously on WB's *Popstars*.

After Diddy ixnayed her for the second edition of MTV's *Making the Band*, **Vonzell Solomon** worked it like a pro by making it all the way to third place in Season 4.

Before she was Fantasia's main competition, Season 3's **Diana DeGarmo** was shown the door on *America's Most Talented Kid* on NBC.

Fans' favorite rocker of 2006, **Chris Daughtry**, didn't feel the love when he auditioned for CBS's *Rock Star: INXS*.

A look at the various locations each *Survivor* install-ment has visited gives some insight into what the castaways must deal with to "outwit, outlast and outplay" their opponents.

Season 1: Borneo

Mild temperatures allowed Season 1 winner Richard Hatch to roam in the buff.

Season 2: Australia

The Australian Outback presented unpleasantries like deadly snakes, torrential rain and chef Keith Famie's rice recipes.

Season 3: Africa

Heat, dehydration and malnutrition faced the gang in Kenya.

Season 4: Marquesas

Biting mosquito-like bugs called "no-nos" were a major pain.

Season 5: Thailand

It was monsoon season!

Season 6: The Amazon

A battle between the sexes ensued in the middle of a tropical rainforest.

Seasons 7, 8 and 12: Pearl Islands

The group of islands off the coast of Panama has a historical connection to pirates, some-thing fan fave Rupert Boneham really got into. So did producers, who used the locale for Season 8, *All-Stars*...and again for Season 12 *Panama: Exile Island*.

Season 9: Vanuatu

Contestants participated in tribal customs and ceremonies.

Season 10: Palau

Beautiful, crystal-clear water gave rise to many water-based challenges.

Season 11: Guatemala

The competition took place among the ruins of Maya civilization.

Season 13: Cook Islands

The location of the famous mutiny on the HMS Bounty inspired this edition's big twist.

Season 14: Fiji

Conditions were hot, rainy and snake-infested.

The Osbourne's

20 Craziest Moments

* The Osbournes' neighbors irritate them by playing loud music late at night. After Sharon's peacemaking attempt is ignored, the family goes on the offensive. Sharon throws bagels and a ham over the fence dividing their properties, resulting in a visit from the police, and Ozzy throws a log through the neighbors' window.

* Ozzy films a "Moulin Rouge"-style promotional video for his album, *Down to Earth*, committing to the part in full costume, including a wig, bustier and stockings.

* After Sharon shows Ozzy the special effects planned for his winter tour (including a sleigh that shoots snow and a bubble machine), the singer angrily protests, "Bubbles? I'm the Prince of f—-ing Darkness, Sharon!"

* Christmas dinner conversation centers on Sharon's hatred for Christina Aguilera's holiday album and the gravy Ozzy continually reminds everyone that he made himself. Discussion further devolves after Jack gives Kelly the finger, and the siblings shout profane insults at one another until Kelly storms out.

* Later on Christmas, Jack receives a pocket knife from one of his friends. But when he tries twice to leave the house with it, Ozzy confiscates it and hides it in a bowl of fruit. In the next episode, Jack is seen stalking around the property wearing Army gear and carrying a rifle.

* Ozzy and Sharon attend the White House Correspondents' Dinner. During his speech, President Bush says, "What a fantastic audience we have tonight: Washington power brokers, celebrities, Hollywood stars, Ozzy Osbourne," prompting an excited Ozzy to stand up and offer a salute.

* A few months after the first-season premiere, Sharon is diagnosed with colorectal cancer, but insists that filming continue. Ozzy doesn't handle the situation well, though, and falls back into his old hard-drinking ways.

* Hoping to cheer Sharon up, Ozzy seeks advice from the fire department on building a fire outside their rented Malibu beach house. However, he digs the pit too close to the water, so the fire keeps going out. Ozzy later wades into the ocean, trying—unsuccessfully—to catch a fish with his bare hands.

* Ozzy is excited to receive a star on the Hollywood Walk of Fame and is praised by the mayor during his induction.

* Ozzy is shown working out to VH-1 classic videos by Tina Turner ("What's Love Got to Do With It?") and Bette Midler ("Wind Beneath My Wings").

* While in New York working on her debut album, *Shut Up*, Kelly meets Sean Combs at a party. After one of Combs' security guards accidentally knocks Kelly down, Combs apologizes by presenting her with a diamond-encrusted watch. This leads Sharon to ponder what life would be like as the mother-in-law of P. Diddy.

* When Sharon and Ozzy decide to renew their wedding vows, he promises not to get drunk at the reception like he did the first time. However, he once again drinks too much and passes out on a couch, leaving Sharon to lament being cheated out of another wedding night.

* The Osbournes take Jack to a medieval-theme restaurant for his birthday, giving him a suit of armor and a sword, which he uses to duel in the street with one of his friends.

* Annoyed by neighbors who play tennis on their private court late into the night, the Osbourne family declares war on them: Ozzy blasts heavy metal and Jack shoots his paintball gun into the tennis court, leading to a visit from the police. Sharon later suspects the neighbors are responsible for the disappearance of three of the family's cats, but is unable to prove the allegation.

* While fulfilling the lifelong dream of taking Jack on a father-son fishing trip, Ozzy and his son are chastised by the charter boat's captain for throwing firecrackers at pelicans.

* Jack becomes concerned about his increasingly violent attacks on the family's pets while sleepwalking. This climaxes with a horror-struck Jack waking up with the dead body of Sharon's beloved dog Minnie and fleeing the house with it—before the director yells "cut" and explains that the entire episode was scripted.

* After Ozzy loses a diamond pinkie ring worth more than $100,000, he forbids Sharon from buying any more expensive jewelry. Instead, she buys his-and-hers Bentleys.

* While riding an ATV on the Osbournes' English estate, Ozzy is nearly killed during a bad accident in which he suffers a broken neck vertebra, collarbone and ribs. He spends three weeks in the hospital recovering.

* When Kelly begins to act strangely, Ozzy and Jack suspect she is on drugs, but Sharon won't believe it. However, Kelly eventually admits to her mother that she is using drugs and agrees to enter rehab.

* In the series' final episode, therapist Dr. Phil McGraw pays a visit to the Osbourne home—in spite of Jack and Kelly's objections—to talk about the issues the family has dealt with and help them repair their fractured relationships.

Survivor's Top Five Alliances

How choosing the right co-conspirator can make one lucky castaway a millionaire.

Rob and Amber—*Survivor: All-Stars*

Victor: Amber (*and* Rob)

Why it worked: Lust. Rob fell for Amber, who rode his coattails.

Speed bump: Rob begging Lex to keep Amber in the game (a move that ultimately cost Rob the win).

Memorable moment: Rob's early observation that Amber has "a smokin' ass."

Jeff Probst's take: "[Their alliance] was strategy. Then they fell in love, and that affected Rob's game. He beat his chest and said, 'I'm runnin' this game with my girl tucked under my arm, and anybody who thinks they're big enough to stop me, bring it.' The only person big enough to stop him was himself."

Richard and Rudy—*Survivor: Borneo*

Victor: Richard

Why it worked: Opposites attract. The gay corporate trainer wisely cozied up to the former Navy SEAL as soon as he recognized that Rudy's word was strong as oak.

Speed bump: Richard's proclivity for getting nekkid; his being so confident in the alliance that, during the final immunity challenge, he stepped down off the pole, leaving Rudy to tough it out.

Memorable moment: Rudy slathering sunscreen on Richard's back.

Probst's take: "The most enjoyable alliance, not just because it was the first but because it [proved] that anybody is a possible partner. It's 'in this situation, who best works for me or with me?'"

Colby and Tina—*Survivor: The Australian Outback*

Victor: Tina

Why it worked: Colby had the strength to win immunity, and Tina had the brains to play up to his mama's boy tendencies.

Speed bump: What speed bump? These two had each other's backs the whole way.

Memorable moment: Colby's decision to honor the alliance and take Tina to the final two instead of Keith, even though it meant he'd likely lose.

Probst's take: "They were strategic. They both picked a person they knew they could count on and [who] was strong enough to make it to the end. People say Colby lost. I don't know. Colby not taking the easy win is the only honorable decision so far in *Survivor*."

4 | Jenna and Heidi—*Survivor: The Amazon*

Victor: Jenna
Why it worked: They considered themselves hot. How could they not bond?
Speed bump: Jenna's whining when she was sick; Heidi's torch getting snuffed before reaching the final four.
Memorable moment: Their infamous decision to strip down to nothing in exchange for some peanut butter.
Probst's take: "Jenna and Heidi are a good example of making the best of what they had out there. I don't know if those two sought each other out as much as then ended up with each other. [But] it worked for them."

5 | Tom and Ian—*Survivor: Palau*

Victor: Tom.
Why it worked: Mutual respect. The 41-year-old firefighter and 23-year-old dolphin trainer clicked even before being picked for the Koror tribe. Both boasted a strong work ethic, brains and strength.
Speed bump: When Ian caught a clam, Tom upstaged him by slaying a shark.
Memorable moment: After catching snakes, the dynamic duo used the reptile blood to lure nearby sharks.
Probst's take: "The bond between Ian and Tim [was] in a father-son way. But Ian [was] not gonna simply listen to Tom because he's older. Ian's got his own mind, and he [fought] to stay on top."

The Amazing Race's

10 Most Memorable Moments

Gutsiest performance:
Little person Charla racing with a 55-pound hunk of meat on her back in Season 5. "She was the smallest person with the biggest heart," says *Race* host Phil Keoghan. "If you look at that, everybody was saying she couldn't do it, and she's probably heard that all her life. But she knew she could do that challenge and she did."

Dumbest mistake:
Four of eight teams putting regular gas into their diesel cars in Portugal in Season 3. By ignoring *all* the signs calling for diesel, the teams proved Keoghan's point that racers "stop thinking about basic things when they rush."

Most disgusting meal:
The live octopus entrée in South Korea during Season 4. As the main course wiggled, contestants had to swallow it. Keoghan reminded the teams that "for the locals, it's a delicacy. It's no different than us loving a hamburger." Except that hamburgers don't walk off your plate.

Oddest mode of transportation:
The bubble-like "zorbs" in Season 5, which teams used to travel down a hill in New Zealand. "I did the guinea pig test of them," says Keoghan. "It was the closest thing to what you imagine floating on a cloud would feel like."

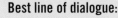

Best line of dialogue:
Kevin yelling, "Swing, you fat bastard, swing!" to Drew as his Season 1 teammate hung on a zip line over a gorge near Victoria Falls. "Watching him hang seemed so funny to me," says Kevin. "People still yell that phrase to us. It's become a term of endearment."

Most dramatic sacrifice:
Joyce getting her head shaved in India in Season 7. "As the hair came off, an internal transformation happened," she says. "I felt liberated. Later we learned that when a woman shaves her head, it's good karma. Maybe that was the key to our success." They won the race.

Most frustrating challenge:

Searching for a clue in a giant bale of hay in a Swedish field during Season 6. The challenge was too much for sisters Lena and Kristy, who struggled so long to find a clue that Keoghan had to come to the hay field to eliminate them. "If Phil hadn't shown up, we might still be out there," Lena says.

Sneakiest maneuver:

Rob taking the four-hour penalty to avoid eating four pounds of icy-looking meat in Season 7. By convincing two other teams to join him, he saved his stomach *and* his place in the race. Recalls Keoghan: "What I loved is he used [his brain] to manipulate the situation."

Saddest moment:

Watching the faces of *Race*'s youngest competitors, like Carissa, 9, when their families were eliminated during the Family Edition. "You're telling a kid he's lost, and he thinks he's not good enough," says Keoghan.

Best Side Trip:

Danny and Oswald going on a Hong Kong shopping spree during Season 2. Even though the other teams stressed about getting to the airport, these friends followed their strategy of asking a travel agency to book their flight, leaving them with enough time to shop for cologne.

1 — Victim: Justin Timberlake

The setup: The pop star arrives home to find his windows boarded up, his belongings on the front lawn, his cars on a flatbed truck, and men claiming to be federal agents seizing his possessions in lieu of an alleged unpaid $9,000,000 tax bill.

Priceless moment: When Justin tearfully calls his mother: "Mom, you gotta get up here, right now!"

Best quote: Justin to the fake feds: "You took my dogs?"

2 — Victim: Beyoncé

The setup: The singer agrees to put the star on top of a Christmas tree at a party for underprivileged children. When she does, the tree topples over, crushing all of the gifts.

Priceless moment: When the event organizer defends Beyoncé to the kids: "She didn't ruin Christmas. She just wrecked it a lot, that's all."

Best quote: Children to Beyoncé: "You broke our presents! You ruined our Christmas!"

3 — Victim: Lara Flynn Boyle

The setup: The actress is invited to a designer's showroom to pick out clothes, which she is led to believe are free. After grabbing 14 shopping bags' worth of goodies, Laura is told she owes $26,000.

Priceless moment: When Laura explains that the clothes are supposed to be freebies for premieres "as long as I said where I got them and so forth," the manager snorts: "Is that what you typically do? That's bizarre."

Best quote: "I cannot afford this! My mother will have a fit! I am in so much trouble."

4 — Victim: Katie Holmes

The setup: Upon arriving at a producer's house for a meeting, Katie briefly meets his departing girlfriend. Moments later, the producer's fiancée arrives, demanding to know if another woman has been in the house.

Priceless moment: After repeatedly lying to the fiancée that she did not see another woman with the producer, Katie swears that she always tells the truth.

Best quote: Katie to the fiancée: "I don't want to be involved in this. I just want to get out of here!"

5 — Victim: Frankie Muniz

The setup: A restaurant valet tells the *Malcolm in the Middle* star that he mistakenly gave Frankie's $250,000 1956 Porsche Speedster to a stranger.

Priceless moment: Frankie calls his cell phone, which is in the car, and when the pretend thief says he's going to sell the car for $100,000 so he and his girlfriend can vacation in Hawaii, Frankie promises them first-class, all expenses-paid trip if they bring the car back.

Best quote: Frankie to valet: "Dude, I'm so @#$%& mad right now!"

Victim: Halle Berry

The setup: Because of overcapacity, the actress is barred from entering the theater where her own movie, "Gothica," is premiering.

Priceless moment: After arguing that her entry will endanger no one because her seat is empty, Halle is shamed into silence by the fire marshal: "After 9/11, I'm a hero. And suddenly, I'm not a hero."

Best quote: "But how can they not let me in? It's my own thing!"

Victim: Jessica Biel

The setup: A father and his 10-year-old son approach Jessica Biel at a restaurant; the dad leaves to get his camera from his car. While he's gone, the child makes crude come-ons to the actress ("You're rip. You should get a little racy on *7th Heaven*—show more skin."). But when dad returns, the son accuses Jessica of being inappropriate toward him.

Priceless moment: The restaurant manager informs Jessica that the dad is going to press charges against her for saying "profane things" to his child.

Best quote: The dad to Jessica: "My son is petrified! I wanna know what happened right now." Jessica to the Dad: "Why would I curse at your son, sir?"

Victim: Missy Elliott

The setup: A jeweler tells Missy that the diamond-encrusted cross and dog tags she left to be cleaned were mistakenly given to a messenger.

Priceless moment: When the rapper clambers atop the glass jewelry case and threatens to break it unless her jewelry is returned "in five seconds."

Best quote: "I'm a big girl; once I jump up on this glass, it ain't gonna be nothing nice because I'm too big to be standing on glass."

Victim: Jennifer Love Hewitt

The setup: *The Ghost Whisperer* star meets with a producer to discuss a role in a film starring Brad Pitt. During the meeting, he confides that he just lost an "obscene" amount of money gambling on the Super Bowl, and some thugs arrive to collect the debt.

Priceless moment: When the producer excuses himself to reason with the thugs, a panicked Jennifer calls her assistant and demands help "immediately. Immediately. I can't even tell you why. Please, I am not kidding around."

Best quote: Jennifer to thugs: "Excuse me, can I step out, please?"

Victim: Nick Lachey

The setup: A bunch of hillbillies arrive at the singer's mansion in a trailer, claiming to be distant relatives of his then-wife Jessica Simpson. When Nick tells them they can't stay, they demand $5000 to leave.

Priceless moment: The look on Nick's face when one of Jessica's "cousins" asks: "Dad is this the Backstreet Boy?"

Best quote: Nick to Jessica: "I'm gonna have to fight this guy because of some white-trash, macho, Texas BS."

The Votes Are In:

Reality Stars

Reality Stars: You love them. You hate Omarosa. At least according to a poll we conducted on 2005 with Bravo, home of *Battle of the Network Reality Stars.*

Who is the most hated reality star of all time?
Omarosa (*The Apprentice*) 50%
Richard Hatch (*Survivor: Borneo*) 23%
Puck (*The Real World: San Francisco*) 19%
Wendy Pepper (*Project Runway*) 8%

Who is the most loved reality star of all time?
Clay Aiken (*American Idol 2*) 35%
Kelly Clarkson (*American Idol*) 34%
Rupert Boneham (*Survivor: Pearl Islands*) 22%
Adam Mesh (*Average Joe*) 8%

Which reality star couple would you entrust to raise your child?
Jessica Simpson and Nick Lachey (*Newlyweds*) 54%
Sharon and Ozzy Osbourne (*The Osbournes*) 26%
Whitney Houston and Bobby Brown (*Being Bobby Brown*) 10%
Britney Spears and Kevin Federline (*Britney & Kevin: Chaotic*) 10%

Which reality star would be your first dodgeball target?
Richard Hatch (*Survivor: Borneo*) 42%
Heidi Bressler (*The Apprentice*) 32%
Will Kirby (*Big Brother 2*) 14%
Wendy Pepper (*Project Runway*) 13%

Which reality star would you most like to see in a Speedo?
Evan Marriott (*Joe Millionaire*) 35%
Burton Roberts (*Survivor: Pearl Islands*) 27%
Mike "the Miz" Mizanin (*The Real World: Back to New York*) 24%
Will Wikle (*Big Brother 5*) 14%

Which reality star deserves his or her own TV series?

William Hung (*American Idol 3*) 31%
Jay McCarroll (*Project Runway*) 27%
Richard Hatch (*Survivor: Borneo*) 23%
Omarosa Manigault-Stallworth (*The Apprentice*) 19%

Which reality show would you like to be a contestant on?

The Amazing Race 31%
The Apprentice 29%
Survivor 23%
The Bachelor/The Bachelorette 17%

10 Most Memorable Dance Moments

1 **Elaine's Little Kicks,** *Seinfeld* (October 10, 1996)

Gettin' jiggy: The spastic, thumbs out and feet-flyin' dance by Elaine Benes (Julia Louis-Dreyfus) to Earth, Wind, and Fire's "Shining Star" at the J. Peterman party—described by George (Jason Alexander) as "a full-body dry heave set to music"—made her coworkers lose all respect for her.
Footnote: She gave a repeat performance the next season while listening to her bedside radio.

2 **Elvis the Pelvis,** *The Ed Sullivan Show* (January 6, 1957)

Gettin' jiggy: Though controversy over his hip swivelin' during earlier appearances led Sullivan to decree that, in this guest spot, the King only be shot from the waist up, viewers knew when Elvis was shakin' his groove thang by the studio audience's screams.
Footnote: Elvis's third and final appearance prompted Sullivan to proclaim Elvis a "real decent, fine boy."

3 **Peanuts Do the Bop,** *A Charlie Brown Christmas* (December 9, 1965)

Gettin' jiggy: In the first Charlie Brown special, the gang bebopped to Vince Guaraldi's classic score and ignored school-play director C.B., who tried to organize them for a Nativity scene.
Footnote: In 2004, 700,000 Web surfers saw the gang shake it like a Polaroid picture in an unauthorized "Hey Ya, Charlie Brown" video set to OutKast's hit song.

4 **The Huxtables' Anniversary Dance,** *The Cosby Show* (October 10, 1985)

Gettin' jiggy: To celebrate Cliff's parents' 49th anniversary, the family danced down the staircase and lip-synched to Ray Charles' "Night Time Is the Right Time" complete with Rudy's rambunctious "Bay-Bay!"
Footnote: They performed to James Brown's "I Got the Feeling" the following season.

5 **The Silver Platters,** *The Brady Bunch* (January 26, 1973)

Gettin' jiggy: The kids got their swerve on and entered an amateur talent show as the Silver Platters in hopes of winning enough cash to pay for their parent's anniversary gift: an engraved silver platter.

Footnote: The Silver Platters' hits—"Keep On" and "It's a Sunshine Day"—were released on a pop album in 1972.

The Moonwalk, *Motown 25: Yesterday, Today, Forever* (May 16, 1983)

Gettin' jiggy: Some 50 million viewers watched Michael Jackson slap on a fedora and, while singing his No. 1 hit "Bille Jean," fluidly slide across the stage backwards in the first public performance of his trademark moonwalk.
Footnote: Michael created the routine just the night before the special, and it propelled *Thriller* to $22 million in sales.

The Urkel, *Family Matters* (February 8, 1991)

Gettin' jiggy: Lovable geek Urkel (Jaleel White) tried to win over his cool classmates when he performed his trademark toe-tapper at a party. Some sample lyrics:
Now point your fingers up to the sky
And talk through your nose way up high
Spin and dip and jump and cavort
And finish it off with a laugh and snort.
Footnote: White also performed The Urkel on the sitcom *Step by Step* in 1991.

The Bartman, *The Simpsons* (December 6, 1990)

Gettin' jiggy: Bratty Bart was the star of a post-episode music video, which found him trying to ruin his school's recital by urging his schoolmates to:
Move your body if you got the notion
Front to back in a rock-like motion
Now thatcha got it if you think you can
Do it to the music, that's the Bartman
Footnote: The video was followed by a *Bartman* comic-book series.

Jack gets 'N Sync, *Will & Grace* (October 11, 2001)

Gettin' jiggy: Jack (Sean Hayes) was supposed to help his son, Elliot (Michael Angarano), get the attention of a pretty girl at his junior-high dance, but when the DJ played 'N Sync's "Pop," Jack pushed Elliot aside (literally!) and re-created the dance routine from the boy band's video.
Footnote: 'N Sync's Justin Timberlake was on the producers' wish list of guest stars to play Jack's boyfriend, though it never happened.

Goldie a Go-go, *Rowan & Martin's Laugh-In* (January 22, 1968)

Gettin' jiggy: Goldie Hawn, who performed on the variety show for two seasons, sported a bikini and gags scrawled all over her body as one of the go-go dancers in the "Mod, Mod World" segments of *Laugh-In*.
Footnote: When Goldie was given a few lines, she giggled and flubbed them—becoming a breakout star of the show.

The Rematch: Dancing With the Stars: Dance Off (September 22, 2005)

When underdogs Kelly Monaco and Alec Mazo edged out favored couple John O'Hurley and Charlotte Jorgensen in the Season 1 finale, a rematch was called. Although the judges offered their critiques, this time viewers' votes determined the winner. O'Hurley and Jorgensen came out on top—but only by one percent of the vote.

Will & Grace

The *Will & Grace* soundtrack CD features "Living With Grace," a song Eric McCormack cowrote with Barry Manilow.

NYPD Blue

Episodes

"True Confessions" (October 12, 1993)

Before David Schwimmer became a household name on *Friends*, he left his mark on this dynamic series in an episode named by TV GUIDE among the 100 Greatest Episodes of All Time. He plays nebbishy lawyer Josh Goldstein, a neighbor of Det. John Kelly's estranged wife. When Goldstein, whom Kelly calls 4B (his apartment number), is mugged, he becomes obsessed with revenge, with tragic consequences. Although Kelly (David Caruso) tries to get him to give up his gun, 4B doesn't listen and, in a shoot-out with a mugger, gets blown away. We, too, were blown away by the emotional finality of losing a character with whom we had empathized so deeply.

"Death in the Family" (May 7, 1996)

This wrenching episode involving the fatal shooting of Sipowicz's son Andy Jr. (Michael DeLuise) showcases some of the finest work of four-time Emmy winner Dennis Franz. The Sipowicz family tragedy comes after a high point—the birth of baby Theo. However, the celebration of the newborn stands in counterpoint to the stunning news of Andy Jr.'s murder. Franz carries off the role of grieving father and hard-nosed detective in an unforgettable tour de force. The show also marks the departure of Gail O'Grady as Donna Abandando, whose swan song is muted by the homicide that stops everything cold at the 15th Precinct.

"Hearts and Souls" (November 24, 1998)

Fifteen million *Blue* fans tuned in to bid farewell to Jimmy Smits' Bobby Simone.The episode shot the show to no. 2 in the ratings for the week, as the cool but caring Simone died of a heart condition after four seasons. "He came into a very fragile situation," said series creator Steven Bochco of Smits, who joined the squad after David Caruso's 1994 exit. And he left a hero. Simone's swan song is one of TV's most affecting depictions of death's impact on a person's loved ones, underscored by emotional turns from costars Dennis Franz and Kim Delaney.

A Dozen *Six Feet Under* Episodes

We Can't Live Without

1   "The Foot"
Season 1, Episode 3 (June 17, 2001)

Ah, the woes of high school. Claire gets called a toe-sucker and puts a dismembered foot in a boy's locker for revenge. Keith comes to the rescue to help her out of the mess and cops to being her brother's boyfriend. Her mother turns her grief into a day at the races and her brothers fight off pressure from a funeral-home corporation.

2   "Back to the Garden"
Season 2, Episode 7 (April 4, 2002)

Claire visits her bohemian aunt and finds a crush-worthy boy amid the unusual arty types. After some sexy fantasies, Keith rekindles his romance with David. And Federico, who's been freaking out that his wife's cheating on him with his cousin, is shocked to learn that his macho cousin is gay.

3   "A Private Life"
Season 1, Episode 12 (August 19, 2001)

A tragic hate crime inspires David to come out to Ruth. A dangerous Billy taunts Nate with pictures of him kissing Claire and later attempts to remove Brenda's tattoo with a knife.

4   "The Trip"
Season 1, Episode 11 (August 12, 2001)

Brenda, Nate and David travel to Las Vegas for a funeral-directors conference where bad behavior abounds. An increasingly psychotic Billy stalks Brenda while David winds up being arrested for soliciting a male prostitute. Back home, the body of a baby haunts Federico.

5   "In the Game"
Season 2, Episode 1 (March 3, 2002)

Nate is diagnosed with a brain defect and David is told he has gonorrhea. Ruth has a dinner party for her kids and their companions, but all goes awry when Nate accidentally takes Ecstasy.

6   "It's the Most Wonderful Time of the Year"
Season 2, Episode 8 (April 21, 2002)

Holiday havoc ensues when Billy's mom frees him from the mental institution. A wounded Nikolai relies on Ruth's care. Nate tells Brenda he's sick, and the family faces the one-year anniversary of Nate Sr.'s death.

7   "Tears, Bones and Desire"
Season 3, Episode 8 (April 20, 2003)

Ruth makes a move on oddball intern Arthur and sparks fly. Keith pits his tough pals against David's chorus buddies in a raucous paintball game. Sarge, a super-buff pot smoker, solicits a threesome with Keith and David. Lisa, concerned about her faltering marriage to Nate, poses as a massage client to see Brenda for the first time. Claire feels her relationship with Russell threatened by art teacher Olivier, especially when Billy confesses that Olivier sometimes likes to have a "boy year" with his male students.

8 "A Coat of White Primer"
Season 5, Episode 1 (June 6, 2005)
Brenda suffers a miscarriage, but she and Nate go ahead with their wedding ceremony. George returns home from the hospital where he's undergone electroshock treatment, and an emotionally strained Ruth slaps Claire for taking an unflattering photograph of George. Claire and Billy move in together.

9 "Ecotone"
Season 5, Episode 9 (July 31, 2005)
Just as Maggie and Nate are locked in an intimate moment, Nate has a seizure and is rushed to the hospital. Claire leans on new love interest Ted for emotional support. Nate wakes from his coma and tells Brenda they should give up on their marriage. He and David have a shared dream that has them at the beach with their father, a dream that ends in David waking up to find Nate dead.

10 "Everyone's Waiting"
Series Finale: Season 5, Episode 12 (August 21, 2005)
Brenda's baby daughter is born prematurely. Claire leaves town for a new life in New York. Frederico buys his own funeral home. The deaths of Ruth, David, Claire, Frederico, Keith and Brenda are shown at the episode's end.

11 "Falling Into Place"
Season 4, Episode 1 (June 13, 2004)
Nate picks up Lisa's body at the morgue and clashes with her family over her burial; he then absconds with Lisa's body and buries it in the desert himself. Claire reveals to an emotional Russell that she had an abortion.

12 "That's My Dog"
Season 4, Episode 5 (July 18, 2004)
While Keith is away on business, David has an alarming encounter with a hitchhiker, who takes him on a brutal night of torment.

Reasons
We Love *Grey's Anatomy*

This sexy medical drama gives us a healthy dose of hot docs, strong women and real relationships.

It's comfortable. Every great television show seems simultaneously fresh and as if it's been on the air forever. From the minute it debuted in March 2005, *Grey's Anatomy* was that kind of success. The five sexy surgical interns—Meredith, Christina, Izzie, Alex and George—felt like they could've been our old high-school friends, and their professional and highly personal adventures at the fictional Seattle Grace Hospital were addictive.

The women rule. Now that 60 percent of medical students have two X chromosomes, the time couldn't be better for a medical drama from the female point of view. It's wonderful to watch competent women engaged in the daily struggle to balance work and life, ambition and affection. Best of all, series creator Shonda Rhimes empowers women without bashing men. Her women want it all. Her show delivers it.

Anything goes. Rhimes effortlessly captures the unpredictable quality of life for career-driven, twentysomething brainiacs. The tone can swing from gross (the removal of a gargantuan tumor) to absurd (a rapist's severed penis goes missing) to mundane (George refuses to buy tampons for his female roommates) to tragic (people die) to romantic (the pillow talk is terrific), often inside 15 minutes. But it never veers from real emotion.

The sex is sexy. *Grey's Anatomy*—you've got to love the title's double meaning—captures the tension of gorgeous singles thrown together in a compelling, intense environment. So when the sparks fly, they feel genuine (who wouldn't fall prey to an adrenaline-charged, post-op, supply-closet tryst?). The soap-opera revelations are perfectly timed (Mrs. Dr. McDreamy?!). And no one can make a line sound as dirty as Sandra Oh's Dr. Cristina Yang. Example: After Cristina's lover Preston won a confrontation with Meredith's lover Derek, Oh nailed the killer retort, "Mine's bigger than yours." Three more factors that ratchet up the lust quotient: Patrick Dempsey, Patrick Dempsey, Patrick Dempsey.

5 **They seem smart enough to be doctors.** An intern who paid for medical school by modeling underwear sounds like a men's magazine fantasy, but Izzie (Katherine Heigl) has just the right amount of world-weariness to pull it off. She and her fellow docs all radiate the quality that whiz kids have, of being the smartest person in any room. So when they get together, their chatter is a pleasure to listen to, as they one-up, vie with, boss around and confide in one another. These junior masters of the universe could be in any high-octane profession (lawyers, bond traders), but their being doctors adds an extra life-and-death charge. They're playing God, they know it—and they like it. We do, too.

Grey's Anatomy

Rob Lowe was originally considered for the role of Derek Shepherd, aka Dr. McDreamy, on *Grey's Anatomy*.

TV's All Time Hottest Doctors

In 2005, TV GUIDE listed the healers who got our hearts racing; they're smart, sexy and, of course, have a great bedside manner.

Dr. Derek Shepherd (Patrick Dempsey), *Grey's Anatomy*

Why our pulses raced: The sexy, flirtatious physician with piercing blue eyes is known as "Dr. McDreamy."
Bedside manner: The first time we meet him he's waking from a night of passion with Dr. Meredith Grey (Ellen Pompeo).
Healing powers: He treats a victim of a brutal attack with tender loving care.

Dr. Gonzo Gates (Gregory Harrison), *Trapper John, M.D.*

Why our pulses raced: A Gifted surgeon who lived in a motor home on hospital grounds, he was the hunk with a heart of gold. He was young, irreverent and rebellious.
Bedside manner: Took a leave from the hospital to care for a rich young woman with a rare medical condition. Luckily, she could still put the moves on him.
Healing powers: Fond of taking on the Establishment, he had a building torn down because it was a health hazard.

Dr. Phillip Chandler (Denzel Washington), *St. Elsewhere*

Why our pulses raced: A dedicated doctor who was a loner and went on to become chief resident. We dreamed about him making house calls.
Bedside manner: Dr. Roxanne Turner (Alfre Woodard) enjoyed his prescription for love.
Healing powers: He worked for free at a clinic for troubled women.

Dr. Jack Shepard (Matthew Fox), *Lost*

Why our pulses raced: Heroic spine specialist is the passionate physician whom survivors turn to on the island.
Bedside manner: Kate (Evangeline Lilly) is seduced by his compassion for the wounded.
Healing powers: He transfused his own blood in a vain attempt to save Boone and made his bride walk again.

Dr. Drake Ramoray (Joey Tribbiani), *Days of Our Lives* (Matt LeBlanc on *Friends*)

Why our pulses raced: He was a suave, sweet-talking neurosurgeon who fell down an elevator shaft. Later came out of a coma and received a brain transplant (from a female).
Bedside manner: Dated gorgeous soap fan Erika Ford (played by Brooke Shields), a stalker who thought Joey really was Dr. Drake.
Healing powers: None, really, because as Chandler once pointed out, "he's not real."

Dr. Doug Ross (George Clooney), *ER*

Why our pulses raced: Caring pediatrician was a stud with a stethoscope—and who can resist a bad boy?
Bedside manner: Doug has as many conquests on-screen as George has had off-screen.
Healing powers: Rescued a boy trapped in a storm drain, and rode off into the sunset with head nurse Carol Hathaway (Julianna Margulies).

Dr. Luka Kovak (Goran Visnjic), *ER*

Why our pulses raced: Having lost his family, he's vulnerable. Plus, he's eye candy in a lab coat, with a sexy accent to boot.
Bedside manner: Enjoys playing doctor with the nurses.
Healing powers: Cares for the sick in war-torn Congo.

Dr. Ben Casey (Vince Edwards), *Ben Casey*

Why our pulses raced: Though he was gruff and bullying—to both patients and colleagues—'60s women swooned over his dark hair, good looks and, believe it or not, his large hairy arms.
Bedside manner: He fell in love with a woman who emerged from a coma after 13 years.
Healing powers: A top-notch neurosurgeon, he was the go-to guy for brain tumors.

Dr. Noah Drake (Rick Springfield), *General Hospital*

Why our pulses raced: Every soap fan wanted to be "Noah's girl, Noah's girl."
Bedside manner: The surgical stud had the pick of the staff, but ended up with lovely Bobbie Spencer (Jackie Zeman).
Healing powers: Having given more mouth-to-mouth to the nurses than the patients, he broke more hearts than he mended.

10   Dr. James Kildare (Richard Chamberlain), *Dr. Kildare*

Why our pulses raced: With his blond, movie-star looks and reputation as an idealistic medical crusader, this sensitive soul was practically a saint.

Bedside manner: Tripped over a cart while looking at a cute nurse's aide and hurt his back. He was girl crazy, but basically chaste.

Healing powers: Befriended patients, bonding emotionally with them and giving them advice on their problems.

Two more hot docs deserve an examination:

Dr. John 'J.D.' Dorian (Zach Braff), *Scrubs*

Why our pulses raced: Sensitive and quirky, his busy little brain is always cooking up strange fantasies around the hospital. Unfortunately, his overactive imagination often causes him relationship troubles.

Bedside manner: Equally neurotic Dr. Elliot Reed (Sarah Chalke) fell hard and got hurt, but they've managed to stay pals.

Healing powers: When a patient needed a kidney, he found the man's estranged son and reunited them.

Dr. Gregory House (Hugh Laurie), *House*

Why our pulses raced: He's crabby and unsociable, but his diagnostic genius and his rare moments of vulnerability make for a dangerous aphrodisiac.

Bedside manner: He rekindled a romance with his ex, Stacy Warner (Sela Ward), but encouraged her to return to her physically handicapped husband, claiming he wouldn't change his tormented ways.

Healing powers: He let down his guard and helped a rape victim as she dealt with her experience.

Lost

J.J. Abrams had originally intended for the character of Jack to be killed in the pilot episode and Kate to become the group's leader, but scrapped the idea.

TV's Top Female Cops

1   Det. Olivia Benson

(Mariska Hargitay), *Law & Order: Special Victims Unit*

Who she is: She's the relentless, dedicated sex-crimes detective who bonds with victims because she herself was born after her mother was raped.

What she does: Though her empathy is often a comfort to victims, it also complicates Benson's career, as in the case where she was torn about prosecuting suspects who had killed a rapist cabbie.

Behind the badge: Mariska's experience on *SVU* led her to start The Joyful Heart Foundation, a nonprofit group that aids victims of sexual assault and domestic abuse.

2   CSI Catherine Willows

(Marg Helgenberger), *CSI*

Who she is: The former stripper manages to balance being a single mom with her job as a senior crime-scene investigator, where she's an expert on blood-spatter analysis.

What she does: She's tough enough to investigate a reported rape, even though her ex-husband is the suspect, and she later learns the true identity of her father, a casino mogul and murder suspect, during another investigation.

Behind the badge: Marg was worried she wouldn't get the role in the Jerry Bruckheimer-produced series after publicly making a negative comment about his flick "Bad Boys." "Thank God he's a forgiving man!" she says.

3   Dep. Chief Brenda Leigh Johnson

(Kyra Sedgwick), *The Closer*

Who she is: Brenda is a former CIA agent who, because of her reputation as one of the leading interrogators, is hired to boost the conviction rate of the LAPD's high-profile homicide division.

What she does: Because of her own quirky neuroses, like her food obsession, Brenda is able to glean the personality quirks of her suspects, and use that information to coax confessions from them.

Behind the badge: Kyra was the show creator's first and only choice for the role.

4   Agent Samantha Spade

(Poppy Montgomery), *Without a Trace*

Who she is: A member of a crack New York City-based FBI team investigating missing-persons cases, she's guilty of a crime of the heart: having an affair with her married boss, Jack (Anthony LaPaglia).

What she does: Though frequently underestimated because of her good looks, Samantha is a smart, thoughtful investigator who's often the one to connect the dots in difficult-to-solve cases.

Behind the badge: Poppy's character is a tribute to the famous Dashiell Hammett detective Sam Spade.

5   Sgt. Suzanne "Pepper" Anderson
(Angie Dickinson), *Police Woman*

Who she is: Sexy blonde Pepper uses her good looks and a sometimes skimpy wardrobe as an undercover agent from LAPD's criminal-conspiracy unit.

What she does: After feminists' protests that the show is too sexual, producers call for fewer miniskirts and undercover gigs for Pepper, and both her coworkers and criminals learn not to underestimate how skilled she is with her gun.

Behind the badge: *Police Woman* originated as an episode of the anthology series *Police Story*.

6   Det. Lilly Rush
(Kathryn Morris), *Cold Case*

Who she is: The only female of the Philadelphia homicide squad tackles "cold cases"—older, sometimes forgotten crimes that remain unsolved.

What she does: Lilly's been-there, seen-that approach belies the fact that she recognizes the continuing impact of the unsolved crimes, like the mother who wants to see the 1960s hate-crime murder of her gay son solved before she dies.

Behind the badge: Producer Jerry Bruckheimer thought Kathryn would make a great television heroine after seeing her play Tom Cruise's wife in "Minority Report."

7   Julie Barnes
(Peggy Lipton), *The Mod Squad*

Who she is: Groovy chick Julie is the heroine (and fashion plate) of the Aaron Spelling-produced *Squad*, about a trio of late-'60s delinquent hipsters-turned-cops working undercover to bust the baddies who prey on other young people.

What she does: Poses as an actress to track down a star's killer; poses as a high-school student to bust a teen car-theft plot; and poses as a hippie to investigate a bombing at an anti-establishment newspaper.

Behind the badge: Spelling says ABC initially balked at the then-controversial interracial kiss between Julie and *Mod* man Linc (Clarence Williams III), but caved when he insisted the young viewing audience would accept it.

8   FBI Agent Nicole Scott
(Vivica A. Fox), *Missing*

Who she is: Special agent Scott is one of the FBI's most talented agents, but she constantly butts heads with her superiors and has been given one last chance to make use of her skills in the Bureau's missing-persons division.

What she does: Teamed up with psychic agent Jess (Caterina Scorsone), Nicole uses her sharp investigative skills to track down kidnapped children and a pregnant woman's stolen fetus while embarking on a new office romance with Antonio (Mark Consuelos).

Behind the badge: Vivica, who underwent real FBI training for the role, is also an executive producer on the show.

9   Lt. Anita Van Buren
(S. Epatha Merkerson), *Law & Order*

Who she is: The tough but caring working mom was a narcotics officer before joining the homicide division of the NYPD.

What she does: As the lieutenant, she's often stuck behind the desk corralling the efforts of the detectives, though she finds herself in the middle of the action in Season 5, when a teen attempts to rob her at an ATM and she shoots and kills him.

Behind the badge: Since the departure from the series of the late Jerry Orbach in 2004, Epatha is now the show's longest-running cast member (she joined *Law & Order* in 1993).

10 Off. Stacy Sheridan
(Heather Locklear), *T.J. Hooker*

Who she is: To step out of her cop father's shadow, feisty Stacy leaves a desk job to become a beat cop, partnering with elder officer Jim Corrigan (James Darren).

What she does: Her willingness to take risks means she often goes undercover or poses as a decoy to nab bad guys, but she also shows a sensitive side when she takes in a stray child and embarks on a romance with Corrigan.

Behind the badge: Heather starred as *Dynasty*'s troublemaking bad girl Sammy Jo throughout *T.J. Hooker*'s run.

Cagney & Lacey

Every year the show was on the air, the Emmy for Best Actress in a Drama Series went to one of the stars of this show: Tyne Daly won four times and Sharon Gless won twice.

Quirky Detectives

What does it take to be a TV detective? An eye for detail helps. A trench coat can't hurt. And a certain personality type is essential. Call them iconoclastic, eccentric or just downright weird, but the best TV snoops prove that although Monk might have perfected the fine art of neurosis, he certainly didn't invent it.

1 Lt. Columbo, *Columbo*, NBC (1971-77)

What six words struck terror into the hearts of high-class criminals with perfect alibis? "There's just one more thing, sir." With that refrain, Lt. Columbo (Peter Falk), who never went anywhere without his rumpled raincoat and purposely naïve nature, kept yammering and hammering his point—when he had one—until ending his cat-and-mouse games with a cockeyed grin. Falk won four Emmys for the role.

2 Adrian Monk, *Monk*, USA Network (2002-present)

Monk hopes to clean up crime, and he has just enough Handi Wipes for the job. The phobic, obsessive-compulsive detective brings new meaning to neat freak (he gets his wallet buffed and dishwashes his doorknobs). The humorous—and vastly human—portrayal of the OCD PI has earned Tony Shalhoub several Emmys.

3 Special Agent Dale Cooper, *Twin Peaks*, ABC (1990-91)

Like many TV detectives, Cooper (Kyle MacLachlan) loved damn fine coffee and cherry pie. But unlike other TV detectives, Cooper was Boy Scout exuberant, dreamed of a backward-talking dancing dwarf and trusted clues he got from a lady who carried a log. He was ideally suited for David Lynch's perverse *Twin Peaks* universe.

4 Jim Rockford, *The Rockford Files*, NBC (1974-80)

"Two hundred dollars a day, plus expenses" bought you the services of Rockford, a man who hated working, never ran without a limp (courtesy of star James Garner's four knee operations) and kept his gun in a cookie jar. He used a roster of offbeat sidekicks he'd met in the joint (before his full pardon) and always got his man.

5 **Dep. Chief Brenda Johnson,** *The Closer,* TNT (2005-present)
To handle its most delicate murder cases, the LAPD turns to Brenda Johnson (Kyra Sedgwick), an abrasively eccentric Southerner with an uncanny skill for eliciting confessions from crooks—and respect from her male colleagues. "If I liked being called a bitch to my face," she says, "I'd still be married."

6 **Det. Arthur Dietrich,** *Barney Miller,* ABC (1976-82)
The philosopher of Precinct 12 waxed sardonic on everything from logarithms to Moe, Larry and Curly. "We have the option of holding you or letting you go," Dietrich (Steve Landesberg) deadpanned to a con. "Come to think of it, we have the power of life and death over you."

7 **David Addison,** *Moonlighting,* ABC (1985-89)
Decades before *CSI*, David (Bruce Willis) and Maddie (Cybill Shepherd) perfected a different type of investigative chemistry on *Moonlighting*. As head of the Blue Moon Detective Agency, Addison preferred making out to staking out, but he won cases and hearts though snappy dialogue. He also earned a unique distinction for Willis: a drama-actor Emmy and a comedy-actor Golden Globe.

8 **Lt. Bookman,** *Seinfeld,* NBC (1991)
No doubt big-time funny boy Jerry Seinfeld thought it was some kind of joke, taking Henry Miller's "Tropic of Cancer" out of the library in high school and not returning it for 20 years. But justice never slept for Bookman (Philip Baker Hall). Writer Larry Charles based his fast-talking library detective on another (unintentionally) hilarious cop: *Dragnet*'s Joe Friday (Jack Webb). And that's just the facts.

9 **Veronica Mars,** *Veronica Mars,* UPN (2004-present)
In a profession dominated by rumpled old men with faces as wrinkled as their overcoats, Veronica (Kristen Bell) is the odd girl out. Part Buffy, part Nancy Drew, the sleuth of Neptune High is as likely to back-talk the town sheriff as the school principal. Too brainy to be popular, Veronica knows what's really important: finding out who killed your best friend—while keeping up your GPA.

10 **Det. Robert Goren,** *Law & Order: Criminal Intent,* NBC (2001-present)
A vastly intelligent Holmes-ian detective, Goren (Vincent D'Onofrio) has a gift for observing the arcane, command of several languages and more hammy tics than a bad Method actor. With the ability to shock a suspect into self-incrimination by simply shouting "Answer!" he's the unleashed master of TV crime drama's great stage: the interrogation room. We pity the perp who lands there.

Great Dramatic Guest Stars

Dennis Hopper. Sally Field. Liza Minnelli. These are some of the big names who have given stellar, unforgettable guest performances on some of our favorite dramas.

Ed Begley Jr. on *Veronica Mars*, as the affable Dean O'Dell, whose life falls apart—and ends tragically—after he learns his wife is cheating on him with a Hearst College professor.

Peter Boyle on *The X-Files*, in an Emmy-winning turn as a psychic whom Mulder believes really can predict the future.

Kate Burton on *Grey's Anatomy*, in the Emmy-nominated role of Meredith's Alzheimer's afflicted mother, a once-great surgeon who now seldom recognizes her own daughter.

Chevy Chase on *Law & Order*, as an anti-Semitic, has-been actor accused of murdering a Jewish TV producer.

Melinda Clarke on *CSI: Crime Scene Investigation*, as Lady Heather, a dominatrix caught up in a murder investigation whom Grissom is inexplicably drawn to.

James Cromwell on *24*, as Phillip Bauer, Jack's father whose warm facade hid his sinister intentions—until he killed Jack's brother and took his own grandson hostage.

Vincent D'Onofrio on *Homicide: Life on the Street*, in an Emmy-nominated turn as a man caught between a subway platform and the train, whose family the detectives race to find before he dies.

Charles S. Dutton on *Without a Trace*, in an Emmy-winning turn as a man who won't give up the search for his missing son years after the boy disappeared.

Sally Field on *ER*, in the Emmy-winning role of Maggie Wyczenski, a suicidal woman who claims to be nurse Abby Lockhart's mother.

Lance Henriksen on *The X-Files*, as Frank Black from Chris Carter's cult favorite *Millennium*, making his final appearance as the character and wrapping up that show's truncated story line.

Dennis Hopper on *24*, as the ruthless Eastern European villain Victor Drazen, who will stop at nothing to exact revenge on Jack Bauer, whom he blames for the deaths of his wife and daughter.

Jerry Lewis on *Law & Order: Special Victims Unit*, as a murder suspect who is also Det. Munch's homeless uncle.

Ray Liotta on *ER*, in an Emmy-winning turn as a dying alcoholic whose final hours are shown in real time.

Liza Minnelli on *Law & Order: Criminal Intent*, playing the unstable mother of a murdered child beauty queen.

Amanda Plummer on *Law & Order: Special Victims Unit*, in an Emmy-winning performance as a schizophrenic woman who helps the detectives catch a serial rapist.

Christina Ricci on *Grey's Anatomy*, in an Emmy-winning turn as a young paramedic who cracks under the stress of keeping her hand inside a man with a bomb in his stomach.

Doris Roberts on *Law & Order: Criminal Intent*, portraying the ailing matriarch of a feuding, wealthy family.

Martin Short on *Law & Order: Special Victims Unit*, as a psychic who butts heads with Det. Stabler when he comes forward claiming to have information on a missing girl.

George Takei on *Heroes*, as Mr. Nakamura, Hiro's disapproving business-executive father.

Forrest Whitaker on *ER*, as a carpenter who sues the arrogant Dr. Kovac after suffering a stroke while being treated for a cough.

Heroes

Cheerleader Hayden Panettiere received a Grammy nomination for Best Spoken Word Album for her work in "A Bug's Life Read-a-Long."

TV's All Time Juiciest Cliffhangers

Who Shot J.R.? *Dallas* (1981)

The Cliffhanger: When hated oil mogul J.R. Ewing (Larry Hagman) was shot, his brother Bobby (Patrick Duffy), rival Cliff (Ken Kercheval), wife Sue Ellen (Linda Gray) and sister-in-law Pam (Victoria Principal) were all suspects.

The Resolution: Sue Ellen was arrested after they found her prints on the gun. The entire cast was shown holding a pistol, but it was finally revealed that J.R.'s mistress Kristin (Mary Crosby) had pulled the trigger.

The Wrong Name, *Friends* (1998)

The Cliffhanger: While reciting his wedding vows to Emily (Helen Baxendale), Ross said Rachel's name instead. The befuddled minister asked: "Should I go on?"

The Resolution: Although she was devastated, Emily went ahead with the wedding to Ross. But she ran off shortly after the ceremony, leaving Rachel (Jennifer Aniston) to go on the honeymoon with the groom.

Missing in Action, *Alias* (2003)

The Cliffhanger: After being missing for two years, Sydney (Jennifer Garner) woke up with no memory and a stomach scar—and found out that Vaughn (Michael Vartan) had gotten married.

The Resolution: Sydney learned she'd been kidnapped, brainwashed and turned into an assassin—and that Vaughn's wife was a double agent.

Tony Moves Out, *The Sopranos* (2002)

The Cliffhanger: Carmela (Edie Falco) was happy Tony (James Gandolfini) bought a beach house—but soon was enraged when Tony's ex-lover called to taunt her about their affair. "I don't love you anymore! I don't want you!" she screamed at Tony, demanding he move out.

The Resolution: The divorce was in motion, but Tony eventually wormed his way back into Carmela's heart—and their home.

The Flesh-eating Disease, *24* (2003)

The Cliffhanger: President Palmer (Dennis Haysbert) collapsed after shaking hands with a crowd of supporters—including an assassin, who had transferred a poisonous flesh-eating disease to his hand.
The Resolution: Three years passed—and President Palmer recovered from the terrorist attack, though he was scarred.

Who Stabbed Lindsay? *The Practice* (1998)

The Cliffhanger: Lindsay (Kelli Williams) was stabbed by an unknown assailant wearing a nun's habit, managing only to say the word "nun" to husband Bobby (Dylan McDermott).
The Resolution: Although there were several suspects, weirdo Vogelman, whom Ellenor (Camryn Manheim) had previously cleared of murder charges, turned out to be the culprit.

Who's Cartman's Dad? *South Park* (1999)

The Cliffhanger: The paternity of the meanest, fattest kid on TV had fans guessing whether it was Mr. Garrison, Jimbo, Off. Barbrady, Chef or a host of others.
The Resolution: It was finally revealed that Eric Cartman's mom was a hermaphrodite, making her both his mother and his father.

Buffy's Big Sacrifice, *Buffy the Vampire Slayer* (2001)

The Cliffhanger: Buffy sacrificed her life to save her sister Dawn and the rest of the world. The final WB episode concluded with a shot of the epitaph on her tombstone.
The Resolution: With the series moving to UPN, Willow secretly performed a powerful spell at Buffy's gravesite to bring the slayer back from the dead.

Abducted by Borgs, *Star Trek: The Next Generation* (1990)

The Cliffhanger: Capt. Jean-Luc Picard (Patrick Stewart) was abducted by the Borg and brainwashed, forcing Cdr. Riker (Jonathan Frakes) to attempt a daring rescue.
The Resolution: Riker saved Earth from a Borg invasion. Enterprise captain Picard was deprogrammed and reinstated.

Massacre in Moldavia, *Dynasty* (1995)

The Cliffhanger: The wedding of Amanda Carrington (Catherine Oxenberg) and Prince Michael (Michael Praed) turned into a bloodbath during a terrorist coup in fictional Moldavia.
The Resolution: Although it was believed producers planned to wipe out half the cast, only guest star Ali MacGraw and bit player Billy Campbell bit the dust.

Bochco's Best

1 — **"Ipso this, you pissy little bitch!"** **(Pilot, September 21, 1993)**
Det. Andy Sipowicz's retort to ADA Sylvia Costas "flew our flag right off the bat," Bochco says.

2 — **Sipowicz Gets Sloshed** **(Pilot, September 21, 1993)**
"Our willingness to look at Andy's alcoholism with an unflinching eye makes in memorable."

3 — **Sipowicz Gets Soul** **("Oscar, Meyer, Wiener," December 7, 1993)**
Lt. Fancy takes Andy to a soul food joint, "giving Sipowicz insight into what it's like to be the guy who's different."

4 — **Medavoy's Eyeful** **("Abandando Abandoned," January 11, 1994)**
Nebbishy Greg Medavoy has a close encounter with bombshell Donna Abandando. "She takes off her robe, Medavoy's eyes lock on her, and he goes, 'Ub, ub, uh-boy!'"

5 — **Andy Meets Bobby** **("Simone Says," November 15, 1994)**
Jimmy Smits "had enormous impact, not only because I adored Jimmy—I'd offered him the role that David Caruso took—but because of our anxieties about whether or not people would respond to the new guy."

6 — **The Last Hug** **("Auntie Maimed," April 30, 1996)**
After second son Theo arrives, Andy tells elder son Andy Jr. he loves him. Andy Jr. is killed shortly after.

7 — **Exit Bobby** **("Hearts and Souls," November 24, 1998)**
"Bobby's death was the most gut-wrenching thing I've seen."

8 — The Last New Guy **("Lie Like a Rug," November 6, 2001)**
"I knew the moment Mark-Paul Gosselaar came in that we'd never see another partner for Sipowicz."

9 — Yep, He's Gay **("Bale Out," December 14, 2004)**
Sipowicz learns that new boss Lt. Thomas Bale is closeted. "For Andy to honor Bale's secret said more about Sipowicz to Bale than any 20 scenes."

10 — Donning the Blues **("Old Man Quiver," February 1, 2005)**
Newly promoted Sipowicz dons his sergeant's uniform. "Every cop in the precinct snaps a salute. It takes your breath away."

NYPD Blue

When *NYPD Blue* premiered in 1993, 57 ABC affiliates refused to carry the show because of its content.

David E. Kelly's
Most Memorable Lawyers

The Craziest: Denny Crane (Emmy-nominated William Shatner), *Boston Legal*

Why we love him: The preening, self-proclaimed courtroom legend actually is as good as he says.

Craziest moment: He tells a distraught, gun-toting client to shoot him so "Denny Crane" can be immortalized in legal folklore.

What William says: "Whatever forces have made him a loon, somewhere in that person, there's humanity, and that humanity commands respect."

The Skinniest: Ally McBeal (Calista Flockhart), *Ally McBeal*

Why we love her: Women can relate to many of her insecurities, neuroses and dating disasters.

Skinniest moment: Equally scrawny guest star Lara Flynn Boyle's character tells Ally she should eat a cookie, to which Ally replies: "Maybe we should share one."

What Calista says: "She's a complex, passionate person who puts herself out there and pays the price. She wears her heart out on her sleeve and cries at the drop of a hat."

The Sexiest: Nelle Porter (Portia de Rossi), *Ally McBeal*

Why we love her: Although she can be cold and aloof, Nelle's the only woman in the office to see the special charm of nerdy John Cage (Peter MacNicol).

Sexiest moment: Whenever Nelle unleashes her shiny flaxen locks—usually because she wants to manipulate a man.

What Portia says: "Nelle's quick-witted and powerful, but also feminine and vulnerable. It's typical of her to not just have hair but also give it a job to do."

The Toughest: Ellenor Frutt (Camryn Manheim), *The Practice*

Why we love her: She's a confident woman with a strong moral compass who doesn't let her weight define her.

Toughest moment: Fed up with obnoxious opposing counsel Hannah Rose (Rebecca De Mornay), scrappy Ellenor decks her.

What Camryn says: "Ellenor fights the good fight for everybody but herself. She needs to lighten up, but she's a good egg."

5 The Wittiest: Shirley Schmidt (Candice Bergen), *Boston Legal*

Why we love her: The ferocious founding partner of Crane, Poole and Schmidt is an expert at putting egomaniacs Denny Crane and Alan Shore in their place.
Wittiest moment: In reaction to Alan's flirting, she says: "Make a list of all the places you'll never visit. Add to those places 'Schmidt'."
What Candice says: "Shirley's a woman of political principles. She's tough, but like Murphy Brown, I try to humanize her. I like to make her a cuddly shark."

6 The Hunkiest: Jonathan Rollins (Blair Underwood) *L.A. Law*

Why we love him: Though he's the youngest and newest member of the firm, it doesn't stop him from being the cockiest.
Hunkiest moment: He rips off his white shirt to reveal his chiseled chest and washboard abs.
What Blair says: "Jonathan would walk over anybody to get where he wanted to be, whereas that's not my style."

7 The Dreamiest: Bobby Donnell (Dylan McDermott), *The Practice*

Why we love him: An idealistic criminal-defense attorney, Bobby always acts in his client's best interest—even if the client is a serial killer.
Dreamiest Moment: It's a dream come true for Lindsay (Kelli Williams) when she marries Bobby at the Boston Red Sox's Fenway Park.
What Dylan says: "He's me, you know. I was more like myself in that role than I've ever been, and maybe that's why people respond to him."

8 The Sleaziest: Arnie Becker (Corbin Bernsen), *L.A. Law*

Why we love him: Deep down inside, the smooth-talking, womanizing divorce lawyer's a softie with a special spot in his heart for devoted secretary Roxanne.
Sleaziest moment: Arnie gets his dream house by convincing a divorcing couple to reconcile—and then rent him the mansion they were fighting over.
What Corbin says: "Arnie's just a common guy who really wants to love and be loved but can't sacrifice his professional status enough to make that work."

9 The Vainest: Alan Shore (James Spader), *Boston Legal*

Why we love him: When Alan breaks the law it's usually in the interest of justice.
Vainest moment: He laps it up when two sexy lawyers in the office (played by Lake Bell and Rhona Mitra) fight for his love.
What James says: "He's a rascal. He's a troublemaker. He has tremendous appetites. But he values truth, even in its most destructive form."

The Wackiest: John Cage (Peter MacNicol), *Ally McBeal*

Why we love him: Cage, aka The Biscuit, has an endearing nose whistle and a touching habit of channeling Barry White when he needs sexual confidence.

Wackiest moment: He unwittingly flushes his beloved pet frog, Stefan, down the toilet with his remote-control flusher.

What Peter says: "The Biscuit is something doughy, warm, not sharply defined, but smooth and inviting."

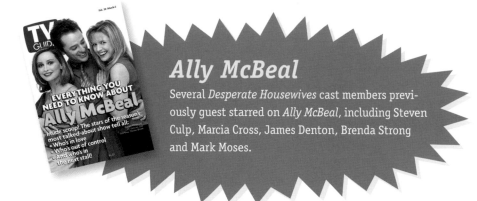

Ally McBeal

Several *Desperate Housewives* cast members previously guest starred on *Ally McBeal*, including Steven Culp, Marcia Cross, James Denton, Brenda Strong and Mark Moses.

Cosmo:
Always Thinking

He had many harebrained schemes over *Seinfeld*'s nine-year run, but these 12 concepts rank up there as Kramer's kookiest.

1
A coffee-table book about coffee tables

2
Beach-scented cologne

3
A roll-out tie dispenser

4
"The Bro" bra for men

5
Chaperoning Miss Rhode Island

6
A make-your-own-pizza place

7
Drying clothes in the oven

8
Operating his own MovieFone

9
A smoking lounge in his apartment

10
The Peterman Reality Bus Tour

11
Shaving with butter

12
A rickshaw service

Famous
Seinfeld Girlfriends

Jerry and Co. have had their share of bad relationships. Here are just a few of the famous faces who became casualties of the gang's endless pursuit of absolute perfection.

Melinda Clarke, as Jerry's girlfriend who convinces him to start shaving his hairy chest.
Episode: "The Muffin Tops"
Better Known For: *The O.C.*

Jennifer Coolidge, as Jerry's masseuse girlfriend who takes Kramer on as a client, but refuses to give Jerry a massage.
Episodes: "The Masseuse"
Better Known For: *Joey*, "American Pie," "Legally Blonde"

Kristin Davis, as Jerry's girlfriend who becomes repugnant to him after she unknowingly uses a toothbrush that fell into the toilet.
Episode: "The Pothole"
Better Known For: *Sex and the City*

Lisa Edelstein, as George's girlfriend who he believes is "faking it."
Episodes: "The Mango," "The Masseuse"
Better Known For: *House*

Janeane Garofalo, as Jerry's girlfriend and—briefly—his fiancée, who is basically a female version of himself.
Episodes: "The Invitations," "The Foundation"
Better Known For: *Saturday Night Live, The Larry Sanders Show*

Jami Gertz, as Jerry's girlfriend who "can't spare a square" for Elaine when they are in neighboring bathroom stalls.
Episodes: "The Stall"
Better Known For: *Still Standing*

Lauren Graham, as Jerry's girlfriend who uses her speed dial to rank the people in her life.
Episode: "The Millennium"
Better Known For: *Gilmore Girls*

Teri Hatcher, Jerry's girlfriend who, after being groped by Elaine, tells Jerry of her breasts, "They're real, and they're spectacular."
Episode: "The Implant"
Better Known For: *Lois & Clark, Desperate Housewives*

Jane Leeves, as Jerry's girlfriend who he is excited to discover is still a virgin.
Episode: "The Virgin"
Better Known For: *Frasier*

Lori Loughlin, as Jerry's girlfriend who—frustrated by his lack of emotion—finally gets to see his temper after she gives away his New York Knicks tickets.
Episode: "The Serenity Now"
Better Known For: *Full House, Summerland*

Marlee Matlin, in an Emmy-nominated turn as Jerry's deaf girlfriend whose lip-reading skills George uses for his own gain.
Episode: "The Lip Reader"
Better Known For: "Children of a Lesser God," *The West Wing, The L Word*

Debra Messing, as one half of a married couple Jerry and Elaine help to break up, then date.
Episode: "The Wait Out," "The Yada Yada"
Better Known For: *Will & Grace*

Justine Miceli, as a woman who dates George, sleeps with Jerry and dumps both of them.
Episode: "The Betrayal"
Better Known For: *NYPD Blue*

Christa Miller, as George's girlfriend who, he's upset to discover, has drawn an unflattering sketch of him.
Episode: "The Doodle"
Better Known For: *The Drew Carey Show, Scrubs*

Christine Taylor, as Jerry's girlfriend who everyone dislikes except for his parents, who think she's perfect.
Episode: "The Van Buren Boys"
Better Known For: "Dodgeball: A True Underdog Story," "Zoolander," *Friends*

All in the Family

Episodes

"Sammy's Visit" (February 19, 1972)

Six months before Sammy Davis Jr. hugged Richard Nixon at the Republican National Convention, he kissed America's most lovable bigot. This episode (named by TV GUIDE among the 100 Greatest Episodes of All Time) captures the feelings someone like Davis might elicit from someone like Archie: Respect and awkwardness mingle with bias. "If you were prejudiced, you'd go around thinking you're better than anyone else in the world, Archie," Sammy says. "But I can honestly say you've proven to me that you ain't better than anybody!" This dis is followed by that kiss—planted on a startled Archie.

"Edith's 50th Birthday" (October 16, 1977)

The provocative sitcom that redefined the genre further pushed the envelope in this episode, which subjects one of TV's most beloved characters—Edith Bunker—to an attack by a rapist at her home on her 50th birthday.

The episode plays out as an edgy blend of drama and suspense as Edith (Jean Stapleton) stalls for time from her would-be attacker (David Dukes), a slick felon posing as a cop. Meanwhile, her family is preparing a surprise birthday party for her next door. Director Paul Bogart won an Emmy for the episode.

"Two's a Crowd" (February 12, 1978)

Archie and "the Meathead"—one on one.

In this memorable episode, originally telecast near the end of the series' eighth season (and only a month before the Stivics, played by Rob Reiner and Sally Struthers, left the show), Archie (Carroll O'Connor) and his liberal son-in-law Mike (Reiner) find themselves accidentally locked in the storeroom of Archie's saloon. It's an ideal setup for verbal sparring, especially after both guys turn to a whiskey bottle for solace from the wintry night...and from one another. They vent hostilities in a seriocomic encounter that ultimately yields to a poignant interlude: Archie's touching reflections of his childhood and memories of his father that lead Mike to feel pity and grudging respect.

Dick Van Dyke Show

Episodes

"It May Look Like a Walnut" (February 6, 1963)

As a rule, Rob (Dick Van Dyke) is the one who keeps his head while everybody else is losing theirs all around him. But in this surreal and wonderfully nutty episode, Rob is the one who seems to be losing not just his head but both his thumbs. He stays up late one night watching a film about an alien (guest star Danny Thomas) with a fondness for walnuts and a plan for world conquest. The next day, Rob finds the living room strewn with walnuts, Laura (Mary Tyler Moore) offering him a walnut omelette and Buddy (Morey Amsterdam) eating walnuts instead of the usual pistachios. No wonder Rob thinks he's cracking up.

"That's My Boy?" (September 25, 1963)

Who could blame Rob Petrie (Dick Van Dyke) for fretting over whether he brought home the right newborn from the hospital? A bumbling nurse and a series of minor mix-ups could shake any first-time dad. But if a brief anxiety attack was all that occurred in this episode, it might not have been such a gem. But put that attack into Van Dyke's brilliant comedic hands and it's a whole other story: Rob takes his fear to hilarious extremes, summoning the parents (Greg Morris and Mimi Dillard) of the child he thinks was switched with Ritchie. Everyone has a laugh at Rob's expense, while Laura (Mary Tyler Moore) is an ocean of calm and the perfect counterpoint to her nervous husband.

"Coast to Coast Big Mouth" (September 15, 1965)

One of the entertainment world's best-kept secrets—that Rob's boss, Alan Brady (series creator Carl Reiner), wears a toupee—is revealed when Laura (Mary Tyler Moore) accidentally blabs it on a game show. "What do you think Alan will do?" asks a frantic, nervous Laura. "It's not what," replies Rob (Dick Van Dyke), "but how."

And indeed, the Emmy-winning script for "Coast-to-Coast Big Mouth" shows that hell hath no fury like an egomaniacal TV star who's had the rug pulled out from over him. What follows is a caustic meditation on male vanity and office etiquette. Not to mention one of the most precise and funny half hours of TV ever produced.

Cosby Show

Episodes

"Goodbye Mr. Fish" (September 27, 1984)

When Rudy's beloved goldfish, Lamont, dies, Cliff is worried that his youngest daughter will take the passing too hard. "Goodbye, Mr. Fish" possesses the kind of warmth and humor that made *The Cosby Show* so consistently endearing—and a long-time NBC Thursday-night ratings juggernaut. Cliff gathers the entire family for a solemn funeral in the bathroom. He has the best of intentions, of course, but Lamont's elaborate send-off is cut short by Rudy (she's bored and wants to watch TV), leaving Cliff alone to flush the fish to its eternal rest.

"Happy Anniversary" (October 10, 1985)

Cliff Huxtable's parents (Earle Hyman, Clarice Taylor) celebrate their 49th wedding anniversary in a classic episode (named by TV GUIDE among the 100 Greatest Episodes of All Time). Cliff and Clair (Bill Cosby, Phylicia Rashad) surprise them with a dinner party, after which Sondra, Denise, Theo, Vanessa and Rudy join their parents and entertain Grandma and Grandpa by lip-synching favorite tunes such as Ray Charles' "Night Time Is the Right Time." By showing the three generations together, "Happy Anniversary" helped define the series' underlying message: Strong, positive children are a parent's greatest legacy.

Taxi

Episodes

"Memories of Cab #804" (November 28 and December 5, 1978)

This two-part gem finds the drivers reminiscing about a beloved old cab that the hapless John (Randall Carver) totaled. The cast shines in a series of clever flashbacks recounting experiences in Cab #804. Danny DeVito's Louie is his gleefully obnoxious self as he matches wits with a smart-aleck rich kid (Chris Barnes) in a series of sucker bets. Marilu Henner also sparkles in a delightfully romantic vignette in which her Elaine character wistfully recounts a whirlwind relationship with a handsome art dealer (Tom Selleck). And look for Mandy Patinkin as a panicky father who leaves it to Alex (Judd Hirsch) to deliver his girlfriend's child in the backseat of 804.

"Reverend Jim: A Space Odyssey" (September 25, 1979)

"Reverend Jim" Ignatowski (Christopher Lloyd), a '60s artifact who's eaten one magic mushroom too many, is sitting at a bar. Bobby comes up and says, "Hey Jim, my friends and I were wondering if you'd like to come over and join us." Jim replies, "What did you decide?"

This classic, named by TV GUIDE among the 100 Greatest Episodes of All Time, is a rolling snowball of laughs that includes Jim's hysterical driver's test. He reads the first question and whispers to the cabbies, "What does a yellow light mean?" "Slow down!" Bobby whispers back. "OK," says Jim, "What...does...a...yellow...light...mean?"

"Guess Who's Coming for Brefnish?" (January 15, 1980)

Carol Kane made her *Taxi* debut in this episode. When Latka (Andy Kaufman) hears the sweet but volatile Simka grumbling—in the same native tongue as his own—after losing out for a job at the garage, he establishes an immediate rapport with her. Their giddy chemistry peppered with pseudo-Eastern European wordplay—added another quirky dimension to the series and an appealingly eccentric romance that endured numerous complications before they finally married. Kane's deft characterization earned her two Emmys.

Frasier

Episodes

"The Matchmaker" (October 4, 1994)

Deftly using assumptions about sexuality as grist for farce, this episode (named by TV GUIDE among the 100 Greatest Episodes of All Time) details a mixed-up first date.

Hoping to fix up Daphne, Frasier (Kelsey Grammer) invites his station manager, Tom (Eric Lutes), to dinner, unaware he's gay. During the meal, delicately used pronouns fuel Tom's misconception that he's dating Frasier, who misreads Tom's interest for an attraction to Daphne. When Frasier learns the truth, he's stunned: "All I did was ask him if he was attached, and then we talked about the theater and men's fashions...Oh, my God!"

"An Affair to Forget" (May 2, 1995)

Originally aired during the series' remarkable second season, this episode features an Emmy-winning script from Chuck Ranberg and Anne Flett-Giordano and a memorable tour de farce performance by David Hyde Pierce as Niles. The perfectly played-out plot is sparked when Frasier (Kelsey Grammer) concludes that there's some "bumsen" going on between Niles' wife, Maris, and her Bavarian fencing instructor (Brian Cousins). Factor in a dip in a sensory-deprivation tank, dialogue in three—no, make that four—languages, and Niles' climactic sword fight with the monolingual German fencer, and the result is a comedic affair to remember.

"The Two Mrs. Cranes" (September 17, 1996)

Few sitcoms have handled farce as deftly as *Frasier*, but this episode rises above the pack. It's sparked by the arrival from England of Daphne's ex-fiancé Clive Roddy (Scott Atkinson). Determined to give Clive a definitive brush-off, Daphne introduces Niles as her husband— a fantasy role Niles is all too eager to play. The ruse escalates into an uproarious charade as Frasier, Roz and Martin get in on the act, and their mountain of lies leave Clive appalled. Believing that Martin had once worked for NASA, Clive turns on Niles and Frasier with these parting words: "I'll never understand how two men like you could have been spawned by that sweet, courageous old astronaut."

4 "Merry Christmas, Mrs. Moskowitz" (December 17, 1998)

Frasier's mixed-up dating life—a year-round affair—makes for a sea-sonal situation in this holiday-themed episode.

The story begins in a department store, where Frasier (Kelsey Grammer) is bailed out of a potential gift-giving faux pas by quick-thinking fellow shopper Helen Moskowitz (Carole Shelley). The friendly exchange begets a blind date with Mrs. Moskowitz's attractive daugh-ter, Faye (Amy Brenneman), and mom couldn't be happier. After all, Frasier is an eligible, single doctor. But who knew that she also thinks he's Jewish? Well, not Frasier, until Faye tells him—on Christmas Eve.

5 "Something Borrowed, Someone Blue" (May 18, 2000)

Surprises abound on the eve of Daphne and Donny's wedding, and nat-urally spell high anxiety for Frasier.

Hors d'oeuvres and seating plans are the least of the flustered bride's worries once she resolves to confess her love to Niles (David Hyde Pierce). After Daphne confides in Frasier, he longs to bring her and his brother together at long last for a candid tête-à-tête—until Niles' shocking revelation about Mel changes everything. In the midst of all this, unexpected sparks fly between Roz and Daph's loutish brother, Simon (Anthony LaPaglia).

Frasier

Kelsey Grammer was nominated for Emmys for the same role on three different series: he played Dr. Frasier Crane on *Cheers* and *Frasier*, as well as a guest stint on *Wings*.

Honeymooners

Episodes

"TV or Not TV" (October 1, 1955)

Alice (Audrey Meadows) is dying to have a TV set. But cheapskate Ralph (Jackie Gleason) lamely claims he's holding off until 3-D TV is developed. He finally agrees to go partners with Norton (Art Carney), rigging a coin toss so the set stays in the Kramden apartment. Soon Ralph becomes a total zombie to the new medium, the very archetype of the couch potato. Named one of TV GUIDE's 100 Greatest Episodes of All Time, this was the first episode of *The Honeymooners'* one and only season. All 38 shows that followed met this brilliantly simple, hilarious standard.

"The Golfer" (October 15, 1955)

Hello, ball!

That memorable salutation—delivered by Norton (Art Carney) as he shows the proper way to "address the ball"—has made "The Golfer" a favorite in the series canon. Ralph's trying to impress his boss by offering to join him in a foursome. Problem is, Ralph's never picked up a club in his life and learning to play in two days, he concedes, won't be easy—"It'd take me at least a week." That doesn't stop him from turning his kitchen into a fairway, using a pin cushion as a ball and, unforgettably, getting into the mood by donning an outlandish golfing outfit that is, to quote Norton, "dee-vine."

"Better Living Through TV" (November 12, 1955)

In this gem, Ralph and Norton go on live TV in an attempt to sell the Handy Housewife Helper.

The inspired (and ad-lib laden) "Better Living Through TV" finds Ralph talking Norton into buying TV time so the two of them can go on the air and sell 2000 of the kitchen gadgets. The idea is for "Chef of the Future" Ralph to demonstrate to "Chef of the Past" Norton the many things the gizmo can do, such as open cans, remove corns and, of course, "core a apple." In the rehearsal, Ralph is the picture of calm, but as they prepare to go on the air, panic sets in and he warns a worrisome Ed: "Stop talking like that, nervous, you're gonna get yourself all Norton."

The Honeymooners

The four main characters of *The Flintstones* were based on the four *Honeymooners* characters.

"The $99,000 Answer" (January 28, 1956)

Ralph Kramden's get-rich-quick schemes were a *Honeymooners* staple, but the pipe dream in "The $99,000 Answer" may be the funniest.

Convinced that he'll triumph on a quiz show, popular-music expert Ralph (Jackie Gleason) intensely prepares at home, aided by piano-playing pal Norton (Art Carney), who warms up for each song with a few bars of a familiar Stephen Foster melody. Of course, the second he's on live TV, Ralph's bravado vanishes. Going into the classic Kramden meltdown—the eyes bugging, the lips quivering, the tongue stuttering "hummina-hummina"—he's asked, for his first question, to identify the composer of "Swanee River."

"On Stage" (April 28, 1956)

"Poloponies."

"On Stage" actually began, says cowriter Leonard Stern, "with that one word...and we built a whole sketch around it." And it's that single word—pronounced by Norton (Art Carney) to rhyme with monopolies—that has almost single-handedly made this a favorite among *Honeymooners* fans. The episode begins with Ralph getting a juicy part in a play being mounted by the Raccoon Lodge's Women's Auxiliary. Suddenly Ralph is strutting around like the Barrymore of Bensonhurst and entertaining dreams that a Hollywood producer in the audience will offer him a contract. But before the actual performance, there's a rehearsal with Norton—and that word—to contend with.

M*A*S*H

Episodes

"Sometimes You Hear the Bullet" (January 28, 1973)

Four months after the show premiered in September 1972, antiwar themes were provocatively addressed in the first *M*A*S*H* episode that, series cocreator Larry Gelbart wrote, "mixed laughter and tragedy" and gave the series its tone and voice.

Hawkeye (Alan Alda) is horrified when an old friend (James Callahan) arrives at the 4077th as a mortally wounded soldier. In a vain attempt to console him, Henry explains: "There are certain rules about war, and rule number one is young men die. And rule number two is...doctors can't change rule number one." In another story line, Ron Howard plays a gung-ho teen who faked his age to enlist.

"Abyssinia, Henry" (March 18, 1975)

McLean Stevenson's last appearance as the 4077th's beloved commander, Lt. Col. Henry Blake, occurred in this episode at the end of the third season. Henry's going home to his family in Illinois. After a night of wine, wontons and song, and a touching good-bye with his surrogate son, Radar (Gary Burghoff), Henry takes off on a plane...which is shot down over the Sea of Japan. When Radar stumbles into the operating theater with the news, it is a shattering moment—a measure of just how precious these characters had become to us.

"Hawkeye" (January 13, 1976)

Alan Alda gives a tour de force in this classic gem, in which a concussive Capt. Pierce delivers an episode-long soliloquy in the company of a Korean family who don't understand a word he's saying.

Driving back to the 4077th, Hawkeye swerves to avoid kids playing and flips his jeep. Waiting for help to arrive and aware that passing out could be fatal, he tries to retain consciousness by entertaining his perplexed hosts with a rambling monologue that is alternately hilarious and touching—and which earned an Emmy nomination for writers Larry Gelbart (who also directed) and Simon Muntner.

4 "The Interview" (February 24, 1976)

In this memorable episode (named by TV GUIDE among the 100 Greatest Episodes of All Time), a TV correspondent (Clete Roberts) visits the 4077th to make a documentary. Shot in black and white, the story line features staff members giving their alternately amusing, moving and painful takes on everything from the madness of war to what they miss most about home. The "film" ends with the arrival of new casualties, described by B.J. (Mike Farrell) as "healthy bodies that have been insulted by ammunition." Once again, the staff mobilizes to do the work they do best, but which they would rather not be doing at all, in a place they would rather not be.

5 "Goodbye, Farewell and Amen" (February 28, 1983)

A TV event for the ages. After 11 seasons, the beloved series came to an eventful end with this episode, which attracted the largest audience ever.

With the end of the Korean conflict imminent, the staff at the 4077th is preparing to say good-bye. But since this is war, there's no such thing as an easy ending. Hawkeye has been under psychiatric evaluation following a traumatic event; Charles is giving classical music lessons to a quartet of Chinese prisoners; Klinger finds himself falling in love with a Korean woman; and Father Mulcahy loses his hearing after an explosion.

M*A*S*H

Gary Burghoff (Radar O'Reilly) was the only cast member to star in both the movie and the TV series.

6 CLASSIC

ER

Episodes

"Going Home" (September 29, 1994)

Less than a month after it premiered on NBC, *ER* produced its first classic episode.

It's fun to watch the early work of two characters who later developed into stalwarts of the series: Nurse Carol Hathaway (future Emmy winner Julianna Margulies), who returns to work after recovering from a suicide attempt, and John Carter (Noah Wyle), then a scout-like intern who needs help diagnosing an Alzheimer's patient (Emmy-nominated guest star Rosemary Clooney). Dubbed "Madame X," Clooney's character thinks it's 1948, but she manages to teach Carter a lesson in compassion when they talk about the music of yesteryear.

"Love's Labor Lost" (March 9, 1995)

The explosive almost-too-painful-to-watch "Love's Labor Lost" (named by TV GUIDE among the 100 Greatest Episodes of All Time) is the most riveting, harrowing and visceral hour of medical drama ever aired. What seems like a routine day in the ER turns sour for Dr. Mark Greene (Anthony Edwards). Distracted by personal and professional problems, he misdiagnoses a pregnant woman and begins a downward spiral of missteps and questionable procedures that continues until all present are in over their heads, panic is thick in the air and, just as in real life, bad things happen to good people—with shocking speed.

"Hell and High Water" (November 9, 1995)

ER fans will look back on George Clooney's outstanding turn on "Hell and High Water" as one of the series' peak moments.

With his professional and personal life at an all-time low, Ross (Clooney) is asked to rescue a 12-year-old trapped in a flooded culvert. He succeeds, but the youngster emerges suffering from hypothermia. Believing the boy needs immediate intensive-care treatment, Ross makes a critical—and highly controversial—decision regarding the boy's care, one that could either salvage his career and reputation or destroy them completely.

ER

In 1984-85, starred in a sitcom titled *E/R*, which was also set in a Chicago hospital.

"The Healers" (February 22, 1996)

Paramedics Shepherd and Raul (Ron Eldard and Carlos Gomez) attempt to rescue three children from a burning apartment building on one of the series' most harrowing episodes.

The medics are the first emergency personnel to arrive on the scene, and although Raul argues that firefighters are "gonna be [there] in seconds," Shep dashes into the inferno. His partner follows in close pursuit, and they quickly realize that there's no escape.

"Gut Reaction" (April 16, 1998)

What the series does so well—blend stories about the ordinary events of life with the extraordinary ones—is exemplified by "Gut Reaction."

As Mark Greene deals with the details of an off-premises bash he's throwing for his staff, two emergent dramas unfold within the hospital. An unsure Morgenstern clashes with Benton as a colleague lays dying because of a botched surgery; and, in the stillness of an oncology isolation unit, Jeanie (Gloria Reuben) helps a young cancer patient who admires her decide if he wants to continue his debilitating treatment. Their memorable scene together still evokes tears.

"Such Sweet Sorrow" (May 11, 2000)

After six seasons as nurse Carol Hathaway, Julianna Margulies made her final appearance as a series regular in this poignant episode, which features a cameo by George Clooney.

The episode finds Hathaway reaching a crossroads in her life after she revives a "do not resuscitate" cancer patient (Rachel Singer) to allow the woman to spend a few last moments with her family. In other story lines, Greene decides to spend more time with his daughter (Yvonne Zima); and Corday assesses Malucci's performance.

Thanks for the Memories...

Bob Hope's Television Milestones

Bob Hope's brilliant career could serve as a time capsule of 20th-century humor. Hope, who died July 27, 2003, at the age of 100, conquered all forms of popular entertainment with seemingly effortless style. As tastes evolved, so did this versatile pioneer: from headlining in vaudeville and Broadway to the arenas of movies and radio, which led to the new and exciting frontier of TV. He helped popularized the medium with his NBC specials and hundreds of guest appearances. Below is a timeline of Hope's TV accomplishments.

1932: Bob Hope's earliest known TV appearance, on CBS's experimental station W2XAB in New York City.

September 26, 1949: The entertainer makes his national TV debut on Ed Sullivan's *Toast of the Town*.

April 9, 1950: *Star Spangled Revue*, a 90-minute Easter Sunday musical-comedy special, begins Hope's nearly 50-year partnership with NBC. The second show's highlight: Frank Sinatra's TV debut.

March 19, 1953: Hope hosts the first televised Academy Awards. It's one of 18 times he hosts from 1940 to 1978.

October 12, 1953: *The Bob Hope Show*, the star's first regular TV series, replaces Milton Berle's *Buick-Berle Show* one Tuesday a month for two seasons; in its third season, the variety hour alternates with Berle, Dinah Shore and Martha Raye.

January 9, 1955: Acting as an ambassador of culture for the State Department, Hope visits the Soviet Union. Upon his return, he puts together a film of Soviet performers, creating the first American special from inside the USSR.

November 29, 1962: Americans get to see filmed portions of Hope's command performance for Queen Elizabeth of England.

September 27, 1963: *Bob Hope Presents the Chrysler Theater*, a mix of dramas and musical-variety shows, begins its four-year run.

November 29, 1967: To kick off his 30th year with NIBC—he signed his first radio contract in 1938—Hope receives a two-hour tribute on *Today*.

October 14, 1975: *The Texaco Bob Hope Specials* premiere. The mix includes two-hour extravaganzas around a single topic, such as *Bob Hope's Bicentennial Star Spangled Spectacular* on July 4, 1976.

October 28, 1977: In a tribute on NBC to friend and partner Bing Crosby, who had died just two weeks before, Hope spends two hours reminiscing, showing clips from movies and TV specials.

November 22, 1978: Demonstrating that he stays current, Hope guest-stars on Steve Martin's first television special, *Steve Martin: A Wild and Crazy Guy*.

September 16, 1979: In another international milestone, Hope hosts *Bob Hope on the Road to China*, the first American special from the People's Republic of China.

February 3 and 10, 1980: NBC devotes six prime-time hours to *Bob Hope's Overseas Christmas Tours*, honoring his more than 30 years of entertaining at military bases and hospitals in the United States and abroad.

May 23, 1983: President Reagan, Lucille Ball, George Burns and a score of others join together in *Happy Birthday Bob*, a televised party at the Kennedy Center celebrating Hope's 80th.

January 15, 1984: Hope returns to the combat zone, this time in the Middle East, enlisting Brooke Shields, Ann Jillian and others to entertain the troops. The result: *Bob Hope's USO Christmas in Beirut*.

December 27, 1985: The entertainer receives a Kennedy Center Honor.

November 9, 1991: In a poll, 2000 adults say Bob Hope can pitch a product better than anyone else. At 88, he beats Bill Cosby, Pope John Paul II and Michael Jordan.

1995-96: For the first time in almost half a century, a television season goes by without a new Bob Hope Christmas special.

November 23, 1996: *Bob Hope: Laughing With the Presidents* marks Hope's TV return, his 285th and final special, and the end of his 46-year relationship with the NBC television network.

October 26, 1997: Kmart begins airing a Penny Marshall-directed commercial featuring a cameo by Hope, who reportedly earns six figures to say, "Big Kmart. Now, that's big!"

April 20, 2003: NBC airs *100 Years of Hope & Humor* in honor of the comedian's centennial.

Guest Stars
Who Made Us Giggle

Who knew that baseball's Keith Hernandez or politico Madeline Albright could make us chuckle so much? Below, check out 28 guest stars who have tickled our funny bones.

Madeline Albright on *Gilmore Girls*, as herself, in a dream had by Rory, who has always wanted to meet the former Secretary of State.

Paul Anka on *Gilmore Girls*, as himself, in a dream Lorelai has after naming her dog after the soft-rock singer.

Christina Applegate on *Friends*, in the Emmy-winning role of Rachel's spoiled, self-absorbed younger sister Amy.

Christine Baranski on *Frasier*, in an Emmy-nominated turn as Dr. Nora Fairchild, a parody of conservative talk-show host/therapist Laura Schlessinger.

Cher on *Will & Grace*, as herself, being mistaken by Jack—supposedly her biggest fan—for a male Cher impersonator.

Matt Damon on *Will & Grace*, as Jack's heterosexual rival for a spot in the Manhattan Gay Men's Chorus.

Brian Dennehy on *Just Shoot Me!*, as Dennis's surprisingly burly and masculine father, who proposes to Nina after knowing her for only a few days.

Chris Elliot on *Everybody Loves Raymond*, as Robert's highly eccentric brother-in-law, Peter, who still lives in his parents' basement.

Keith Hernandez on *Seinfeld,* as himself, being accused by Kramer of spitting on him at a Mets game where he was being heckled for errors.

Sir Derek Jacobi on *Frasier*, in an Emmy-winning turn as a Shakespearean actor Niles and Frasier idolized as children, but who, after trying to help revive his career, they discover is an untalented hack.

Christopher Lloyd on *Cheers*, as a bohemian painter who becomes obsessed with creating a portrait of Diane, much to Sam's dismay.

Kevin McDonald on *That '70s Show*, as Pastor Dave, the clueless head of the Foremans' church who is always trying—and failing—to relate to "kids today."

Brad Pitt on *Friends*, as a formerly overweight high-school pal of Ross's who still harbors a grudge against Rachel for teasing him about being fat.

Julia Roberts on *Friends*, as a girl Chandler embarrassed in grade school, and who now goes out with him only to take her humiliating revenge.

Winona Ryder on *Friends*, as a sorority sister who Rachel "experimented with" in college, and who has harbored an undying love for her ever since.

William Shatner on *3rd Rock From the Sun*, in an Emmy-nominated performance as The Big Giant Head, the Solomon family's imposing alien boss.

Ben Stiller and Mel Brooks on *Curb Your Enthusiasm*, as themselves, with Stiller playing Larry's incredulous costar in the latest Broadway version of Brooks' acclaimed musical "The Producers."

Mary Lynn Rajskub, and **Thurston Moore and Kim Gordon of Sonic Youth** on *Gilmore Girls*, as folk musicians who come to Stars Hollow seeking fame after the town troubadour (singer-songwriter Grant-Lee Phillips) lands a gig opening for Neil Young.

French Stewart on *That '70s Show*, as Kelso's arrogant opponent in a radio-station contest to win a new van.

Jay Thomas on *Murphy Brown*, in the Emmy-winning role of tabloid talk-show host Jerry Gold, who Murphy falls for despite her professional disdain for him.

Marisa Tomei on *Seinfeld*, as herself, rejecting George's advances after she finds out that he hit on her while he was engaged.

Mel Tormé on *Seinfeld*, as himself, serenading a doped-up Kramer who has been mistaken for a mentally challenged man.

John Turturro on *Monk*, in an Emmy winning turn as Ambrose, the agoraphobic brother of the OCD-afflicted detective.

Wayne Wilderson on *The Office*, as a new employee and former convict who convinces the Dunder-Mifflin staff that prison life was more fun than working there.

Bruce Willis on *Friends*, in an Emmy-winning turn as Rachel's macho-but-sensitive boyfriend who openly hates Ross for dating his coed daughter.

Entertainment Tonight's

Biggest Moments

When the show celebrated its 25th year in 2006, Mary Hart and Co. revealed their Top 10 stories of all time.

The Michael Jackson Scandals

Jackson's talent was eclipsed by his personal dramas: that bizarre marriage to Lisa Marie, the mysteriously sired kids, the child molestation trial. "The controversies snuffed out the flame," said anchor Mark Steines. "We're all left scratching our heads going, *'What happened?'*"

The Death of Princess Di

"Her death united the world in grief—it was as if we all emotionally imploded," said Steines, who covered the funeral. The dark tragedy shone a harsh light on a still-growing problem. Noted Steines: "Diana would still be with us today—and having a huge global impact—if it wasn't for some guys trying to get a picture."

Madonna Mania

ET tracked her from Material Girl to Kabbalah peddler. But the ultimate Madonna moment? Said Mary Hart, "That [2003 VMA] kiss with Britney and Christina had us all going, 'That's carrying it too far!'"

"Titanic" Fever

The epic tearjerker sank all box-office records—nearly $2 billion worldwide—and might never be topped. "Two months after it opened, the grosses were *still* growing," recalled film expert Leonard Maltin. "It attracts 10-year-olds and 80-year-olds. That breadth of appeal will be hard to match."

Rock Hudson Diagnosed with AIDS

In July 1985, the movie idol entered a Paris hospital for treatment. Said Maltin, "It triggered a sea change in AIDS awareness."

The End of *Friends*

We missed *Cheers*. We mourned *Seinfeld*. But losing *Friends* was, well, like losing friends. "America felt a deep and intimate connection to the characters," said *ET* executive producer Linda Belle Blue. "But they were smart to end the show."

The O.J. Trial

If you watched a bit, you could not quit. "America was addicted to the trial like it was a soap opera," said Blue. "We had to stay on the story—to the point of reporting on Marcia Clark's hairdos—because that's all the public wanted.

The Deaths of John and Carolyn Kennedy

We were all part of this story, as we waited and prayed for a miracle. "It didn't matter if you were Democrat or Republican," said Hart. "John's death left a big hole in everyone's heart."

Ellen Comes Out

First she came out as a lesbian in a 1997 *Time* magazine cover story, then DeGeneres's character did the same on her sitcom. "Ellen broke down walls," said Blue. "It was good for the country."

Brad Pitt: The Love Chronicles

"Loni and Burt, Arnold and Maria, Tom and Katie—our fascination with star romances never wanes," said anchor Jann Carl. But no one has fueled female frenzy like Brad Pitt and his lady loves: Gwyneth, Jennifer and now, Angelina. "We love when he falls in love. We're mad when it's not forever. But even if we can't have him, we want him to be happy."

Friends

Chandler Bing's middle name was Muriel.

Mary's Most Memorable Hart-to-Hearts

She lost her virginity to Eddie Murphy—her *Entertainment Tonight* virginity, that is. In 2006, when Mary Hart approached her quarter-century mark with the show, she looked back to her first celebrity chat (Murphy was still a regular on *SNL*). And since then, she says, "it seems like I've interviewed the world." Though she'll never forget her first, these are the ones Hart recalled the most vividly.

Michael Jackson (February 24, 1988)

"I'd gone to Pensacola, Florida, to watch him in rehearsals for his concert tour. I spent a couple of days watching a master at work. Whatever you think of him today, he was in total control of every aspect of the production back then. Three weeks later I flew to Kansas City, and as we walked from backstage into a stadium of 40,000, this shy, quiet guy held my hand nervously. Then, in an instant, he transformed into this wild, magical, larger-than-life superstar. It was stunning to see."

Gloria Estefan (February 4, 1991)

"It was her first interview after the terrible bus accident that broke her back. I was the first person to talk about it in her home in Miami. She was in physical therapy so torturous it made her cry, but we had a great time. She even cooked me Cuban food. Her strength of will was inspirational. She displayed such determination, courage, and love and appreciation for her fans, who had really helped carry her through it. The doctors said she'd never walk again, but she was determined to prove them wrong."

Richard Pryor (October 7, 1992)

"He was my best and my worst interview. Prior to *ET*, I interviewed him for an Oklahoma City talk show and he was so angry, foulmouthed and obnoxious, it wasn't airable. When I went to see him after his MS diagnosis, his eyes teared up, and he apologized for his horrible behavior. He said 'I am so sorry that I made that day so difficult for you, I was horrible to a lot of people and I feel very badly for that.' I was like *'Whaat?'* Then he gave me the interview of a lifetime. I appreciated that so much because he touched me personally."

Caroline Kennedy (November 18-19, 2005)

"We talked about her mother, her brother, her days in the White House with her father. And she had a great perspective on it. I was so impressed: I expected her to be reserved, given the tragedies she's had to bear, but she was very funny and forthcoming. She dreads the spotlight and for years she thought, 'Great, let my brother represent the family—*he's* the glamour boy!' Now she knows it's up to her. She wanted to stay private, but that's not going to happen because she's the only one left."

George Clooney:

Paying His Dues

Before this heartthrob hit it big as Doug Ross on *ER* and a multitude of big-screen hits, his was a journeyman's career, with dues paid on shows of varying quality.

E/R (1984-85)
Not to be confused with the current phenom, this short-lived CBS sitcom, also set in Chicago, featured Clooney in the Dr. John Carter role, as a green young doctor named Ace.

The Facts of Life (1985-86)
Joined the teen-com as carpenter George Burnett, who helped rebuild the fire-damaged Edna's Edibles into the novelty shop Over Our Heads.

Roseanne (1988-89)
In the first season, played plastics-plant foreman Booker Brooks, who got in Roseanne's face while hitting on her sister, Jackie.

Sunset Beat (1990)
Blink, and you missed it. Lasting only two episodes, this *Miami Vice* clone about undercover cops posing as bikers starred Clooney as Chic Chesbro, who moonlighted as a rock guitarist.

Baby Talk (1991-92)
In this troubled adaptation of "Look Who's Talking," he played Joe, a construction worker in the orbit of single mom Julia Duffy. He split the crib over "creative differences," as did Duffy.

Bodies of Evidence (1992)
Played emotionally vulnerable detective Ryan Walker in this short-lived police drama.

Sisters (1993-94)
Joined the sibling soap opera as Det. James Falconer, who married Sela Ward's Teddy before getting murdered by a drug dealer. Warner Bros., which produced *Sisters* and *ER*, clearly noticed his potential. He debuted on the hospital drama in the fall of '94.

The Secret Stars of *The Simpsons*

In the October 21, 2000, issue of TV GUIDE, the magazine honored our favorite Springfield family with an unprecedented 24 separate covers, each showcasing one of two dozen memorable Simpsons characters.

Apu Nahasapeemapetilon
Kwik-E-Mart clerk

Barney Gumble
Moe's Tavern regular

Bumblebee Man
Television personality

Comic Book Guy
Owner of The Android's Dungeon comic-book store

Dr. Julius Hibbert
The unconventional doc at Springfield General Hospital

Ned Flanders
Homer's ever-cheerful, ever-faithful holy-rollin' neighbor

Grampa Abraham Simpson
Homer's dad and Sringfield Retirement Castle resident

Itchy & Scratchy
The legendary cartoon duo

Kang
Drooling alien from the "Treehouse of Horror" episodes

Edna Krabapple
Bart's divorced, bitter fourth-grade teacher

Krusty the Klown (aka Herschel Krustofski)
Kids-show host and entrepreneur

Sea Captain McAllister
Inept sailor and owner of The Frying Dutchman restaurant

Millhouse Van Houten
Bart's nerdy best friend

Moe Szyslak
Proprietor of Moe's Tavern and recipient of Bart's prank phone calls

C. Montgomery Burns
Homer's boss at the Springfield Nuclear Power Plant and the Most Despised Man in Springfield

Professor John Frink
Mad scientist

Ralph Wiggum
Lisa's dim-witted second-grade classmate

Santa's Little Helper
The family's dog

Selma Bouvier
Marge's older, chain-smoking, Homer-hating sister, twin to Patty

Sideshow Bob
Krusty the Klown's maniacal sidekick

Seymour Skinner
The much-maligned principal of Springfield Elementary

Waylon Smithers
Mr. Burns' overly dedicated personal assistant

Chief Clancy Wiggum
Head of the Springfield PD

Groundskeeper Willie
Springfield Elementary's handyman

The Simpsons:

Schticks and Stones

Over its many seasons, the classic cartoon comedy has offered a few punch lines that were taken a little too seriously...

 After "Blame It on Lisa" aired on March 31, 2002, Ritour, the official tourism bureau of Rio de Janeiro, claimed defamation and threatened to file a civil lawsuit against the show for its story line, wherein the Simpsons go to Brazil. While in the South American country, Homer is kidnapped for a $50,000 ransom, Bart is eaten by a boa constrictor and the family is attacked by monkeys on the street.

 Following the "Streetcar Named Marge" episode (October 1, 1992), New Orleans protested about lyrics in a *Simpsons* song in which the city is referred to as the "home of pirates, drunks and whores." The next week, Bart wrote "I WILL NOT DEFAME NEW ORLEANS" on the blackboard.

 Oy, Carumba! Several Jewish groups protested "Like Father, Like Clown" (October 24, 1991), the "Jazz Singer"-like episode in which Krusty reveals that his real name is Krustofski and that he is estranged from his rabbi father (Jackie Mason).

 In 1990, an Ohio principal banned children from wearing a *Simpsons* T-shirt emblazoned with "UNDERACHIEVER" and featuring Bart, brandishing a slingshot, declaring in a cartoon bubble: "And proud of it, man!"

 Among the many excuses Bart used to get out of a test ("Marge Gets a Job," November 5, 1992) was that he had Tourette's syndrome ("Shove it, witch!"). After complaints to the network, the Tourette's reference is replaced with "rabies" in repeats.

Reasons
We Love *American Dad*

This outrageous toon from the *Family Guys* keeps us on the alert—and in hysterics.

CIA agent Stan Smith breaks the TV-dad mold—think Archie Bunker with high security clearance. Like Archie, Stan means well. But he takes his love for God, country and the right to bear arms *way* too far. (This is a guy who'll pull a gun on a lasagna when it shows up unannounced on casserole night.) Still, the antiterrorist nut married a woman who appreciates him. "Francine knows she's safe in an unsafe world," says *Dad* cocreator Mike Barker. "If it means dealing with his vigilance, it's a trade she's willing to make." Of course, not everyone is a fan. Stan's radical-feminist daughter, Hayley, once slept with a guy because he claimed to be an al-Qaeda member.

It's political, but wackier than C-SPAN. "President Bush" has made an appearance. After an accidental serving of alcohol, the president falls off the wagon and back into the partying ways of his youth.

Roger reminds us of Paul Lynde. Seth MacFarlane's voice for the alcoholic alien who hides in the Smith home brings back memories of the late funnyman with the killer lines on *Hollywood Squares*. It's no accident, says Barker: "The kids who watch don't know we've robbed an entire man's essence for our own gain."

What's funnier than a German-speaking goldfish? It may not be easy to write gags for Klaus, who hangs out in a bowl all day. But he has had major story lines. He once got stuck in a freezer, in a parody of "Alive." Barker notes: "Eventually he realizes that to survive, he [had] to eat fish sticks."

It dares to take on *Desperate Housewives*. Competing against one of prime-time's hottest shows sucks. But the show took dead aim with a send-up of Wisteria Lane. Francine joined a secret society of housewives who cheat and kill—using supermarket shopping carts as their weapons. "We're not averse to trying to take some of the *Desperate Housewives* audience," Barker says. "One way to do that is to ridicule and try to suggest that the entire idea for their show is flawed." Stan would surely approve.

20 Carrot Diamonds:
The Best Bugs Bunny Cartoons

1 *The Wild Hare*, 1940, Tex Avery
Bugs's first use of, "What's up, Doc?"

2 *Tortoise Beats Hare*, 1941, Tex Avery
Cecil the turtle wins the race

3 *Wabbit Twouble*, 1941, Robert Clampett
Elmer goes west for "west and rewaxation"

4 *Super-Rabbit*, 1943, Chuck Jones
Bugs eats fortified carrots and acquires superpowers

5 *A Corny Concerto*, 1943, Robert Clampett
Bugs waltzes away from Porky Pig in this ballet

6 *Little Red Riding Rabbit*, 1944, Friz Freleng
A spoof on the classic tale

7 *Baseball Bugs*, 1946, Friz Freleng
Bugs stars as a baseball player who triumphs over the Gashouse Gorillas

8 *What's Up, Doc?* 1950, Robert McKimson
Bugs shares his showbiz story in true Hollywood style

9 *Rabbit of Seville*, 1950, Chuck Jones
Bugs and Elmer act in "The Barber of Seville"

10 *Operation: Rabbit*, 1952, Chuck Jones
The first meeting between Bugs and Wile E. Coyote

11 *Rabbit Seasoning*, 1952, Chuck Jones
Daffy Duck tries to convince Elmer that it's rabbit season, not duck season

12 *Duck Amuck*, 1953, Chuck Jones
Bugs annoys Daffy as an unseen animator

13 *Bugs and Thugs*, 1954, Friz Freleng
Two crooks are outsmarted

14 *To Hare Is Human*, 1956, Chuck Jones
Wile E. Coyote assembles a do-it-yourself electronic brain to help him capture Bugs Bunny

15 *What's Opera, Doc?* 1957, Chuck Jones
Bugs and Elmer star in an opera parody

16 *Show Biz Bugs*, 1957, Friz Freleng
Daffy puts dynamite on a xylophone and urges Bugs to play

17 *Hare-way to the Stars*, 1958, Chuck Jones
Bugs must stop Marvin the Martian from destroying Earth

18 *Baton Bunny*, 1959, Chuck Jones and Abe Levitow
Maestro Bugs conducts a symphony

19 *Blooper Bunny*, 1991, Greg Ford and Terry Lennon
A mockumentary about the jealousy and antipathy for Bugs Bunny from Daffy and Yosemite Sam

20 *Carrotblanca*, 1995, Douglas McCarthy
A Looney Toons spin on the classic film

Greatest Cartoon Characters of All Time

1 Bugs Bunny

2 Homer Simpson

3 Rocky and Bullwinkle

4 Beavis and Butt-Head

5 The Grinch

6 Fred Flintstone and Barney Rubble

7 Angelica Pickles

8 Charlie Brown and Snoopy

9 SpongeBob SquarePants

10 Cartman

11 Bart and Lisa Simpson

12 Fat Albert

13 The Powerpuff Girls

14 Daffy Duck

15 Pikachu

16 Gumby

17 Betty Boop

18 Top Cat

19 Mickey Mouse

20 Popeye

21 Gerald McBoing-Boing

22 Scooby-Doo

23 Underdog

24 Josie and the Pussycats

25 Heckle and Jeckle

26 Arthur

27 Winnie the Pooh

28 Felix the Cat

29 Mr. Magoo

30 George of the Jungle

31 Ren and Stimpy

32 Tom Terrific

33 Tweety and Sylvester

34 Bill (on Capitol Hill)

35 Space Ghost

36 Yogi Bear and Boo Boo

37 Mighty Mouse

38 Wile E. Coyote and Road Runner

39 Superman

40 Batman

41 Daria

42 Wonder Woman

43 Donald Duck

44 Alvin the Chimpunk

45 Boris Badenov and Natasha Fatale

46 Woody Woodpecker

47 Porky Pig

48 Bobby Hill

49 Speed Racer

50 Tom and Jerry

Since this list was published on August 3, 2002, 10 more characters have come to mind who we think are worthy, including...

Bender (*Futurama*)

Blue (*Blue's Clues*)

Clifford the Big Red Dog

Dora the Explorer and her cousin, Diego

Foghorn Leghorn

Hong Kong Phooey

Pepe Le Pew

The Smurfs

Stewie Griffin (*Family Guy*)

Angel's High Points

The most memorable moments from a show with real bite.

"I Will Remember You" (November 23, 1999)
Angel rekindles his passion for Buffy after suddenly becoming mortal. But when he realizes he's no longer an effective warrior against evil, he sacrifices his happiness to save her and arranges for the day to be erased from her memory—after they share a final kiss.

"Hero" (November 20, 1999)
Plagued by guilt over allowing his own clan to be slaughtered years before, Doyle (Glenn Quinn), Angel's half-demon sidekick, gives his life to save another demon tribe. Doyle's final gesture: kissing Cordelia, transferring his curse/gift of receiving psychic messages from The Powers That Be.

"To Shanshu in L.A." (May 23, 2000)
Occult scholar Wesley translates a prophecy that includes the word *shanshu*, which means that Angel will become human after fulfilling his destiny. "That'd be nice," Angel says, offering a rare smile. Finally, a ray of hope for the future.

"Reunion" (December 19, 2000)
Bloodthirsty vamps Darla (Julie Benz) and Drusilla (Juliet Landau) trap Wolfram & Hart attorneys in a wine cellar and Angel locks the doors, sealing the lawyers' doom. Then Angel returns to his Angel Investigation buddies and—surprise!—fires them all.

"There's No Place Like Plrtz Glrb" (May 22, 2001)
Lorne (Andy Hallett) looks very John the Baptist when his head is delivered on a platter to Cordelia, the new princess of Lorne's homeland, Pylea. As she weeps, his eyes open: "Oh, honey. I'm right there with ya."

"Lullaby" (November 19, 2001)
Darla is in labor with Angel's child—don't ask—while being chased by Holtz, an ancient vampire hunter. Darla realizes that the baby, the only thing she's loved in 400 years, is dying, so she drives a stake into her heart and dissolves into dust, leaving an infant boy behind on the wet pavement.

"Sleep Tight" (March 4, 2002)
Concerned for the safety of Angel's son, Connor, Wesley kidnaps the infant to give to a woman who promises to keep him safe. In a shocking betrayal, she cuts Wesley's throat and delivers the baby to the enemy, Holtz. "He'll never know you existed," Holtz tells Angel as he jumps with Connor through a time-space portal.

"The Price" (April 29, 2002)
Connor returns from the alternate dimension—and is now a teen (Vincent Kartheiser) with hate in his heart for the father he never knew. He's become "The Destroyer," looking for Angel. Arriving in a flash of light, along with a horned creature he coolly beheads, Connor points a weapon at Angel and says, "Hi, Dad!"

"Supersymmetry" (November 3, 2002)
Brainiac Fred and her lover, Gunn, confront an evil professor who once banished Fred to Pylea. "You know what they say about payback? Well, I'm the bitch!" Fred says. But Gunn steps in and kills the prof instead, snapping his neck. Fred is not pleased by Gunn's chivalry.

"Apocalypse, Nowish" (November 17, 2002)
As signs of the apocalypse abound—plagues of rats and snakes, earthquakes and a fearsome Beast that wreaks havoc—Cordelia takes Connor to bed. Horrified fans go "eww" as a rain of fire falls on L.A. and Angel watches his son and the considerably older Cordelia make love during war.

"Home" (May 7, 2003)
Having saved the world from the messianic, flesh-eating baddie Jasmine, our heroes are rewarded for *ending* world peace by Wolfram & Hart's evil attorneys. The lawyers turn over their L.A. offices to Angel and Co., where they can now fight evil from within. "There's no way this is going to go well," Angel mutters.

"Destiny" (November 19, 2003)
When a mysterious package renders vampire-turned-ghost Spike whole, the universe is thrown for a loop by the existence of two vampires with souls. Spike and Angel fight to be the first to drink from the Cup of Perpetual Torment   which turns out to be a fake. Still, Angel, the loser, broods: "What if it means I'm not the one?"

"Smile Time" (February 18, 2004)
Angel investigates an epidemic of comatose kids, which leads him to a popular children's show. After visiting the set, he mysteriously turns into a puppet, causing him to lament, "I'm made of felt—and my nose comes off."

"A Hole in the World" (February 25, 2004)
Angel must choose between saving one friend's life and the lives of thousands when Fred falls desperately ill after examining a mysterious sarcophagus that arrives in the lab.

"The Girl in Question" (May 5, 2004)
A Buffy-centric episode that doesn't actually feature Buffy, but gives one last glance of Dru and Darla, and tells of the one vampire who actually gets one up on Angel and Spike.

"Not Fade Away" (Series finale: May 19, 2004)
The gang wages war on the Circle of the Black Thorn, living the day out as if it's their last before each of them takes on separate fights with a different bigwig. The final battle started, the remains of the team gather in a back alley to end the fight together, looking to their leader, Angel, for a plan. "Personally? I kinda want to slay the dragon. Let's go to work."

35 Famous Guest Stars
on *Star Trek: The Next Generation*

Majel Barrett as Lwaxana Troi, the mother of Counselor Deanna Troi
Episode: "Haven" (first of several appearances)
Better Known For: *Star Trek* (Nurse Christine Chapel)

Corbin Bernsen as Q2
Episode: "Deja Q"
Better Known For: *L.A. Law*

Billy Campbell as Capt. Thadiun Okona
Episode: "The Outrageous Okona"
Better Known For: *Dynasty, Once and Again, The 4400*

Nikki Cox as Sarjenka
Episode: "Pen Pals"
Better Known For: *Nikki, Las Vegas*

James Cromwell as Jaglom Shrek
Episodes: "The Hunted"; "Birthright: Part 1 and 2"
Better Known For: "L.A. Confidential," "Babe," *Six Feet Under, 24*

Daniel Davis as Professor Moriarty
Episodes: "Elementary, Dear Data"; "Ship in a Bottle"
Better Known For: *The Nanny*

James Doohan as Montgomery "Scotty" Scott
Episode: "Relics"
Better Known For: *Star Trek* ("Scotty")

Kirsten Dunst as Hedril
Episode: "Dark Page"
Better Known For: "Bring It On," "Spider-Man" movies

Mick Fleetwood as an Antedian dignitary
Episode: "Manhunt"
Better Known For: Founding classic-rock band Fleetwood Mac

Susan Gibney as Dr. Leah Brahms
Episodes: "Booby Trap"; "Galaxy's Child"
Better Known For: *Diagnosis Murder, Crossing Jordan*

Kelsey Grammer as Capt. Morgan Bateman
Episode: "Cause and Effect"
Better Known For: *Cheers, Frasier*

Teri Hatcher as Chief B.G. Robinson
Episode: "The Outrageous Okona"
Better Known For: *Lois & Clark, Desperate Housewives*

Stephen Hawking as himself, in hologram form
Episode: "Descent: Part 1"
Better Known For: "A Brief History of Time"

Jennifer Hetrick as Vash
Episodes: "Captain's Holiday"; "QPid"
Better Known For: *L.A. Law*

Famke Janssen as Kamala
Episode: "The Perfect Mate"
Better Known For: "The X-Men" movies, *Nip/Tuck*

Ken Jenkins as Dr. Paul Stubbs
Episode: "Evolution"
Better Known For: *Wiseguy, Scrubs*

Renée Jones as Lt. Aquiel Uhnari
Episode: "Aquiel"
Better Known For: *L.A. Law, Days of Our Lives*

DeForest Kelley as Adm. Leonard McCoy
Episode: "Encounter at Farpoint" (pilot episode)
Better Known For: *Star Trek*

Sabrina Le Beauf as Ensign Giusti
Episodes: "Gambit: Parts 1 and 2"
Better Known For: *The Cosby Show*

Carolyn McCormick as Minuet
Episodes: "11001001"; "Future Imperfect"
Better Known For: *Cracker, Law & Order*

Star Trek

Martin Landau was originally offered the role of Spock, but turned it down.

Matt McCoy as Devinoni Ral
Episode: "The Price"
Better Known For: "Police Academy 5," "Police Academy 6," "L.A. Confidential"

Christopher McDonald as Lt. Richard Castillo
Episode: "Yesterday's Enterprise"
Better Known For: "Happy Gilmore," *Veronica's Closet*

Bebe Neuwirth as Lanel
Episodes: "First Contact"
Better Known For: *Cheers, Frasier, Law & Order: Trial by Jury*

Leonard Nimoy as Mr. Spock
Episodes: "Unification: Parts 1 and 2"
Better Known For: *Star Trek* (Mr. Spock)

David Ogden Stiers as Timicin
Episode: "Half a Life"
Better Known For: *M*A*S*H, The Dead Zone*

Terry O'Quinn as Adm. Eric Pressman
Episode: "The Pegasus"
Better Known For: *Millennium, Alias, Lost*

Joe Piscopo as The Comic
Episode: "The Outrageous Okona"
Better Known For: *Saturday Night Live*

Saul Rubinek as Kivas Fajo
Episode: "The Most Toys"
Better Known For: "Wall Street," *Frasier*

Dwight Schultz as Lt. Reginald Barclay, a role he later reprised on *Star Trek: Voyager*
Episodes: "Hollow Pursuit"; "The Nth Degree"; "Realm of Fear"; "Ship in a Bottle"; "Genesis"
Better Known For: *The A-Team*

Armin Shimerman as Qwark, who later became a regular character on *Star Trek: Deep Space Nine*
Episodes: "The Last Outpost"; "Haven"; "Peak Performance"; "Firstborn"
Better Known For: *Beauty and the Beast, Buffy the Vampire Slayer*

Paul Sorvino as Dr. Nikolai Rozhenko
Episode: "Homeward"
Better Known For: "Goodfellas," *Law & Order*

John Tesh as a Klingon warrior (uncredited)
Episode: "The Icarus Factor"
Better Known For: Hosting *Entertainment Tonight*

Ray Walston as Boothby
Episode: "The First Duty"
Better Known For: *My Favorite Martian, Picket Fences*

David Warner as Gul Madred
Episodes: "Chain of Command: Parts 1 and 2"
Better Known For: "Tron," "Time Bandits"

James Worthy as Klingon Koral
Episode: "Gambit: Part 2"
Better Known For: Participating in three Los Angeles Lakers championship wins

Things We Miss About *Xena*

I — THE GRRRL POWER:

We don't mean to bash Buffy or alien-ate Scully, but Xena (Lucy Lawless) put every other sci-fi fantasy dame to shame. Think about it: Xena battled cannibals, vampires and killer Valkyries, survived shipwrecks and tsunamis, fought as a gladiator at the Colosseum, kicked Caligula's keister in a chariot race and single-handedly defeated the entire Persian army. Oh, and in what surely was a first for a TV drama queen, she also contracted head lice.

II — THE STUNTS:

Xena's aerodynamic, sword-swinging acrobatics rivaled any you'll find on the big screen.

III — THE FASHIONS:

We were always suckers for a gal in a wrought-iron bra.

IV — THE BLOOD! THE GUTS!:

Tony Soprano has nothing on Xena, who has personally whacked thousands and, in the finale, was found responsible for 40,000 more. And she herself died more times than we can remember. Our favorite Xena demise: the time she was crucified by Julius Caesar, went to heaven and became an archangel (we're not making this up).

V — THE SUBVERSITY:

You have to admire a show that played so fast and loose with history (didn't you know it was Xena who killed Cleopatra's love Marc Antony?) and the Bible (which seems to have left out the part where Xena helped David slay Goliath). Anything goes in the Xena-verse.

VI — THE CAST:

That oh-so-kinky breastplate wasn't the only thing supporting La Lawless. She was backed by the stellar Ted Raimi as the bumbling, fumbling Joxer, Hudson Leick as the witchy Callisto and Renee O'Connor as Xena's bosom buddy, Gabrielle, whose costumes got skimpier with each passing season.

VII — THE CHEESE FACTOR:

Even a bad Xena is a good Xena, though the all-musical episode, "Lyre, Lyre, Hearts on Fire," did put our loyalty to the test. Draco (Jay Laga'aia) and his army did a water ballet. Xena sang "Sisters Are Doin' It for Themselves." Joxer's flamingly gay brother

Jace (also played by Raimi) did a disco version of "Dancing in the Moonlight." The episode ended with Lawless—who at the time was so pregnant she couldn't see her feet—dancing in a bare-midriff go-go outfit. Oh, baby.

VIII THE MESSAGE:

The show's plea for tolerance and its timeless advice—be true to yourself—were the ultimate in cool.

IX THE LESBIAN SUBTEXT:

Did Xena have a thing for Gabrielle? Yes, claimed legions of lesbian fans, who launched a massive mail campaign begging the producers to let our warrior princess lay a big, sloppy, soulful kiss on Gabby before the saga came to an end. Xena execs played up the speculation, titillating the "believers" with double entendres, meaningful glances and an all-girl hot-tub scene. And Lawless publicly credited the lesbian community with putting her show on the map.

X THE STAR:

As a rule, women who cross swords don't cross paths with Emmy, but make no mistake: Lawless was an actress of great depth and humor and a classic beauty who proved indisputably that blondeness is way overrated. But why go on and on when three words say it all? We Loved Lucy.

Greatest Sci-Fi Legends

1 Rod Serling
The Twilight Zone, CBS (1959-64)

2 *Star Trek* Crews
Star Trek, NBC, Syndicated, UPN (1966-2006)

3 Uncle Martin
My Favorite Martian, CBS (1963-66)

4 George Jetson
The Jetsons, ABC (1962-63)

5 Diana
V, NBC (1983-85)

6 David Vincent
The Invaders, ABC (1967-68)

7 Fox Mulder
The X-Files (1993-2002)

8 ALF
ALF, NBC (1986-90)

9 Capt. John Sheridan
Babylon 5, Syndicated (1992-97); TNT (1998)

10 Jack O'Neill
Stargate SG-1, Showtime (1997-2001); Sci-Fi Channel (2002-06)

11 Duncan MacLeod
Highlander, Syndicated (1992-98)

12 Sam Beckett
Quantum Leap, NBC (1989-93)

13 *MST3K* Crew
Mystery Science Theater 3000, Comedy Central (1989-96); Sci-Fi Channel (1997-99)

14 Robot
Lost in Space, CBS (1965-68)

15 The Coneheads
Saturday Night Live, NBC (1977-79)

Allie Keys
Taken, Sci-Fi Channel (2002)

 Max Guevara
Dark Angel, Fox (2000-02)

 Capt. Malcolm "Mal" Reynolds
Firefly, Fox (2002)

 Steve Austin and Jaime Sommers
The Six Million Dollar Man, ABC (1973-78),
The Bionic Woman, ABC (1976-77); NBC (1977-78)

 John Crichton
Farscape, Sci-Fi Channel (1999-2003)

 Starbuck
Battlestar Galactica, ABC (1978-79)

 Doctor Who
Doctor Who, BBC/Syndicated (various years, from 1963 to the present)

Ultraman
Ultraman, Syndicated (1966)

Dick Solomon
3rd Rock From the Sun, NBC (1996-2001)

Captain Video
Captain Video (1949-55)

Top 25
Cult Shows Ever

1 *Star Trek*

2 *The X-Files*

3 *Buffy the Vampire Slayer*

4 *Farscape*

5 *Monty Python's Flying Circus*

6 *The Simpsons*

7 *The Prisoner*

8 *The Twilight Zone*

9 *Xena: Warrior Princess*

10 *Pee-Wee's Playhouse*

11 *Mystery Science Theater 3000*

12 *Family Guy*

13 *Babylon 5*

14 *Beauty and the Beast*

15 *Quantum Leap*

16 *My So-Called Life*

17 *The Avengers*

18 *Doctor Who*

19 *Dark Shadows*

20 *Twin Peaks*

21 *Mary Hartman, Mary Hartman*

22 *H.R. Pufnstuf*

23 *Forever Knight*

24 *Absolutely Fabulous*

25 *Freaks and Geeks*

On Second Thought...

Let's not forget these fan favorites:

Battlestar Galactica

Firefly

Futurama

Heroes

Kids in the Hall

Millennium

The Outer Limits

10 Best Family Holiday Specials

Dr. Seuss' How the Grinch Stole Christmas

A Charlie Brown Christmas

Rudolph the Red-Nosed Reindeer

Frosty the Snowman

The Year Without a Santa Claus

Winnie the Pooh and Christmas Too

Rugrats Chanukah

A Muppet Family Christmas

Santa Claus Is Comin' to Town

A Garfield Christmas Special

Top 10 Holiday Episodes

It's a tradition dating back to the Ricardos and Kramdens—special episodes that warm hearts (and boost ratings). How did we choose our favorites? Well, we love originality, which explains the absence of any "Christmas Carol" knockoffs.

1

The Mary Tyler Moore Show: "Christmas and the Hard-Luck Kid II"
(December 19, 1970, CBS)
Christmas-loving Mary is forced to work a lonely holiday shift at WJM-TV. When Lou, Murray and Ted pay a surprise visit, who needs Santa? Aired only three months into this series' run, the episode proved that *MTM* was beginning to look a lot like a classic.

2

thirtysomething: "The Mike Van Dyke Show"
(December 20, 1988, ABC)
Leave it to Michael Steadman to turn the holidays into an existential crisis. When his wife and daughter are in a car accident, he longs for the simpler days when life was like a *Dick Van Dyke*-style sitcom. The touching fantasy episode was nominated for two Emmys.

3

Seinfeld: "The Strike"
(December 18, 1997, NBC)
Frank Costanza takes a break from collecting TV GUIDEs to celebrate Festivus, the holiday "for the rest of us." But the Airing of Grievances and Feats of Strength were too "out there" even for Kramer. Trivia: Festivus was invented by the father of *Seinfeld* writer Daniel O'Keefe.

4

The Honeymooners: "'Twas the Night Before Christmas"
(December 24, 1955, CBS)
A take on O. Henry's "The Gift of the Magi" finds Ralph hocking his bowling ball to buy something for Alice. Taped before a live audience, Jackie Gleason interrupted the applause to give his cast a curtain call for their bang-zoom performances.

Friends: "The One with the Holiday Armadillo"
(December 14, 2000, NBC)
Nothing says "happy holidays" like a burrowing, nocturnal, armor-plated mammal. Ross hilariously dresses up as the Holiday Armadillo (they're all out of Santa costumes at the store) to help teach his Saint Nick-obsessed son, Ben, about Hanukkah.

I Love Lucy: "The 'I Love Lucy' Christmas Episode"
(December 24, 1956, CBS)
As they trim the tree, the Ricardos and Mertzes take a loving look back at how Little Ricky changed their lives. This was the first TV episode ever to use the clip-show device that audiences love—and actors cherish for the reduced working hours!

ER: "A Miracle Happens Here"
(December 14, 1995, NBC)
The second (and best) entry in what would become a tradition of holiday *ER* episodes celebrates the power of everyday miracles: finding a lost child, the appearance of a toymaker named "Stan Calaus" (notice the anagram?) and a dying priest's plea to turn the other cheek.

The O.C.: "The Chrismukkah That Almost Wasn't"
(December 16, 2004, Fox)
The gang gathers at the Cohen house for "Chrismukkah," and the melodrama really snowballs. Tempers flare (and one vase flies), but at its heart, the episode celebrates the warmth—and humor—of the blended family. No "Oy, humbug!" from us.

The Simpsons: "Miracle on Evergreen Terrace"
(December 17, 1989, Fox)
"If TV has taught me anything, it's that miracles always happen to poor kids at Christmas," declares Bart Simpson in this first-ever full episode of the series. In this case, miracles involve Marge spending all her money for Bart's tattoo removal.

South Park: "Mr. Hankey, the Christmas Poo"
(December 17, 1997, Comedy Central)
Who else but the folks at South Park could redefine the phrase "Yule log." If you don't already know about Mr. Hankey, we're not going to be the ones to tell you. Plus, it's the first episode of the series in which Kenny doesn't die. Who says South Park has no heart?

30 Sirens
Who Posed For *Playboy*

Some women bare their assets to jump-start a stalled career, others to launch a new one. Still others figure while they've got it, they might as well flaunt it.

1. Drew Barrymore
2. Kim Basinger
3. Brooke Burke
4. Charisma Carpenter
5. Joan Collins
6. Shannen Doherty
7. Carmen Electra
8. Erika Eleniak
9. Linda Evans
10. Farrah Fawcett
11. Sherilyn Fenn
12. Deborah Gibson
13. Robin Givens
14. Daryl Hannah
15. Tricia Helfer
16. Mariel Hemingway
17. Pamela Sue Martin
18. Jenny McCarthy
19. Donna Mills
20. Kelly Monaco
21. Dana Plato
22. Teri Polo
23. Jaime Pressly
24. Victoria Principal
25. Denise Richards
26. Suzanne Somers
27. Charlize Theron
28. Tiffany
29. Vanna White
30. Peta Wilson

20 Celebrities
Who Appeared in *Playgirl*

If the girls can take it all off, so can the guys. Sports stars, singers and actors have all graced the pages of the mag.

1 **Christopher Atkins** ("Blue Lagoon")

2 **Steve Bond** (*General Hospital*)

3 **Jim Brown** (football player)

4 **Fabian** (singer)

5 **Christopher George** (*The Rat Patrol*)

6 **Tyrese Gibson** (model/actor/singer)

7 **Peter Lupus** (*Mission: Impossible*)

8 **George Maharis** (*Route 66*)

9 **Shawn Michaels** (wrestler)

10 **Dan Pastorini** (football player)

11 **Burt Reynolds** ("Smokey and the Bandit")

12 **Adam Rich** (*Eight Is Enough*)

13 **Sylvester Stallone** ("Rocky")

14 **Peter Steele** (singer for band Type O Negative)

15 **Don Stroud** ("License to Kill")

16 **Keith Urban** (country singer)

17 **Lyle Waggoner** (*The Carol Burnett Show*)

18 **Victor Webster** (*Days of Our Lives*)

19 **Fred Williamson** (football player/actor)

20 **Steve Yeager** (baseball player)

The O.C.'s
Top 10 Moments

After four seasons and countless fistfights, the soap headed into the sunset, and TV GUIDE looked back on its juiciest twists.

1
"Welcome to the O.C., Bitch!"
"Premiere" (August 5, 2003)
Luke's bon mot to new punching-bag-in-town Ryan (Benjamin McKenzie) quickly became the signature line of the series. Says Schwartz, "Kids from Orange County say they're from 'the O.C.' like it's 'the Ukraine.' I always found it funny so I gave Luke that line."

2
Marissa Dies
"The Graduates" (May 18, 2006)
Marissa (Mischa Barton) died in Ryan's arms after being run off the road by her bad-boy ex Volchok in Season 3's shocking finale. Despite what the rumor mill would have you think, Schwartz contends that the tragedy was not dictated by anyone's off-set antics: "Losing Marissa—and Mischa—was a big loss for the show."

3
Julie's Affair With Luke
"The Telenovela" (February 25, 2004)
Jaws dropped—and temperatures soared—when Julie (Melinda Clarke) bedded her teenage daughter's ex-beau (Chris Carmack) while also romancing her best friend's father, Caleb. Talk about multitasking.

4
Chrismukkah Is Born
"The Best Chrismukkah Ever" (December 3, 2003)
Seth's Festivus-like mixed-faith holiday was almost called something else. "A lot of names were tossed around," recalls Schwartz. "Han-ukas being one of them." Oy to the world!

5

Marissa Goes Lesbian

"The Lonely Hearts Club" (February 10, 2005)

Coop's Sapphic fling with Bait Shop babe Alex (Olivia Wilde) was too hot to handle—at least by Fox standards. "It was post-Janet Jackson/Super Bowl FCC time," Schwartz says. "And we were forced to end the story line much sooner."

6

Seth and Summer's Spider-Man Kiss

"Rainy Day Women" (February 24, 2005)

Ever the pop-culture avatar, *The O.C.* scored with this cinematic nod to beauties and their comic-book fanboy toys everywhere. "After the episode aired, we got called from then-Marvel head Avi Arad and 'Spider-Man' director Sam Raimi saying how much they loved it," Schwartz says.

7

Marissa ODs in Tijuana

"The Escape" (September 16, 2003)

The kids' ill-fated run for the border stands as one of Schwartz's favorites eps. "It sums up what I think the show was capable of: feeling real, heightened, funny and, at times, operatically tragic," he says.

8

Oliver Goes Nuts

"The Links" (January 14, 2004)

Although Schwartz calls Marissa's friendship with the unhinged interloper (played by Taylor Handley) "the single most passionately hated story line," he gives the kid props for being creatively crazy. "C'mon people! He broke a plate then punched himself in the head—twice!"

9

Sandy Serenades Kirsten on Their 20th Anniversary

"The Power of Love" (January 13, 2005)

Solomon Burke's "Don't Give Up on Me" never sounded so sweet. "It embodies their crazy love for each other," remembers Schwartz. Plus, "after Peter Gallagher serenaded Kelly Rowan, he got a record deal out of it."

10

Cage-fighting Ryan Falls for Taylor Townsend

"The Sleeping Beauty" (November 30, 2006)

"Like a lot of people, I originally thought it was an odd pairing," Autumn Reeser reveals of the romance that juiced the lighter, quirkier final season. It also—finally!—gave Ryan (the best thing to happen to muscle tees since Marlon Brando) a reason to smile. And that's the happiest ending we could ask for.

Greatest Shows of All Time

Mike Wallace and a vampire slayer? Andy Griffith and the Sopranos? On one list? What were we thinking? Simply put, the best of the best, from Day 1 to our 50th anniversary celebration in 2002: quality, innovation and the ability to stay in our lives year after year. A touch of sentiment? Sure, but nostalgia alone couldn't make the cut (sorry, Beav). These are the series we watched regularly—and will watch again. And again.

1 *Seinfeld*

2 *I Love Lucy*

3 *The Honeymooners*

4 *All in the Family*

5 *The Sopranos*

6 *60 Minutes*

7 *Late Show With David Letterman*

8 *The Simpsons*

9 *The Andy Griffith Show*

10 *Saturday Night Live*

11 *The Mary Tyler Moore Show*

12 *The Tonight Show* Starring Johnny Carson

13 *The Dick Van Dyke Show*

14 *Hill Street Blues*

15 *The Ed Sullivan Show*

16 *The Carol Burnett Show*

17 *Today*

18 *Cheers*

19 *Thirtysomething*

20 *St. Elsewhere*

21 *Friends*

22 *ER*

23 *Nightline*

24 *Law & Order*

25 *M*A*S*H*

26 *The Twilight Zone*

27 *Sesame Street*

28 *The Cosby Show*

29 *Donahue*

30 *Your Show of Shows*

31 *The Defenders*

32 *An American Family*

33 *Playhouse 90*

34 *Frasier*

35 *Roseanne*

36 *The Fugitive*

37 *The X-Files*

38 *The Larry Sanders Show*

39 *The Rockford Files*

40 *Gunsmoke*

41 *Buffy the Vampire Slayer*

42 *Rowan & Martin's Laugh-In*

43 *Bonanza*

44 *The Bob Newhart Show*

45 *Twin Peaks*

46 *Star Trek: The Next Generation*

47 *Rocky and His Friends*

48 *Taxi*

49 *The Oprah Winfrey Show*

50 *Bewitched*

On Second Thought...

In the years since this list was first published, some extraordinary series have been produced, which we feel belong on this exalted list. For your consideration...

24

The Amazing Race

American Idol

Arrested Development

The Daily Show

Gilmore Girls

Lost

The Office

The West Wing

The Dick Van Dyke Show

Carl Reiner originally created this sitcom as a vehicle for himself, basing the main characters of Rob Petrie and Buddy Sorrell on himself and Mel Brooks.

Worst Shows of All Time

1 *The Jerry Springer Show* (Syndicated, September 30, 1991-present)

2 *My Mother the Car* (NBC, September 14, 1965-April 5, 1966)

3 *XFL* (NBC, UPN, TNN, February 3, 2001-April 21, 2001)

4 *The Brady Bunch Hour* (January 23, 1977-May 25, 1977)

5 *Hogan's Heroes* (CBS, September 17, 1965-July 4, 1971)

6 *Celebrity Boxing* (Fox, March 13, 2002)

7 *AfterMASH* (CBS, September 26, 1983-December 18, 1984)

8 *Cop Rock* (ABC, September 26, 1990-December 26, 1990)

9 *You're in the Picture* (CBS, January 20, 1961-January 27, 1961)

10 *Hee Haw Honeys* (Syndicated, 1978-79)

11 *The Secret Diary of Desmond Pfeiffer* (UPN, October 5, 1998-October 26, 1998)

12 *Hello, Larry* (NBC, January 26, 1979-April 30, 1980)

13 *Twenty-one* (NBC, September 12, 1956-October 16, 1958)

14 *Baby Bob* (CBS, March 18, 2002-June 20, 2003)

15 *Manimal* (NBC, September 30, 1983-December 31, 1983)

16 *The Chevy Chase Show* (Fox, September 7, 1993-October 15, 1993)

17 *Casablanca* (NBC, April 10, 1983-September 3, 1983)

18 *The Ugliest Girl in Town* (ABC, September 26, 1968-January 30, 1969)

19 *The P.T.L. Club* (Syndicated, 1976-87)

20 *The Pruitts of Southampton* (ABC, September 6, 1966-April 7, 1967)

21 *Baywatch* (NBC/Syndicated, September 22, 1989-May 19, 2001)

22 *The Powers of Matthew Star* (NBC, September 17, 1982-April 15, 1983)

23 *Sammy and Company* (Syndicated, 1975-77)

24 *One of the Boys* (NBC, January 23, 1982-August 20, 1982)

25 *Who Wants to Marry a Multi-Millionaire?* (Fox, February 15, 2000)

26 *Life With Lucy* (ABC, September 20, 1986-November 15, 1986)

27 *Turn-on* (ABC, February 5, 1969)

28 *Supertrain* (NBC, February 7, 1979-July 28, 1979)

29 *Howard Stern* (E!, June 20, 1994-present)

30 *Unhappily Ever After* (WB, January 11, 1995-May 2, 1999)

31 *Homeboys in Outer Space* (UPN, August 27, 1996-May 13, 1997)

32 *Co-ed Fever* (CBS, February 4, 1979)

33 *Holmes and Yoyo* (ABC, September 25, 1976-December 11, 1976)

34 *Alexander the Great* (ABC, January 26, 1968)

35 *Pink Lady...And Jeff* (NBC, March 1, 1980-April 11, 1980)

36 *The Misadventures of Sheriff Lobo* (NBC, September 18, 1979-May 5, 1981)

37 *Saturday Night Live With Howard Cosell* (ABC, September 20, 1975-January 17, 1976)

38 *Hell Town* (NBC, September 11, 1985-December 25, 1985)

39 *Still the Beaver* (Disney Channel, 1985-86)

40 *Makin' It* (ABC, February 1, 1979-March 19, 1979)

41 *The Tom Green Show* (MTV, 1999 2000)

42 *The Flying Nun* (ABC, September 7, 1967-April 3, 1970)

43 *Woops!* (Fox, September 27, 1992-December 6, 1992)

44 *She's the Sheriff* (Syndicated, 1987-89)

45 *A.K.A. Pablo* (ABC, March 6, 1984-April 17, 1984)

46 *Me and the Chimp* (CBS, January 13, 1972-May 18, 1972)

47 *Rango* (ABC, January 13, 1967-September 1, 1967)

48 *Bless This House* (CBS, September 11, 1995-January 1, 1996)

49 *The Ropers* (ABC, March 13, 1979-May 22, 1980)

50 *Barney & Friends* (PBS, April 6, 1992-present)

The stinkers just keep coming...

Jackass (MTV, October 2000-April 2002)

Temptation Island (Fox, January 10, 2001-September 29, 2003)

Fear Factor (NBC, June 11, 2001-September 12, 2006)

Joe Millionaire (Fox January 16, 2003-February 17, 2003)

Are You Hot? (ABC, February 13, 2003-April 5, 2003)

The Mullets (UPN, September 11, 2003-March 17, 2004)

The Swan (Fox, March 29, 2004-December 20, 2004)

Stacked (Fox, April 13, 2005-January 11, 2006)

Britney and Kevin: Chaotic (UPN, May 17, 2005-June 14, 2005)

Being Bobby Brown (Bravo, June 30, 2005-December 21, 2005)

Top Miniseries

Of course, *The Thorn Birds*, *Roots* and *Band of Brothers* are widely recognized as three of the top miniseries of all time. Check out these other classic limited series that have aired throughout the decades.

1970s

Rich Man, Poor Man (1976)
I, Claudius (1977)
Jesus of Nazareth (1977)
Roots (1977)

1990s

Armistead Maupin's Tales of the City (1994)
Jane Austen's `Pride and Prejudice' (1996)
George Wallace (1997)
Armistead Maupin's More Tales of the City (1998)
From the Earth to the Moon (1998)

1980s

Edward & Mrs. Simpson (1980)
Shogun (1980)
Tinker, Tailor, Soldier, Spy (1980)
John Steinbeck's East of Eden (1981)
Masada (1981)
A Woman Called Golda (1982)
Brideshead Revisited (1982)
Marco Polo (1982)
The Thorn Birds (1983)
The Winds of War (1983)
North and South (1985)
Peter the Great (1986)
The Singing Detective (1988)
Lonesome Dove (1989)
War and Remembrance (1989)

2000s

Armistead Maupin's Further Tales of the City (2001)
Band of Brothers (2001)
Angels in America (2003)

Greatest Episodes of All Time

1   "Chuckles Bites the Dust" *The Mary Tyler Moore Show* (October 25, 1975)

2   **"Lucy Does a TV Commercial"** *I Love Lucy* (May 5, 1952)

3   "Love's Labor Lost" *ER* (March 9, 1995)

4   **"The Boyfriend"** *Seinfeld* (February 12, 1992)

5   "Password" *The Odd Couple* (December 1, 1972)

6   **"The $99,000 Answer"** *The Honeymooners* (January 28, 1956)

7   "Thanksgiving Orphans" *Cheers* (November 27, 1986)

8   **"Coast to Coast Big Mouth"** *The Dick Van Dyke Show* (September 15, 1965)

9   "Over the River and Through the Woods" *The Bob Newhart Show* (November 22, 1975)

10   **"Clyde Bruckman's Final Repose"** *The X-Files* (October 13, 1995)

11   "To Serve Man" *The Twilight Zone* (March 2, 1962)

12   **"The Germans"** *Fawlty Towers* (1980, US)

13   "Sammy's Visit" *All in the Family* (February 19, 1972)

14   **"Blood Dance"** *Wiseguy* (February 22, 1988)

15   "It May Look Like a Walnut" *The Dick Van Dyke Show* (February 6, 1963)

16   **"Murder by the Book"** *Columbo* (September 15, 1971)

17   "The Crepes of Wrath" *The Simpsons* (April 15, 1990)

18   **"Lucy's Italian Movie"** *I Love Lucy* (April 16, 1956)

19   "Latka the Playboy" *Taxi* (May 21, 1981)

20   **"Abyssinia Henry"** *M*A*S*H* (March 18, 1975)

21   "A Stash From the Past" *Roseanne* (October 5, 1993)

22   **"The Towers of Zenith"** *thirtysomething* (May 15 and 22, 1990)

23   "The Judgment, Part II" *The Fugitive* (August 29, 1967)

24   **"Opie the Birdman"** *The Andy Griffith Show* (September 30, 1963)

25   "Twin Peaks" *Twin Peaks* (April 8, 1990)

26 **"TV or Not TV"** *The Honeymooners* (October 1, 1955)

27 **"The Lars Affair"** *The Mary Tyler Moore Show* (September 15, 1973)

28 **"The Jailer"** *Gunsmoke* (October 1, 1966)

29 **"My Father's Office"** *The Wonder Years* (March 29, 1988)

30 **"Requiem for a Heavyweight"** *Playhouse 90* (October 11, 1956)

31 **"It's a Good Life"** *The Twilight Zone* (November 3, 1961)

32 **"Prison Riot"** *Homicide: Life on the Street* (October 18, 1996)

33 **"The Parking Garage"** *Seinfeld* (October 30, 1991)

34 **"The Dream Sequence Always Rings Twice"** *Moonlighting* (October 15, 1985)

35 **"The Puppy Episode"** *Ellen* (April 30, 1997)

36 **"True Confessions"** *NYPD Blue* (October 12, 1993)

37 **"Getting Davy Jones"** *The Brady Bunch* (December 10, 1971)

38 **"Life of Brian"** *My So-Called Life* (November 10, 1994)

39 **"Everybody Loves Larry"** *The Larry Sanders Show* (November 13, 1996)

40 **"Turkeys Away"** *WKRP in Cincinatti* (October 30, 1978)

41 **"Man From the South"** *Alfred Hitchcock Presents* (January 3, 1960)

42 **"Captain Jack"** *Leave It to Beaver* (October 11, 1957)

43 **"The Matchmaker"** *Frasier* (October 4, 1994)

44 **"Time Heals"** *St. Elsewhere* (February 19 and 20, 1986)

45 **"Home Is the Sailor"** *Cheers* (September 24, 1987)

46 **"When Irish Eyes Are Smiling"** *Brooklyn Bridge* (September 20, 1991)

47 **"How to Be Absolutely Fabulous"** *Absolutely Fabulous* (January 6, 1995)

48 **"Divided He Falls"** *Bewitched* (May 5, 1966)

49 **"Grace Under Pressure"** *Hill Street Blues* (February 2, 1984)

50 **"Death Be My Destiny"** *The Bob Newhart Show* (February 12, 1977)

51 **"The Case of the Deadly Verdict"** *Perry Mason* (October 17, 1963)

52 **"The Producer"** *Gilligan's Island* (October 3, 1966)

53 **"The Eating Contest"** *The Phil Silvers Show* (November 15, 1955)

54 **"Happy Anniversary"** *The Cosby Show* (October 10, 1985)

55 **"Fall Out"** *The Prisoner* (September 21, 1968)

56 **"Columbia Pictures Doing Burns & Allen Story"**
The George Burns and Gracie Allen Show (March 29, 1954)

57 "The Lester Guy Show" *On the Air* (June 20, 1992)

58 **"Fat Farm"** *The Odd Couple* (November 12, 1971)

59 "A Star Named Arnold Is Born" *Green Acres* (April 3 and 10, 1968)

60 **"Chapter 1"** *Murder One* (September 19, 1995)

61 "How Smart Can You Get" *Car 54, Where Are You?* (February 25, 1962)

62 **"Hedda Hopper's Hollywood"** *The Beverly Hillbillies* (October 14, 1964)

63 "Reverend Jim: A Space Odyssey" *Taxi* (September 25, 1979)

64 **"The Best Dressed Man"** *The Many Loves of Dobie Gillis* (October 6, 1959)

65 "The Aurora Borealis" *Northern Exposure* (August 30, 1990)

66 **"Krusty Gets Kancelled"** *The Simpsons* (May 13, 1993)

67 "The Groovy Guru" *Get Smart* (January 13, 1968)

68 **"'A' My Family Name Is Alex"** *Family Ties* (March 12, 1987)

69 "Jerry Lewis Week" *Buffalo Bill* (January 5, 1984)

70 **"The Best of Both Worlds, Part I"** *Star Trek: The Next Generation* (June 18, 1990)

71 "The Cousins" *The Patty Duke Show* (May 24, 1964)

72 **"Small Potatoes"** *The X-Files* (April 20, 1997)

73 "Leo Durocher Meets Mr. Ed" *Mister Ed* (September 29, 1963)

74 **"Survival"** *Combat!* (March 12, 1963)

75 "Hotel Dick" *3rd Rock From the Sun* (September 29, 1996)

76 **"The Great Vegetable Rebellion"** *Lost in Space* (February 28, 1968)

77 "Hash" *Barney Miller* (December 30, 1976)

78 **"Soul Club"** *The Partridge Family* (January 29, 1971)

79 "Sanctuary" *Law & Order* (April 13, 1994)

80 **"The Interview"** *M*A*S*H* (February 24, 1976)

81 "Shady Deal at Sunny Acres" *Maverick* (November 23, 1958)

82 **"The 200th Episode"** *The Love Boat* (October 12, 1985)

83 "Hey Boy's Revenge" *Have Gun, Will Travel* (April 12, 1958)

84 **"The Alan Brady Show"** *Mad About You* (February 16, 1995)

85 "Masked Bandits" *Dragnet* (January 12, 1967)

86 **"The Purr-fect Crime"** *Batman* (March 16 and 17, 1966)

87 "Tet '68" *China Beach* (January 25, 1989)

88 **"Richie Fights Back"** *Happy Days* (October 14, 1975)

89 "Who Is Racer X" *Speed Racer* (Fall 1967)

90 **"Out Where the Buses Don't Run"** *Miami Vice* (October 18, 1985)

91 "Good to the Last Drop" *L.A. Law* (March 21, 1991)

92 **"City on the Edge of Forever"** *Star Trek* (April 6, 1967)

93 "Sweet Prince of Delancy Street" *Naked City* (June 7, 1961)

94 **"Mork's Mixed Emotions"** *Mork & Mindy* (February 22, 1979)

95 "Mother of Sorrow" *The Mod Squad* (February 17, 1970)

96 **"Heart of Saturday Night"** *Picket Fences* (October 27, 1995)

97 "I'll Be Waving As You Drive Away" *Little House on the Prairie* (March 6, 1978)

98 **"The Zanti Misfits"** *The Outer Limits* (December 30, 1963)

99 "The Rusty Heller Story" *The Untouchables* (October 13, 1960)

100 **"The One With the Prom Video"** *Friends* (February 1, 1996)

On Second Thought...

Who can forget these classic episodes?

"The Two Mrs. Cranes" *Frasier* (Sept. 17, 1996)

"The College Visit" *The Sopranos* (July 8, 1999)

"Hush" *Buffy the Vampire Slayer* (December 14, 1999)

"Pine Barrens" *The Sopranos* (May 6, 2001)

"Pilot Episode" *Six Feet Under* (June 3, 2001)

"Identity Crisis" *CSI* (January 17, 2002)

"Day 1 - 11:00 PM-12:00 AM" (Season 1 finale) *24* (May 21, 2002)

"Baggage" *Everybody Loves Raymond* (May 5, 2003)

Greatest TV Stars of All Time

1 Lucille Ball

2 Johnny Carson

3 Jackie Gleason

4 James Garner

5 Mary Tyler Moore

6 Oprah Winfrey

7 Carol Burnett

8 Michael Landon

9 Bill Cosby

10 Dick Van Dyke

11 Lassie

12 Andy Griffith

13 George Burns and Gracie Allen

14 Milton Berle

15 Walter Cronkite

16 Dinah Shore

17 Bob Newhart

18 Richard Chamberlain

19 Tom Selleck

20 James Arness

21 Peter Falk

22 Edward R. Murrow

23 Miss Piggy

24 Robert Young

25 Bob Hope

26 Farrah Fawcett

27 Don Knotts

28 Roseanne

29 Sid Caesar

30 Jerry Seinfeld

31 Phil Silvers

32 Rocky and Bullwinkle

33 Telly Savalas

34 Barbara Walters

35 Fred Rogers

36 David Janssen

37 Susan Lucci

38 Carroll O'Connor

39 Micheal J. Fox

40 Patty Duke

41 Alan Alda

42 Phil Donahue

43 Lawrence Welk

44 Raymond Burr

45 David Letterman

46 Julia Child

47 Howard Cosell

48 Bart Simpson

49 Ricky Nelson

50 Ed Sullivan

It's been six years since we chose the personalities on this list. Since then, even more stars have left their mark, changing the television landscape in all areas: comedy, drama, news, reality and children's programming.

Simon Cowell

Tyne Daly

Elmo

Dennis Franz

James Gandolfini

Kelsey Grammer

Martin Sheen

Jon Stewart

Kiefer Sutherland

The Tonight Show Starring Johnny Carson

Groucho Marx introduced Johnny on his first show.

Greatest Characters

1 **Louie De Palma**
Taxi

2 **Ed Norton**
The Honeymooners

3 **Lucy Ricardo**
I Love Lucy

4 **Fonzie**
Happy Days

5 **Archie Bunker**
All in the Family

6 **Mr. Spock**
Star Trek

7 **Lt. Columbo**
Columbo

8 **Emma Peel**
The Avengers

9 **Barney Fife**
The Andy Griffith Show

10 **George Costanza**
Seinfeld

11 **J.R. Ewing**
Dallas

12 **Felix Unger & Oscar Madison**
The Odd Couple

13 **Ralph Kramden**
The Honeymooners

14 **Homer Simpson**
The Simpsons

15 **Lilly Harper**
I'll Fly Away

16 **Sgt. Bilko**
The Phil Silvers Show

17 **Alex P. Keaton**
Family Ties

18 **Theo Kojak**
Kojak

19 **Maxwell Smart**
Get Smart

20 **Eddie Haskell**
Leave It to Beaver

21 **Mary Richards**
The Mary Tyler Moore Show

22 **Maynard G. Krebs**
The Many Loves of Dobie Gillis

23 **Andy Sipowicz**
NYPD Blue

24 **Paladin**
Have Gun, Will Travel

25 **Jim Rockford**
The Rockford Files

26 **Roseanne**
Roseanne

27 **Steve Urkel**
Family Matters

28 **Edina Monsoon**
Absolutely Fabulous

29 **Ted Baxter**
The Mary Tyler Moore Show

30 **Frank Pembleton**
Homicide: Life on the Street

31 **Niles Crane**
Frasier

32 **Jim Ignatowski**
Taxi

33 **Diane Chambers**
Cheers

34 **Mork**
Mork & Mindy

35 **Kramer**
Seinfeld

36 **Fred Sanford**
Sanford and Son

37 **Hawk**
Spenser: For Hire

38 **Jane Hathaway**
The Beverly Hillbillies

39 **Artie**
The Larry Sanders Show

40 **Alexis Carrington**
Dynasty

41 **Dr. Mark Craig**
St. Elsewhere

42 **Bill Bittinger**
Buffalo Bill

43 **Adam**
Northern Exposure

44 **David Addison**
Moonlighting

45 **Jane Tennison**
Prime Suspect

46 **Xena**
Xena: Warrior Princess

47 **Douglas Wambaugh**
Picket Fences

48 **Miles Drentel**
thirtysomething

49 **Elliot Carlin**
The Bob Newhart Show

50 **Maurice "Buddy" Sorrell**
The Dick Van Dyke Show

On Second Thought...

These favorites were chosen in 1999. Since then, several more characters have changed the landscape of TV, including quirky detectives, a spy, a gangster, a sex-pot, a castaway and a vampire.

Samantha Jones, *Sex and the City*

Buffy Summers, *Buffy the Vampire Slayer*

Sydney Bristow, *Alias*

Jack McFarland, *Will & Grace*

Karen Walker, *Will & Grace*

Lorelai Gilmore, *Gilmore Girls*

Tony Soprano, *The Sopranos*

Jack Bauer, *24*

Adrian Monk, *Monk*

Denny Crane, *Boston Legal*

John Locke, *Lost*

Dr. Greg House, *House*

Veronica Mars, *Veronica Mars*

Ari Gold, *Entourage*

Earl Hickey, *My Name Is Earl*

Joy Turner, *My Name Is Earl*

Dwight Schrute, *The Office*

Michael Scott, *The Office*

Jack Donaghy, *30 Rock*

Game Show Hosts
We Love The Most

Allen Ludden
The G.E. College Bowl
and *Password*

Bob Barker
The Price Is Right
and *Truth or Consequences*

Gene Rayburn
The Sky's the Limit
and *Match Game*

Alex Trebek
The Wizard of Odds
High Rollers
and *Jeopardy!*

Bob Eubanks
The Newlywed Game

Bill Cullen
Place the Face
The Price Is Right
Name That Tune
and *The $25,000 Pyramid*

Peter Marshall
Hollywood Squares

Groucho Marx
You Bet Your Life

Guy Smiley
Sesame Street

Regis Philbin
Who Wants to Be a Millionaire

Richard Dawson
Family Feud

Pat Sajak
G.E. College Bowl
and *Wheel of Fortune*

Howie Mandel
Deal or No Deal

Marc Summers
Double Dare

Greatest Game Shows

1 *The Price Is Right*

2 *Jeopardy!*

3 *The G.E. College Bowl*

4 *Password*

5 *What's My Line?*

6 *$25,000 Pyramid*

7 *Who Wants to Be a Millionaire?*

8 *Masquerade Party*

9 *To Tell the Truth*

10 *Match Game*

11 *The Newlywed Game*

12 *Survivor*

13 *Queen for a Day*

14 *Family Feud*

15 *Twenty-one*

16 *The Gong Show*

17 *Video Village*

18 *Let's Make a Deal*

19 *The Hollywood Squares*

20 *Concentration*

21 *Truth or Consequences*

22 *The $64,000 Question*

23 *Beat the Clock*

24 *You Bet Your Life*

25 *Wheel of Fortune*

On Second Thought...

The Question:
Since this list was first published on January 27, 2001, what are other game shows that would make the grade?

The Answers:
- *Remote Control* (MTV)
- *The Weakest Link*
- *Win Ben Stein's Money*
- *Deal or No Deal*

Teen Idols

1 **David Cassidy** as Keith Partridge on *The Partridge Family* (1970-74)

2 **Ricky Nelson** on *The Adventures of Ozzie and Harriet* (1952-66)

3 **John Travolta** as Vinnie Barbarino on *Welcome Back, Kotter* (1975-79)

4 **Johnny Depp** as Off. Tom Hanson on *21 Jump Street* (1987-90)

5 **Edd Byrnes** as Gerald Lloyd Kookson III (aka Kookie) on *77 Sunset Strip* (1958-63)

6 **Luke Perry** as Dylan McKay on *Beverly Hills, 90210* (1990-95; 1998-2000)

7 **Richard Chamberlain** as Dr. James Kildare on *Dr. Kildare* (1961-66)

8 **Bobby Sherman** as Logger Jeremy Bolt on *Here Come the Brides* (1968-70)

9 **Davy Jones** as Davy on *The Monkees* (1966-68)

10 **Troy Donahue** as Sandy Winfield II on *Surfside 6* (1960-62)

11 **Jason Priestley** as Brandon Walsh on *Beverly Hills, 90210* (1990-98)

12 **Rick Springfield** as Dr. Noah Drake on *General Hospital* (1981-83)

13 **Leif Garrett** as Endy Karras on *Three for the Road* (1975)

14 **Donny Osmond** on *Donny and Marie* (1976-79)

15 **Will Smith** as Will Smith on *The Fresh Prince of Bel-Air* (1990-96)

16 **Scott Baio** as Chachi on *Happy Days* (1977-84) and *Joanie Loves Chachi* (1982-83)

17 **Ashton Kutcher** as Michael Kelso on *That '70s Show* (1998-2006)

18 **Clay Aiken** on *American Idol* (Season 2; 2003)

19 **Kirk Cameron** as Mike Seaver on *Growing Pains* (1985-92)

20 **Ricky Schroder** as Ricky Stratton on *Silver Spoons* (1982-87)

21 **David Boreanaz** as Angel on *Buffy the Vampire Slayer* (1997-99) and *Angel* (1999-2004)

22 **Chad Michael Murray** as Lucas Scott on *One Tree Hill* (2003-Present)

23 **Michael J. Fox** as Alex P. Keaton on *Family Ties* (1982-89)

24 **Carson Daly** as the host of *Total Request Live* (1998-2002)

25 **Joey Lawrence** as Joey Russo on *Blossom* (1991-95)

American Idol

Season 1 is the only year the runner-up did not release a single following the show's finale.

TV's All-Time Greatest Moms

1 **Marge Simpson** (voiced by Julie Kavner), *The Simpsons*
Juggling bratty Bart, precocious Lisa and pacifier-addicted moppet Maggie while reining in hubby Homer's scheming makes Marge our queen mother.
Why she rocks: She's the modern-day June Cleaver, with her own string of pearls and a well-stocked hairdo that hides cash and spare pacifiers.
Why we'd want her in our corner: She'll defend her tribe no matter what. "If Maggie could talk, I'm sure she'd apologize for shooting you," Marge tells mean Mr. Burns.
Words of wisdom: "Let's forget our troubles with a bowl of strawberry ice cream."

2 **June Cleaver** (Barbara Billingsley), *Leave It to Beaver*
She not only dishes out pearls of wisdom, but she's also never without her trademark string of pearls or a warm hug for her boys.
Why she rocks: The woman wears fancy dresses and high heels to vacuum, for goodness sake! Not to mention, her hair always looks like she just stepped out of a beauty salon.
Why we'd want her in our corner: She's a woman who isn't afraid to exact punishment, as Wally and the Beav—who are denied after-school milk and cookies when they misbehave—know all too well.
Words of wisdom: "I wish Wally wouldn't use words like 'flaky' and 'kooky'."

3 **Clair Huxtable** (Phylicia Rashad), *The Cosby Show*
This feisty lawyer with five kids is the super mom of the '80s.
Why she rocks: She plans special, girls-only days with her daughters and sends killer care packages to Denise at college.
Why we'd want her in our corner: Knows how to stand her ground—with Cliff, Elvin and even teen Vanessa in a battle of wills over wearing makeup.
Words of wisdom: (to the guys in the family) "If you don't get it together and drop these macho attitudes, you are never gonna have anybody bringing you anything, anyplace, anytime, ever!"

4 **Olivia Walton** (Michael Learned), *The Waltons*
Mama Walton battles polio, tuberculosis, the Depression and World War II, but keeps her seven kids happy, healthy and loved.
Why she rocks: Olivia has the chance to be a singer, a painter and a dressmaker, but gives them all up to raise her clan.
Why we'd want her in our corner: She wins the cake-baking contest at the county fair...with icing made from whiskey!
Words of wisdom: "I think you could be anything you want to be, doll."

5 Lorelai Gilmore (Lauren Graham), *Gilmore Girls*

She's a sassy single mom who's also her daughter's best pal (she had her at age 16).

Why she rocks: She shares her life experiences, sense of humor and a killer wardrobe with Rory.

Why we'd want her in our corner: She eggs (using deviled eggs) Jess's car when he's a jerk to Rory.

Words of wisdom: "I'm afraid once your heart is involved, it all comes out in Moron."

6 Marion Cunningham (Marion Ross), *Happy Days*

This ditzy but nurturing mom helped turn surrogate son Fonzie from a thug to a loveable lug.

Why she rocks: She cooks, keeps a spotless house, dotes on Richie and Joanie and still finds time to get "frisky" with Howard.

Why we'd want her in our corner: She's the only person brave enough to call Fonzie "Arthur" and one of the few who ever told him to "Sit on it!"

Words of wisdom: "Life would be so much more pleasant if we just had more closet space."

7 Caroline Ingalls (Karen Grassle), *Little House on the Prairie*

She's an infinitely patient mom, even with all the tribulations of prairie life.

Why she rocks: The Ingalls are poor, but Caroline still whips up pretty party dresses for the girls.

Why we'd want her in our corner: No one in Walnut Grove stands up to snobby Mrs. Oleson like Caroline does!

Words of wisdom: "I'm sure Nellie has her good qualities somewhere."

8 Carol Brady (Florence Henderson), *The Brady Bunch*

Lovely lady who's a loving mom and step mom.

Why she rocks: She cooks—er, helps Alice cook—tasty meals like pork chops and applesauce.

Why we'd want her in our corner: Teaches, but ever-so-gently. When Marcia injures her nose, her nose, her nose, a sympathetic Carol reminds her that she wasn't nice in dissing Charlie.

Words of wisdom: "The times might have changed, but people haven't."

9 Elyse Keaton (Meredith Baxter), *Family Ties*

Her '60s hippie sensibilities make her an understanding mom.

Why she rocks: Doesn't agree with rabid Republican son Alex, but supports his right to be different.

Why we'd want her in our corner: Saves her Nixon-loving offspring from himself by putting him in his place when he gets too obnoxious for his britches.

Words of wisdom: "I bet Skippy didn't stay up all night worrying about Watergate."

10 Bree Van De Kamp (Marcia Cross), *Desperate Housewives*

She's obsessed with cooking and cleaning, but beneath those sweater sets lives the heart of a gun-wielding mama who'll do anything to protect her family.

Why she rocks: She does bake a tasty muffin.

Why we'd want her in our corner: The law-abiding lady hides her son's hit-and-run accident to keep him from going to the slammer.

Words of wisdom: "I would love you even if you were a murderer."

Greatest TV Dads
of All Time

This list of first-rate fathers was published in 2004, as TV GUIDE looked back on 50 years of covering the television industry.

1 **Cliff Huxtable** (Bill Cosby), *The Cosby Show*

2 **Ben Cartwright** (Lorne Greene), *Bonanza*

3 **John Walton** (Ralph Waite), *The Waltons*

4 **Charles Ingalls** (Michael Landon), *Little House on the Prairie*

5 **Danny Williams** (Danny Thomas), *Make Room for Daddy/The Danny Thomas Show*

6 **Jim Anderson** (Robert Young), *Father Knows Best*

7 **Steve Douglas** (Fred MacMurray), *My Three Sons*

8 **Andy Taylor** (Andy Griffith), *The Andy Griffith Show*

9 **Howard Cunningham** (Tom Bosley), *Happy Days*

10 **Ray Barone** (Ray Romano), *Everybody Loves Raymond*

11 **Rev. Eric Camden** (Stephen Collins), *7th Heaven*

12 **Steven Keaton** (Michael Gross), *Family Ties*

13 **Dan Conner** (John Goodman), *Roseanne*

14 **Mike Brady** (Robert Reed), *The Brady Bunch*

15 **Tom Corbett** (Bill Bixby), *The Courtship of Eddie's Father*

16 **Dr. Alex Stone** (Carl Betz), *The Donna Reed Show*

17 **Forest Bedford** (Sam Waterston), *I'll Fly Away*

18 **George Lopez**, *George Lopez*

19 **Herman Munster** (Fred Gwynne), *The Munsters*

20 **Tim Taylor** (Tim Allen), *Home Improvement*

21 **Ozzie Nelson**, *The Adventures of Ozzie and Harriet*

22 **Rob Petrie** (Dick Van Dyke), *The Dick Van Dyke Show*

23 **Tony Micelli** (Tony Danza), *Who's the Boss?*

24 **Archie Bunker** (Carroll O' Connor), *All in the Family*

25 **Sandy Cohen** (Peter Gallagher), *The O.C.*

26 **Doug Lawrence** (James Broderick), *Family*

27 **Michael Kyle** (Damon Wayans), *My Wife and Kids*

28 **Ward Cleaver** (Hugh Beaumont), *Leave It to Beaver*

29 **Jack Bristow** (Victor Garber), *Alias*

30 **Chester Riley** (William Bendix), *The Life of Riley*

31 **Andy Sipowicz** (Dennis Franz), *NYPD Blue*

32 **Lucas McCain** (Chuck Conners), *The Rifleman*

33 **Tom Bradford** (Dick Van Patten), *Eight Is Enough*

34 **Philip Banks** (James Avery), *The Fresh Prince of Bel-Air*

35 **Homer Simpson**, *The Simpsons*

36 **Rick Sammier** (Billy Campbell), *Once and Again*

37 **Jason Seaver** (Alan Thicke), *Growing Pains*

38 **John Robinson** (Guy Williams), *Lost in Space*

39 **Martin Lane** (William Schallert), *The Patty Duke Show*

40 **Will Girardi** (Joe Mantegna), *Joan of Arcadia*

41 **Jim Walsh** (James Eckhouse), *Beverly Hills, 90210*

42 **Fred Sanford** (Redd Foxx), *Sanford and Son*

43 **Andy Brown** (Treat Williams), *Everwood*

44 **George Jefferson** (Sherman Hemsley), *The Jeffersons*

45 **Joseph "Rocky" Rockford** (Noah Beery), *The Rockford Files*

46 **Michael Steadman** (Ken Olin), *thirtysomething*

47 **Bernie Mac**, *The Bernie Mac Show*

48 **Paul Hennessy** (John Ritter), *8 Simple Rules for Dating My Teenage Daughter*

49 **Graham Chase** (Tom Irwin), *My-So-Called Life*

50 **Benjamin Sisko** (Avery Brooks), *Star Trek: Deep Space Nine*

On Second Thought...

A few more standouts have emerged over the last few years...

Martin Crane (John Mahoney), *Frasier*

Tom Scavo (Doug Savant), *Desperate Housewives*

Michael Dawson (Harold Perrineau), *Lost*

Alan Eppes (Judd Hirsch), *Numb3rs*

Keith Mars (Enrico Colantoni), *Veronica Mars*

Sexiest Stars of All Time

1 **(tie) George Clooney** as Dr Doug Ross, *ER* (1994-99)

1 **(tie) Diana Rigg** as Mrs. Emma, *The Avengers* (1966-68)

3 **Angie Dickinson** as Suzanne "Pepper" Anderson, *Police Woman* (1974-78)

4 **Denzel Washington** as Dr. Philip Chandler, *St. Elsewhere* (1982-88)

5 **Peggy Lipton** as Julie Barnes, *The Mod Squad* (1968-73)

6 **Richard Chamberlain** as Dr. Kildare, *Dr. Kildare* (1961-66)

7 **Tom Selleck** as Thomas Magnum, *Magnum, P.I.* (1980-88)

8 **Kim Cattrall** as Samantha Jones, *Sex and the City* (1998-2004)

9 **Henry Simmons** as Det. Baldwin Jones, *NYPD Blue* (2000-05)

10 **Farrah Fawcett** as Jill Munroe, *Charlie's Angels* (1976-77)

11 **Clint Eastwood** as Rowdy Yates, *Rawhide* (1959-66)

12 **Don Johnson** as Sonny Crockett, *Miami Vice* (1984-89)

13 **Cher**, *The Sonny and Cher Comedy Hour* (1971-74)

14 **Dean Martin**, *The Dean Martin Show* (1965-74)

15 **Jennifer Aniston** as Rachel Green, *Friends* (1994-2004)

16 **Linda Evans** as Audra Barkley, *The Big Valley* (1965-69)

17 **Jimmy Smits** as Victor Sifuentes, *L.A. Law* (1986-91) AND Det. Bobby Simone, *NYPD Blue* (1994-98)

18 **Anne Francis** as Honey West, *Honey West* (1965-66)

19 **Benjamin Bratt** as Det. Reynaldo "Rey" Curtis, *Law & Order* (1995-99)

20 **Jennifer Garner** as Sydney Bristow, *Alias* (2001- 06)

21 **James Garner** as Bret Maverick, *Maverick* (1957-60)

22 **Burt Reynolds** as Quint Asper, *Gunsmoke* (1962-65)

23 **Jill Hennessy** as Claire Kincaid, *Law & Order* (1993-96) AND Jordan Cavanaugh, *Crossing Jordan* (2001-present)

24 **Pierce Brosnan** as Remington Steele, *Remington Steele* (1982-87)

25 **Heather Locklear** as Amanda Woodward, *Melrose Place* (1993-98)

26 **Steve McQueen** as Josh Randall, *Wanted—Dead or Alive* (1958-61)

27 **Catherine Bach** as Daisy Duke, *The Dukes of Hazzard* (1979-85)

28 **James Gandolfini** as Tony Soprano, *The Sopranos* (1999-2007)

29 **Diahann Carroll** as Julia Baker, *Julia* (1968-71)

30 **Julie Newmar** as Catwoman, *Batman* (1965)

31 **The Men of *Soul Food*: Darrin DeWitt Henson** as Lem, **Boris Kodjoe** as Damon and **Rockmond Dunbar** as Kenny, *Soul Food* (2000-04)

32 **The Women of *Baywatch*: Pamela Anderson** as C.J. Parker, **Carmen Electra** as Lani McKenzie and **Yasmine Bleeth** as Caroline Holden, *Baywatch* (1990s)

33 **Michael Landon** as Joe Cartwright, *Bonanza* (1959-73)

34 **Tuesday Weld** as Thalia Menninger, *The Many Loves of Dobie Gillis* (1959-60)

35 **David Duchovny** as Agent Fox Mulder, *The X-Files* (1993-2000)

36 **Michael Michele** as Cleo Finch, *ER* (1999-2001)

37 **Troy Donahue** as Sandy Winfield II, *Surfside Six* (1960-62)

38 **Katie Holmes** as Joey Potter, *Dawson's Creek* (1998-2003)

39 **Barbara Eden** as Jeannie, *I Dream of Jeannie* (1965-70)

40 **Luke Perry** as Dylan McKay, *Beverly Hills, 90210* (1990-95; 1998-2000)

41 **Jeri Ryan** as Seven of Nine, *Star Trek: Voyager* (1997-2001)

42 **Ashton Kutcher** as Michael Kelso, *That '70s Show* (1998-2006)

43 **John Forsythe** as Blake Carrington, *Dynasty* (1981-89)

44 **Dorothy Malone** as Constance MacKenzie, *Peyton Place* (1964-69)

45 **Jessica Alba** as Max Guevara/X-452, *Dark Angel* (2000-02)

46 **Lucy Liu** as Ling Woo, *Ally McBeal* (1998-2001)

47 **David Cassidy** as Keith Partridge, *The Partridge Family* (1970-74)

48 **Alyssa Milano** as Phoebe Halliwell, *Charmed* (1998-2006)

49 **John Schneider** as Bo Duke, *The Dukes of Hazzard* (1979-85)

50 **Dawn Wells** as Mary Ann Summers, *Gilligan's Island* (1964-67)

The TV industry has no shortage of sexy stars. Here are a few more recent celebs that get us all hot and bothered.

Kristen Bell as Veronica Mars, *Veronica Mars* (2004-present)

Jessica Biel as Mary Camden, *7th Heaven* (1996-2001)

Patrick Dempsey as Dr. Derek Shepherd, *Grey's Anatomy* (2005-present)

James Denton as Mike Delfino, *Desperate Housewives* (2004-present)

Taye Diggs as Kevin Hill, *Kevin Hill* (2004-05)

Matthew Fox as Jack, *Lost* (2004-present)

Josh Holloway as Sawyer, *Lost* (2004-present)

Evangeline Lilly as Kate, *Lost* (2004-present)

Eva Longoria as Gabrielle Solis, *Desperate Housewives* (2004-present)

Jennifer Love Hewitt as Sarah Reeves, *Party of Five* (1995-99) AND Melinda Gordon, *Ghost Whisperer* (2005-present)

Vanessa Marcil as Brenda Barrett, *General Hospital* AND Samantha Jane, *Vegas* (2003-present)

Kiefer Sutherland as Jack Bauer, *24* (2001-present)

Vanessa Williams as Wilhelmina Slater, *Ugly Betty* (2006-present)

Sex and the City

Sarah Jessica Parker had a no-nudity clause in her contract.

Memorable Catchphrases

In 2005, TV GUIDE chose TV's Top 20 Catchphrases. So come on down as we count down the sayings that swept the nation.

1 **"Yada, yada, yada,"** Jerry Seinfeld, *Seinfeld*

2 **"To the moon, Alice!"** Ralph Kramden, *The Honeymooners*

3 **"Eat my shorts,"** Bart Simpson, *The Simpsons*

4 **"How *you* doin'?"** Joey Tribbiani, *Friends*

5 **"Live long and prosper,"** Spock, *Star Trek*

6 **"Let's hug it out, bitch,"** Ari Gold, *Entourage*

7 **"Come on down!"** Johnny Olson and Rod Roddy, *The Price Is Right*

8 **"Sit on it!"** Fonzie, *Happy Days*

9 **"The truth is out there,"** *The X-Files*

10 **"Sock it to me,"** various people, *Rowan & Martin's Laugh-In*

11 **"We are two wild and crazy guys,"** Dan Aykroyd and Steve Martin, *Saturday Night Live*

12 **"Stifle, Edith,"** Archie Bunker, *All in the Family*

13 **"He's just not that into you,"** Berger, *Sex and the City*

14 **"Dyn-o-mite!"** J.J. Evans, *Good Times*

15 **"Up your nose with a rubber hose,"** Vinnie Barbarino, *Welcome Back, Kotter*

16 **"The devil made me do it!"** Geraldine Jones, *The Flip Wilson Show*

17 **"Whatchoo talkin' 'bout Willis?"** Arnold Drummond, *Diff'rent Strokes*

18 **"Who loves ya, baby?"** Lt. Theo Kojak, *Kojak*

19 **"You look mah-velous,"** Billy Crystal as Fernando, *Saturday Night Live*

20 **"Homey don't play that,"** Homey the Clown, *In Living Color*

On Second Thought...

Below are 40 more unforgettable (and highly quotable) phrases made famous by TV characters.

"Jane, you ignorant slut," Dan Aykroyd, *Saturday Night Live*

"Oh, my nose!" Marcia Brady, *The Brady Bunch*

"Legen-...wait for it....-dary," Barney Stinson, *How I Met Your Mother*

"What's up, doc?" Bugs Bunny, *Looney Tunes*

"O-tay!" Buckwheat, *Saturday Night Live*

"Crikey!" Steve Irwin, *The Crocodile Hunter*

"Va-jay-jay," Miranda Bailey, *Grey's Anatomy*

"Bam!" Emeril Lagasse

"Kiss my grits," Florence "Flo" Castleberry, *Alice*

"Whoa!" Joey Russo, *Blossom*

"Cowabunga" *Teenage Mutant Ninja Turtles* AND Bart Simpson, *The Simpsons*

"Baby, you're the greatest!" Ralph Kramden, *The Honeymooners*

"Holy crap!" Frank Barone, *Everybody Loves Raymond*

"Schwiiing!" Wayne Campbell, *Saturday Night Live*

"You're fired," Donald Trump, *The Apprentice*

"How rude!" Stephanie Tanner, *Full House*

"Don't be ridic-u-lous" Balki Bartokomous, *Perfect Strangers*

"I know you are but what am I?" Pee-wee Herman, *Pee-wee's Playhouse*

"I pity the fool," Mr. T, *The A-Team*

"Let's be careful out there," Sgt. Phil Esterhaus, *Hill Street Blues*

"Let's ROCK!" Al Bundy, *Married...With Children*

"Do you smell what the Rock is cookin'?" The Rock, *WWF*

"Aaaaaaayyyyyyyyy," Fonzie, *Happy Days*

"Here it is, your moment of zen," Jon Stewart, *The Daily Show*

"And that's the way it is," Walter Cronkite, *The CBS Evening News*

"Whassup?" Budweiser commercial

"You rang?" Lurch, *The Addams Family*

"Heeeeeeeere's Johnny!" Ed McMahon, *The Tonight Show Starring Johnny Carson*

"You are not the biggest loser," Caroline Rhea, *The Biggest Loser*

"The tribe has spoken," Jeff Probst, *Survivor*

"I want my MTV," MTV slogan

"Tastes great, less filling," Miller Lite slogan

"I'm listening," Dr. Frasier Crane, *Frasier*

"D'oh!" Homer Simpson, *The Simpsons*

"Somebody's in trouuuubbble," Tootie Ramsey, *The Facts of Life*

"Let's get ready to rumble!" Boxing announcer Michael Buffer

"Are you ready for some football?" Hank Williams Jr., *Monday Night Football*

"Well, excuuuuuuse me!" Steve Martin, *Saturday Night Live*

"For me to poop on," Triumph, the Insult Comic Dog, *Late Night With Conan O'Brien*

"Truthiness," Stephen Colbert, *The Colbert Report*

Kojak

Telly Savalas was Jennifer Aniston's godfather and Nicollette Sheridan's stepfather.

The 10 Most **Romantic Couples**

In TV History

There's no doubt about it—TV love is a many-splendored thing. As Valentine's Day 1999 drew near, TV GUIDE and Romance Classics partnered to present TV's most passionate pairings. Some of these dynamic duos seemed destined to be together, while others, at least at first, appeared incredibly mismatched. But all of our favorite twosomes have one thing in common: they've loved each other through the best and worst of circumstances—and we, of course, have loved them for it.

1 Partners in Crime
Diane Russell and Bobby Simone, *NYPD Blue*

We're still not over Bobby's shocking death but at least we've got the memory (and reruns) of TV's most romantic couple of all time. This loving and very sexy couple had just begun to find true happiness balancing life inside and outside the 15th Precinct when tragedy struck. When widower Bobby Simone (Jimmy Smits) fell for newcomer Diane Russell (Kim Delaney), the pair embarked on a relationship that brought out the best in their emotionally wounded characters. He helped her battle alcoholism and overcome her fear of commitment; she made him feel he could love—and be loved—again. Smits believed the dysfunctional nature of the characters contributed to their appeal. "That kind of stuff in the closet, that baggage, really made the relationship interesting." Whether they went under the covers or soaked in the bathtub, they generated enough passion to make *NYPD Blue* red-hot. "It was sexy when it needed to be," said Smits. But we'll never forget the many tender moments between Diane and Bobby, from their city-hall wedding to their heartbreaking bedside good-byes.

2 Supernatural Soul Mates
Catherine and Vincent, *Beauty and the Beast*

The outwardly capable but emotionally fragile Catherine (Linda Hamilton) toiled as an assistant district attorney by day but lived for those precious nighttime hours when Vincent (Ron Perlman) emerged from his secret world below New York City. In 1989, Catherine received a lethal injection from an evil crime lord shortly after giving birth to a son: We wept as Vincent watched helplessly while she died in his arms. "Most of the letters I got at the time were from people who wanted to share their pain," said Perlman. "Vincent represented the vulnerability in all of us. His life was a metaphor for what is unacceptable in all of us, and to have a woman like Catherine giving him her unconditional love—that's the stuff romance is really made of."

3 Opposites Attract
Lucy and Ricky Ricardo, *I Love Lucy*

It has been more than a half-century since we first met Lucy and Ricky Ricardo, and we still love the wacky redhead and her perpetually exasperated husband. What could be more romantic than Ricky singing "I Love Lucy"? Or Lucy giving birth to Little Ricky on January 19, 1953—the same night Lucille Ball and Desi Arnaz welcomed Desi Jr. into the world? (The event was heralded on TV GUIDE's first cover.) We treasure this TV couple because we know that even behind the scenes, their romance was the real thing.

4 Love in the Afternoon
Luke and Laura Spencer, *General Hospital*

For more than 25 years (even with extended absences from *General Hospital*), Lucas Lorenzo Spencer and Laura Webber Baldwin Spencer have reigned supreme as the supercouple of soap-dom. The undeniable magic between actors Genie Francis and Anthony Geary—and some of the most seductive story lines in daytime (they even made saving the world from a deep freeze enticing)—have earned them a permanent spot in the hearts of soap-opera fans everywhere. "She is his angel, he is her hero," said Geary. "That's basically the formula of Luke and Laura." More than 16 million viewers tuned in for their November 1981 nuptials, a two-day celebration attended by none other than fan Elizabeth Taylor (as wicked Helena Cassadine). Since then, they have continued to prove that the path to true love never runs smooth. We wouldn't want it any other way.

5 For Love and Money
Bobby and Pam Ewing, *Dallas*

Here's a recipe for one Texas-size romance: Take a headstrong heir to an oil fortune and a beautiful woman from the wrong side of the tracks, mix in several overheated story lines, add a dash of feuding families and watch the fireworks. The impassioned pairing of Pam and Bobby Ewing (Victoria Principal and Patrick Duffy) kept viewers tuning in throughout their make-ups and break-ups until his death in 1985 and her subsequent marriage to Mark Graison. Luckily the two latter events turned out to be just a dream. The pair reconciled, but then Pam, disfigured in a car accident, disappeared from the hospital and never returned.

6 Young Hearts
Kevin Arnold and Winnie Cooper, *The Wonder Years*

When Kevin (Fred Savage) and Winnie (Danica McKellar) shared their first kiss on the show's first episode (which premiered after the Super Bowl in 1988) the sweetest adolescent romance in TV history was born. "Kevin and Winnie's first kiss was both our real first kiss as well," recalled McKellar. "It was a significant event in my life." At the time life was imitating art. "I had a crush on Fred and I found out he had one on me, "she says. "We did six takes and the director used the last one, I remember because after we kissed for the last time, Fred touched my hair." Whether they were dealing with peer pressure at a "make-out party" (they pretended to participate) or were just trying to survive junior high, they poignantly reminded us of the wonders and woes of a first love. And throughout their coming-of-age ups and downs, one thing remained constant—they were always there for each other and for their legions of fans.

7 Domestic Bliss
Cliff and Clair Huxtable, *The Cosby Show*

Married life never seemed more appealing. Cliff and Clair Huxtable (Bill Cosby and Phylicia Rashad) balanced kids, careers and their incredibly egalitarian relationship with witty, self-effacing humor and a dignity that made their altared state must-see TV. While the children were always their first priority, their desire never died. "The most romantic moment I remember is the night Clair and Cliff reenacted their high-school prom night," said Rashad. "They carried the beauty of the beginning of their romance [through] all those years." When they waltzed off the set and into TV history on the final episode, we knew they'd inspire future sitcom unions. As it turned out, the two inspired their own reunion on *Cosby*.

8 Will They or Won't They?
Maddie Hayes and David Addison, *Moonlighting*

"What contributed to Maddie and David being attracted to each other was Cybill Shepherd and Bruce Willis being attracted to each other," said Shepherd of this pair of private detectives. "I don't believe you can fake it. The chemistry of the actors comes through." Amid nonstop wise-cracks and car chases, the couple shared some of TV's most passionate moments, including a dream sequence in which Maddie seduces David in a Stanley Nonen-directed dance number set to Billy Joel's "Big Man on Mulberry Street." After two years of sexually charged sparring, the dueling duo became lovers in the 1987 episode aptly titled "The Big Bang." When the couple who couldn't live with—or without—each other finally consummated their stormy relationship to the strains of "Be My Baby," we could feel the heat right through the TV screen. Of course, on-screen is exactly where the romance stayed. Despite Shepherd's admission of their undeniable heat (evident even during their later on-set discord), she insists that "Bruce and I were never intimate, and that helped, because that kills [the chemistry]."

9 Yuppie Love
Hope and Michael Steadman, *thirtysomething*

Hope and Michael Steadman (Mel Harris and Ken Olin) knew enough about life and love to be confused by both, yet they were committed to figuring things out together. Though he wanted to be a good husband, father and provider, sometimes the burden seemed overwhelming. She side-lined her publishing career to be a full-time wife and mother and felt guilty about her guilt. They seemed to have it all—a good marriage, kids, a great house and loving (if somewhat dysfunctional) friends—but their search for something more kept us tuning in for four years. In an episode titled "The Mike Van Dyke Show," Michael suffers a crisis of faith when Hope is in a car accident. Faced with the prospect of losing her and later learning she's pregnant with their second child, he is drawn back to his religion, and we are drawn to believe in the power of love.

10 Working-Class Heroes
Ralph and Alice Kramden, *The Honeymooners*

The blustery bus driver (Jackie Gleason) with the dashed dreams and ill-fated schemes proclaimed himself "king of the castle" but knew that without his long-suffering wife (Audrey Meadows) he couldn't shift out of first gear. Despite Ralph and Alice's bickering (his threats to send her "right to the moon" were usually met with a withering comment about his weight), when he cried "Baby, you're the greatest," "we knew their love was here to stay. In "'Twas the Night Before Christmas," Ralph finds Alice what he thinks is the perfect present—a box fashioned from 2,000 match-sticks—until she receives the same tacky trinket from a neighbor. In a panic, he sells his bowling ball to buy an orange-juice maker. Then Alice surprises him with a new bowling ball bag. When a choked-up Ralph tells her the best part of the holidays is knowing there's "somebody you're nuts about," they show us that love is always the best gift.

The 5 Best TV Crossovers

Sometimes when great TV series pool their resources, viewers are treated to a truly special event. Other times, when not-so-great sitcoms or dramas team up, the "event" is far less stellar. Here is our take on the best and worst crossover episodes.

Ally McBeal and *The Practice*: This crossover event played on the shows' differences for laughs. The law firm where Ally McBeal (Calista Flockhart) works takes on the case of a woman who has killed her husband with an axe, and claims to have been Lizzy Borden in a past life. Fearing they're not up to the challenge, Ally and Co. call in some help from *The Practice*'s Bobby Donnell and Eugene Young (Dylan McDermott and Steve Harris), who find *Ally*'s wacky law firm (unisex bathrooms, etc.) more than a little strange.

Buffy the Vampire Slayer and *Angel*: In the episodes "Pangs" (*Buffy*) and "I Will Remember You" (*Angel*), Angel (David Boreanaz) returns to Sunnydale and—unbeknownst to Buffy (Sarah Michelle Gellar)—helps the Scoobies in their battle against a group of angry Native American spirits. After Buffy finds out that Angel was there, she heads to Los Angeles, on what happens to be the same day a demon has made Angel human. The bittersweet conclusion finds the former lovers spending one wonderful day together—before Angel gets the Oracles to rewind time and erase the whole thing.

Crossing Jordan and *Las Vegas*: The episode "What Happens in Vegas Dies in Boston" began a series of crossovers between these two seemingly unrelated shows. On that *Crossing Jordan* episode, Dr. Jordan Cavanaugh and Det. Woody Hoyt (Jill Hennessy and Jerry O'Connell) travel to Las Vegas to investigate the death of a gambler, in which Montecito executives Danny McCoy and Sam Marquez (Josh Duhamel and Vanessa Marcil) are suspected. While there, Woody becomes involved with Sam, which subsequently brings him back to *Las Vegas*—and Sam to *Jordan*—on multiple occasions, establishing a permanent link between the series.

ER and *Third Watch*: When *ER*'s Dr. Susan Lewis (Sherry Stringfield) gets a frantic call from her 6-year-old niece, who's in a New York City hotel room with her former drug-addict mother, she immediately heads east in search of the girl. Once in the Big Apple, she goes on a series of ride-alongs with some *Third Watch* cops to track down her sister—beating the answers out of whomever gets in their way and bringing some gritty, NYC-style reality to the more high-minded *ER*.

Law & Order and *Homicide: Life on the Street*: In 1996's "Charm City"/"For God and Country," Dets. Lenny Briscoe and Rey Curtis (Jerry Orbach and Benjamin Bratt) reluctantly pair up with Baltimore detectives Frank Pembleton and Tim Bayliss (Andre Braugher and Kyle Secor) to catch a man accused of setting gas bombs in New York and Baltimore. The two teams butt heads throughout, demonstrating that equally skilled cops can have very different approaches to getting the job done.

The 5 Worst TV Crossovers

Family Matters and *Step by Step*: When *Family Matters*' resident nerd, Steve Urkel (Jaleel White), must beat a jock in a rope-climbing contest to win the girl of his dreams (seriously), he builds a rocket pack that inadvertently shoots him through the roof. Flying more than 100 miles from Illinois to Wisconsin, he crash-lands right in the middle of a *Step by Step* family barbecue. Unfortunately for viewers, everyone survives.

Grace Under Fire, Coach, The Drew Carey Show and *Ellen*: For a while there, ABC really had a knack for these painfully awkward crossovers. This one, billed as "Viva Las Vegas," found characters from all four previously unconnected series in Las Vegas at the same time, basically wandering through each other's shows. While people from all of the other shows found their way onto *Drew Carey*, the stars of *Ellen* and *Coach* (Ellen DeGeneres and Craig T. Nelson, respectively), sat out the whole crossover thing altogether, with the latter even titling its episode "Viva Las Ratings."

Martial Law and *Walker: Texas Ranger*: What do you get when two acclaimed karate-cop shows team up? This classic crossover in which *Martial Law*'s Sammo Law (Sammo Hung Kam-Bo) and the "Texas Ranger" himself, Cordell "Cord" Walker (Chuck Norris), work together to track down a criminal who murdered a Lone Star state ranger. The kung-fu-fighting finale practically defines the phrase "poetry in motion."

Millennium and *The X-Files*: When Chris Carter's *Millennium* wrapped up its final season in 1999, psychic investigator Frank Black (Lance Henriksen) had quit his job and gone into hiding with his daughter. But, since the show ended a year before the titular event, Carter decided to use *The X-Files* to wrap things up—a nice idea in theory. But in execution, what fans got was an institutionalized Black reluctantly helping Mulder and Scully thwart a plan by four Millennium Group members to be resurrected on New Year's Eve as all-powerful zombies. Why, Chris, why?

Sabrina the Teenage Witch, Boy Meets World, You Wish and *Teen Angel*: The wacky "TGIF" "fun" starts when Salem, a talking cat owned by Sabrina (Melissa Joan Hart), eats a magical "time ball," sending her back to the 1960s. Though the hippy decade seems fun at first, Sabrina soon tires of the lack of equality for women (truly a hot-button issue—30 years earlier). But when she tries to get the ball back, Salem takes off—and Sabrina ends up chasing him through the entire ABC Friday-night lineup, wreaking zany, time-warping havoc on every sitcom they pass through.

The Best Shows

You're Not Watching... *THROUGH THE YEARS*

As television lover, watchdog and critic, TV GUIDE feels strongly about quality programs. Case in point: its goal for several years to save exceptional but low-rated shows from the chopping block. Below are the series that the magazine dubbed "The Best Show You're Not Watching" and the results of our pleas.

Party of Five 1995

We Made the Case: A blend of soap opera and family drama, with an appealing cast dealing with a multitude of wrenching issues.

The Outcome: After its initial slow start, the show enjoyed a six-year run.

Homicide: Life on the Street 1996

We Made the Case: An arresting, gritty police series that stressed plot complexity and character development, not car chases or shoot-outs.

The Outcome: The crime drama saw numerous cast changes and a 1998 Emmy for Andre Baugher, and ran for six years,

The Practice 1998

We Made the Case: TV's toughest legal drama had realistic, strong and quirky lawyers fighting tough cases that did not always end with a tidy wrap-up.

The Outcome: Our readers listened: Not only did the show survive for six more years, but it spun off the acclaimed courtroom drama *Boston Legal*.

7th Heaven 1999

We Made the Case: There's no denying that, at its core, *7th Heaven* is a '50s show—albeit one significantly modified to deal frankly (and often humorously) with the harsh realities of family life in the '90s. The show makes a quiet but convincing argument that traditional values are still applicable to contemporary problems.

The Outcome: The show is still on the air 10 years after its debut.

Sports Night 2000

We Made the Case: The show was an acquired taste: its innovative style and verbal volleys were Aaron Sorkin at his best. But the razor-sharp dialogue and quirky characters got short shrift from ABC, being bounced around the schedule, thus dashing any hopes of ensuring solid ratings.

The Outcome: Sadly, the show was canceled just two months after our piece ran.

Once and Again 2001

We Made the Case: Lily and Rick worked hard to give love and marriage a second chance. Not easy to do when dealing with the tangled dynamics of extended and broken families. But the series handled its familial and relationship issues with poignance, wisdom and humor, and boasted one of TV's most impressive ensembles.

The Outcome: The show got a reprieve...but only for one more year.

Gilmore Girls 2002

We Made the Case: This dramedy has scintillating wit, genuine heart and the snappiest comebacks around. And let's not forget romantic intrigue. With help from its network, the show has done admirably in its quest for new viewers but is continually ignored by Emmy.

The Outcome: The Girls have been going strong ever since.

Everwood 2003

We Made the Case: A smart, if at times sudsy, multigenerational drama.

The Outcome: Our plea was heard...the series lasted until its network (WB) was taken over and renamed CW.

Angel 2003

We Made the Case: A supernatural *Buffy* spin-off with plenty of bite.

The Outcome: Boreanaz and Co. continued fighting the dark forces for just another year.

Without a Trace 2003

We Made the Case: The missing-person mystery is as engrossing as *CSI* but not as gross.

The Outcome: This dedicated team is still going strong as they work to reunite victims and their families

American Dreams 2003

We Made the Case: Feel-good nostalgia with kicky cameos of current pop stars re-creating '60 icons.

The Outcome: The '60s lived on for another two years.

Alias 2003

We Made the Case: Great spy intrigue, with a lighter, more escapist touch than *24*.
The Outcome: Sydney's complicated secret-agent life carried on for three more years, while Jennifer Garner made headlines, with her film career and love life.

Boomtown 2003

We Made the Case: The best new network crime drama in years, though a bit gimmicky.
The Outcome: Sorry, but the show survived just eight additional months.

Gilmore Girls

In the 2005 episode titled "But I'm a Gilmore," TV GUIDE editor Michael Ausiello can be seen in the background as a customer.

TV's 10 Biggest Brats

1. **Bart Simpson**
   The Simpsons

2. **Eddie Haskell**
   played by Ken Osmond
   Leave It to Beaver

3. **Nellie Oleson**
   played by Alison Arngrim
   Little House on the Prairie

4. **The Scavo Brothers**
   played by Brent and Shane Kinsman
   and Zane Huett
   Desperate Housewives

5. **Dee Thomas**
   played by Danielle Spencer
   What's Happening!!

6. **Danny Partridge**
   played by Danny Bonaduce
   The Partridge Family

7. **Wayne Arnold**
   played by Jason Hervey
   The Wonder Years

8. **Dennis Mitchell**
   played by Jay North
   Dennis the Menace

9. **Reese Wilkerson**
   played by Justin Berfield
   Malcolm in the Middle

10. **A.J. Soprano**
    played by Robert Iler
    The Sopranos

On Second Thought...

Here are a few more kids who will really grate on our nerves...

Darlene Conner played by Sara Gilbert, *Roseanne*

Bud Bundy played by David Faustino, *Married...With Children*

Eric Cartman voice of Trey Parker, *South Park*

Vicky the baby sitter voiced by Grey DeLisle, *The Fairly Oddparents*

Stewie Griffin voice of Seth MacFarlane, *Family Guy*

Cranky Characters

Mr. Wilson
Dennis the Menace

Mel Cooley
The Dick Van Dyke Show

Theodore J. Mooney
The Lucy Show

Sgt. Vince Carter
Gomer Pyle, USMC

Col. Wilhelm Klink
Hogan's Heroes

Oscar the Grouch
Sesame Street

Lucy Van Pelt
Charlie Brown specials

Lou Grant
The Mary Tyler Moore Show

Archie Bunker
All in the Family

Maude Findlay
Maude

Fred Sanford
Sanford and Son

Col. Sherman Potter
*M*A*S*H*

Ed Brown (The Man)
Chico and the Man

Mel Sharples
Alice

Stabler and Waldorf
The Muppet Show

Mr. Roper
Three's Company

Jonathan Higgins
Magnum, P.I.

Det. Mick Belker
Hill Street Blues

Dr. Mark Craig
St. Elsewhere

Carla Tortelli-LeBec
Cheers

Dr. Lilith Sternin-Crane
Cheers

Bill Bittinger
Buffalo Bill

Sophia Petrillo
The Golden Girls

Douglas Brackman Jr.
L.A. Law

Roseanne Conner
Roseanne

Darlene Conner
Roseanne

Murphy Brown
Murphy Brown

Jack Arnold
The Wonder Years

Coach Hayden Fox
Coach

Groundskeeper Willie
The Simpsons

Agnes Skinner (Principal Skinner's mother)
The Simpsons

Geoffrey
The Fresh Prince of Bel-Air

Andy Sipowicz
NYPD Blue

Loren Bray
Dr. Quinn, Medicine Woman

George Feeney
Boy Meets World

Angela Chase
My So-Called Life

Mr. Heckles
The downstairs neighbor on *Friends*

Frank Martin
ER

Dr. Robert Romano
ER

Eric Cartman
South Park

John Becker
Becker

Ken Titus
Titus

Det. Odafin `Fin' Tutuola
Law & Order: Special Victims Unit

Lois Wilkerson
Malcolm in the Middle

Dr. Perry Cox
Scrubs

Chloe O'Brian
24

Mrs. McCluskey
Desperate Housewives

Dr. Greg House
House

Stanley Hudson
The Office

Joy Turner
My Name Is Earl

All in the Family

The first toilet flush ever heard on TV was aired on *All in the Family*.

It's Murder Out There:
TV's Greatest Detectives

1 **Jim Rockford** (James Garner), *The Rockford Files*

2 **Lt. Columbo** (Peter Falk), *Columbo*

3 **Frank Pembleton** (Andre Braugher), *Homicide: Life on the Street*

4 **Mary Beth Lacey and Chris Cagney** (Tyne Daly and Sharon Gless), *Cagney & Lacey*

5 **Theo Kojak** (Telly Savalas), *Kojak*

6 **Thomas Magnum** (Tom Selleck), *Magnum, P.I.*

7 **Jane Tennison** (Helen Mirren), *Prime Suspect*

8 **David Addison and Maddie Hayes** (Bruce Willis and Cybill Shepherd), *Moonlighting*

9 **Steve McGarrett** (Jack Lord), *Hawaii Five-O*

10 **Andy Sipowicz** (Dennis Franz), *NYPD Blue*

11 **Tony Baretta** (Robert Blake), *Baretta*

12 **Joe Mannix** (Mike Connors), *Mannix*

13 **Jessica Fletcher** (Angela Lansbury), *Murder, She Wrote*

14 **Ricardo Tubbs and Sonny Crockett** (Philip Michael Thomas and Don Johnson), *Miami Vice*

15 **Lennie Briscoe** (Jerry Orbach), *Law & Order*

16 **Kelly Garrett, Sabrina Duncan and Jill Munroe** (Jaclyn Smith, Kate Jackson and Farrah Fawcett), *Charlie's Angels*

17 **Hercule Poirot** (David Suchet), *Agatha Christie Mysteries: Poirot*

18 **Robert T. Ironside** (Raymond Burr), *Ironside*

19 **Peter Gunn** (Craig Stevens), *Peter Gunn*

20 **Ken Hutchinson and Dave Starsky** (David Soul and Paul Michael Glaser), *Starsky and Hutch*

21 **Spenser** (Robert Urich), *Spenser: For Hire*

22 **Amos Burke** (Gene Barry), *Burke's Law*

23 **Frank Drebin** (Leslie Nielsen), *Police Squad!*

24 **Mick Belker** (Bruce Weitz), *Hill Street Blues*

25 **Honey West** (Anne Francis), *Honey West*

On Second Thought...

We've hunted down four more to add to our list.

Robert Goren (Vincent D'Onofrio), *Law & Order: Criminal Intent*

Gil Grissom (William Petersen), *CSI*

Veronica Mars (Kristen Bell), *Veronica Mars*

Adrian Monk (Tony Shalhoub), *Monk*

Starsky & Hutch

Starsky's red two-door Ford Torino was nicknamed the "Striped Tomato."

Wacky SideKicks

Every great sitcom character needs a silly sidekick to help them out with their crazy schemes and get them deeper into trouble. Sometimes these pals steal show (like Kramer or Urkel), and at times even got shows of their own (remember *Grady* or *Rhoda*?).

Ed Norton
(Art Carney), *The Honeymooners*

Ethel Mertz
(Vivian Vance), *I Love Lucy*

Barney Fife
(Don Knotts), *The Andy Griffith Show*

Barney Rubble
(voice of Mel Blanc), *The Flintstones*

Eddie Haskell
(Ken Osmond), *Leave It to Beaver*

Maynard G. Krebs
(Bob Denver), *The Many Loves of Dobie Gillis*

Dick Grayson/Robin
(Burt Ward), *Batman*

Shaggy
(voice of Casey Kasem),
Scooby-Doo: Where Are You?

Rhoda Morgenstern
(Valerie Harper), *The Mary Tyler Moore Show*

Howard Borden
(Bill Dailey), *The Bob Newhart Show*

Fred "Rerun" Stubbs
(Fred Berry), *What's Happening!!*

Grady Wilson
(Whitman Mayo), *Sanford and Son*

Larry Dallas
(Richard Kline), *Three's Company*

Potsie Weber and Ralph Malph
(Anson Williams and Donny Most), *Happy Days*

George Utley
(Tom Poston), *Newhart*

Erwin "Skippy" Handelman
(Marc Price), *Family Ties*

Kimmy Gibler
(Andrea Barber), *Full House*

Steve Urkel
(Jaleel White), *Family Matters*

"Screech" Powers
(Dustin Diamond), *Saved by the Bell*

Anthony Bouvier
(Meshach Taylor), *Designing Women*

Maryann Thorpe
(Christine Baranski), *Cybill*

Sideshow Bob
(voice of Kelsey Grammer), *The Simpsons*

Millhouse
(voice of Pamela Hayden), *The Simpsons*

Cosmo Kramer
(Michael Richards), *Seinfeld*

Jack McFarland and Karen Walker
(Sean Hayes & Megan Mullally), *Will & Grace*

Patrick Star
(voice of Bill Fagerbakke),
SpongeBob SquarePants

Fez
(Wilmer Valderrama), *That '70s Show*

Barney Stinson
(Neil Patrick Harris), *How I Met Your Mother*

Randy Hickey
(Ethan Suplee), *My Name Is Earl*

Dwight Schrute
(Rainn Wilson), *The Office*

Terrible Bosses

> You think your boss is unbearable? At least you don't have to work for one of these nutcases...

Alan Brady (Carl Reiner), *The Dick Van Dyke Show*

Mr. Slate (voiced by John Stephenson), *The Flintstones*

Cosmo G. Spacely (voiced by Mel Blanc), *The Jetsons*

George Jefferson (Sherman Hemsley), *The Jeffersons*

Jerry Davenport (Charles Siebert), *One Day at a Time*

Louie De Palma (Danny DeVito), *Taxi*

Jefferson Davis "Boss" Hogg (Sorrell Booke), *The Dukes of Hazzard*

Bill Bittinger (Dabney Coleman), *Buffalo Bill*

Leon Carp (Martin Mull), *Roseanne*

Charles Montgomery Burns (voiced by Harry Shearer), *The Simpsons*

Mr. Pitt (Ian Abercrombie) and J. Peterman (John O'Hurley), *Seinfeld*

Amanda Woodward (Heather Locklear), *Melrose Place*

Nigel Wick (Craig Ferguson), *The Drew Carey Show*

Kerry Weaver (Laura Innes), *ER*

Ian Maxtone-Graham (Eric Idle), *Suddenly Susan*

Richard Wright (James Remar), *Sex and the City*

Nina Fletcher (Joely Fisher), *Desperate Housewives*

David Brent (Ricky Gervais), *The Office*, British version

Michael Scott (Steve Carell), *The Office*, U.S. version

Jack Donaghy (Alec Baldwin), *30 Rock*

TV's Nuttiest Neighbors

1 — Cosmo Kramer (**Michael Richards**), *Seinfeld*
Wild and crazy Kramer was the freeloading neighbor across the hall who dreamed up harebrained schemes that often turned out disastrously for his friend Jerry.
Pesky Behavior: Had a bad habit of bursting into Jerry's apartment uninvited, which led to Jerry's place being burglarized when Kramer forgot to close the door.
Nuttiest Moment: Kramer put a garbage disposal in his shower and began washing his produce there—much to the subsequent horror of his dinner guests.

2 — Rose (**Melanie Lynskey**) *Two and a Half Men*
Rose is Charlie Harper's zany next-door neighbor, who mistook their one-night stand for true love and now stalks him with unbridled devotion.
Pesky Behavior: She thinks nothing of sneaking into Charlie's house (usually after climbing over his fence), once even slipping under the sheets with him.
Nuttiest Moment: Rose created the website charlieharpersucks.com—a forum for other women who have been dumped by the object of her desire.

3 — Felicia Tilman (**Harriet Sansom Harris**), *Desperate Housewives*
Felicia arrived on Wisteria Lane after her sister, Martha Huber, disappeared, and immediately began stirring things up.
Pesky Behavior: Began sniffing around the truth after realizing that the late Mary Alice Young was actually her former coworker Angela.
Nuttiest Moment: When her sister's body was found, a cold and unfeeling Felicia announced the gruesome details of her murder to the neighbors. Then she added: "In lieu of a memorial service, I'll be holding an estate sale the day after tomorrow. Please, no personal checks."

4 — Ralph Furley (**Don Knotts**) *Three's Company*
Chrissy and Janet's landlord Furley, who frequently misinterpreted normal conversations as "gay talk," liked to call their roommate Jack "Tippytoes."
Pesky Behavior: Fancying himself a playboy, Furley—who favored leisure suits with colorful scarves—constantly introduced Jack to sexy women to get him to switch teams.
Nuttiest Moment: Furley tried to impress an old rival by pretending that Chrissy was his wife.

5 — Phyllis Lindstrom (**Cloris Leachman**), *The Mary Tyler Moore Show*
Phyllis, Mary's landlady, adored her but never had a kind word to say about her other tenant, Mary's best friend Rhoda.

Pesky Behavior: After Mary's TV station produced the documentary "What's Your Sexual IQ?" Phyllis begged Mary to explain the facts of life to Phyllis's 11-year-old daughter, Bess.

Nuttiest Moment: The minute she got her real-estate license, Phyllis barged into Mary's office to solicit business, and ended up badgering Mary's boss, Lou, into selling his house.

6 — Gladys Kravitz **(Alice Pearce & Sandra Gould),** *Bewitched*

Poor Gladys Kravitz: Living across from Samantha and Darrin Stephens gave her a bird's-eye view of the witchy goings-on, but whenever she reported them back to her husband, Abner, he told her to take a pill.

Pesky Behavior: Gladys was always calling the authorities, trying to convince them that something strange was going on at the Stephens' house.

Nuttiest Moment: After Samantha convinced Gladys that the things she saw at Sam's home were the result of Gladys's own ESP, Gladys made a fool of herself trying to use her power to do things like stop the rain.

7 — Wilson W. Wilson Jr. **(Earl Hindman),** *Home Improvement*

Wilson, whose full face we never saw (until the series finale) because he talked to neighbor Tim Taylor from behind the fence they shared, always had sage advice for Tim, his wife and their kids.

Pesky Behavior: When the Taylors kept setting off their new security alarm, Wilson drew up a petition to stop them from using it.

Nuttiest Moment: After winning $10,000 at a hockey game Tim took him to, Wilson made plans to build a giant greenhouse that would block the Taylors' view.

8 — Steve Urkel **(Jaleel White),** *Family Matters*

The socially inept Urkel became famous for uttering "Did I do that?" whenever he inadvertently caused problems for the Winslows, which was often.

Pesky Behavior: Urkel practically moved in with the Winslows after they became indebted to him for saving Carl's life with CPR.

Nuttiest Moment: The Gumby-like teen created an embarrassing dance called The Steve Urkel in an ill-conceived attempt to make himself more popular at school.

9 — Lenny & Squiggy **(Michael McKean and David L. Lander),** *Laverne & Shirley*

Laverne and Shirley's upstairs neighbors were also Shotz Brewery employees, giving them opportunities to annoy the ladies both at work and at home.

Pesky Behavior: They always entered the girls' apartment with a nasal, nails-on-chalkboard "Hellooooo."

Nuttiest Moment: The boys crashed the girls' cruise by becoming stowaways, then pretended to be part of the ship's band.

10 — Dale Gribble **(voiced by Johnny Hardwick),** *King of the Hill*

A conspiracy theorist, clueless Dale likes to know what everyone is up to—but doesn't realize that his son was fathered by another man.

Pesky Behavior: Annoyed at being axed as the Hills' exterminator, Dale released dozens of fire ants onto their lawn.

Nuttiest Moment: Convinced the raccoon that bit him was rabid, he moved into the woods and lived on wild mushrooms which made him hallucinate.

TV's Most Memorable Teachers

We pay tribute to the classroom leaders who really make the grade.

1

Gabe Kotter (Gabe Kaplan), *Welcome Back, Kotter*

Head of the class: Mr. Kotter bonds with his class—the remedial students known as the Sweathogs at Brooklyn's James Buchanan High—because he was once a Sweathog himself.

School days: Though he helps with serious problems, it's his corny family stories and compassion that inspire the Sweathogs—including breakout star John "Barbarino" Travolta—to stay in school.

Class notes: *Kotter* was initially banned by the ABC affiliate in Boston, which feared the show's integrated classroom would cause problems during the city's busing crisis. The show eventually aired without incident.

2

Edna Krabappel (voice of Marcia Wallace), *The Simpsons*

Head of the class: Mrs. Krabappel does her best "to supply her students with the minimal educational stimulus legally required by the Springfield Board of Education."

School days: Keeping Bart in line takes up much of Mrs. Krabappel's time, which may account for some of her weariness with the job. Her signature punishment: making him write sentences on the board, like "I will not torment the emotionally frail," "I will not charge admission to the bathroom" and "I will not hide the teacher's Prozac."

Class notes: Though *Simpsons* creator Matt Groening admits that she's named after the sour crabapple fruit, Mrs. Krabappel's name is pronounced "Cra-bappel."

3

Laura Ingalls (Melissa Gilbert), *Little House on the Prairie*

Head of the class: Laura is a lazy student who becomes motivated by her kind teacher, Miss Beadle. She develops a love for reading and learning that inspires her to follow in her beloved instructor's footsteps.

School days: Strict but caring Laura—whose sister Mary also goes into the profession—stands up for the rural students when Mrs. Oleson wants to make them learn French instead of practical lessons they'll need to run their family farms.

Class notes: Melissa was at her own school when she was told by a classmate, the daughter of Michael Landon, that she had won the role of Laura.

4 Ross Geller (David Schwimmer), *Friends*

Head of the class: Ross gets a forum for sharing the dinosaur lectures that bore his friends when he becomes a professor at New York University.
School days: When cute Elizabeth calls him the "hottie of the paleontology department," Ross risks all to begin a clandestine fling with her.
Class notes: David has said that, since *Friends* ended, he's considered becoming a public-school teacher.

5 Charlie Moore (Howard Hesseman), *Head of the Class*

Head of the class: Teaches the honors program at Manhattan's Millard Fillmore High.
School days: Helps his genius students see there's more to life than academics, especially in the musical episodes featuring reenactments of "Hair" and "Little Shop of Horrors."
Class notes: When Brad Pitt guest-starred in 1989, he met and began dating *Class* star Robin Givens

6 Mark Cooper (Mark Curry), *Hangin' With Mr. Cooper*

Head of the class: Mr. Cooper returns to his alma mater to teach and coach basketball after his pro hoops career ends.
School days: Mark is a substitute teacher at Oakland High, which means he does everything from helping an athlete pass algebra and prepping a history class for a trivia competition, to taking a group of students camping and burning his eyebrows when he subs for the home-ec teacher.
Class notes: In a crossover episode, his first-grade class includes Michelle Tanner (Mary-Kate and Ashley Olsen) from *Full House*.

7 Arthur "The Fonz" Fonzarelli (Henry Winkler), *Happy Days*

Head of the class: The high-school dropout secretly takes night classes to graduate with pals Richie, Potsie and Ralph, and later becomes a shop teacher at Jefferson High.
School days: Tries to persuade Howard to hire his class to add on a bathroom to the Cunninghams' house. Later, he becomes the dean of boys at the tough George S. Patton Vocational High School.
Class notes: The day after a 1977 episode in which The Fonz proclaims getting a library card cool, librarians all over the country report a major jump in applications.

8 Carol Vessey (Julie Bowen), *Ed*

Head of the class: The "It Girl" while she was a student at Stuckeyville High, aspiring writer Carol returns to her alma mater as an English teacher.
School days: Though she was best-known as the head cheerleader who dated jocks during her Stuckeyville High days, teacher Carol has a soft spot for her geekier students and even battles the gym teacher when he threatens the college scholarship of one of her gifted students.
Class notes: During *Ed*, Julie tutored high-school students in her spare time.

Debbie Allen (Lydia Grant), *Fame*

Head of the class: She's the no-nonsense but caring dance instructor at New York City's High School for the Performing Arts.

School days: Even the prize student, Leroy, isn't immune to Lydia's tough work ethic. "You want fame? Well, fame costs. And right here is where you start paying. With sweat," she says.

Class notes: Debbie was Paula Abdul's dance instructor.

 Max Medina (Scott Cohen), *Gilmore Girls*

Head of the class: Rory's Chilton English teacher mixes business with pleasure when he starts dating her mom, Lorelai.

School days: He continues to be kind to Rory even after her mom plays runaway bride the night before their scheduled wedding.

Class notes: On the show, Max tells Rory his childhood ambition was to become a clown. In real life, Scott took a clowning class in college that made him decide he wanted to become a performer.

Happy Days

Originated as a segment on *Love, American Style*.

TV's Most Magical Witches

We've brewed up a list of the 10 best broom-jockeys to ever cast a spell...

1 Samantha Stephens
(Elizabeth Montgomery), *Bewitched*

Sweet witch Samantha's mortal hubby, Darrin, was against her using her "witch twitch" nose to conjure up magic unless it was to get him out of a jam!

Spell Check: Samantha's many memorable spells included turning Darrin into a giant fish to keep him from kissing another woman. But our favorite bit of Stephens magic? That automatic vacuum cleaner and the levitating furniture.

Secret Ingredient: Samantha's famous nose twitch was an illusion. Elizabeth was actually twitching her upper lip, which made her nose wrinkle, too.

2 Amanda Tucker
(Catherine Hicks), *Tucker's Witch*

Her P.I. hubby, Rick (Tim Matheson), had the sleuthing skills, but Amanda possessed something even better: witchcraft, including the ability to communicate telepathically with her cat, Dickens.

Spell Check: Her skills could be erratic. And when tracking down bad guys, like an international assassin who was out to bump off a celebrity hairdresser, conjuring up a bit of misinformation was often a dangerous thing.

Secret Ingredient: *Sex and the City*'s Kim Cattrall starred in the pilot of the '80s series but was later replaced by *7th Heaven*'s Catherine Hicks.

3 Wilhelmina W. Witchiepoo
(Billy Hayes), *H.R. Pufnstuf*

Witchiepoo was Living Island's resident baddie, flying on her Vroom Broom (a tricked out broomstick equipped with a steering wheel), trying to steal Freddie the magic talking flute.

Spell Check: Jimmy, Freddie's owner was lured to Living Island by Witchiepoo, who turned Jimmy into a mechanical boy and cast other spells to keep him, and the coveted Freddie, trapped far from home.

Secret Ingredient: The original McDonaldland characters—including Grimace, the Hamburglar and Mayor McCheese—were based on the *H.R. Pufnstuf* characters, which led to a lawsuit in which McDonald's was forced to pay $50,000 for infringement.

4 Willow Rosenberg
(Alyson Hannigan), *Buffy the Vampire Slayer*

Willow was a kind, gentle, loyal friend to Buffy. But her witchy powers were strong, and when she was properly motivated, her sweet temperament could turn deadly.

Spell Check: When her girlfriend and fellow witch Tara was murdered, Willow exacted a gruesome revenge, and it was her awesome powers that eventually doomed Sunnydale's Hellmouth.

Secret Ingredient: Riff Regan played Willow in the original *Buffy* pilot, but the role was recast with Alyson after the WB green-lighted the show.

5 Prue, Piper and Phoebe Halliwell, and Paige Matthews

(Shannon Doherty, Holly Marie Combs, Alyssa Milano, Rose McGowan), *Charmed*

The "Charmed Ones" are the San Franciscan Halliwells, a trio of prophesied witches. After sister Prue is killed by Sax, the women discover they have a half sister, Paige, who helps them restore the "power of three."

Spell Check: Guided by the Book of Shadows, the women cast various spells to thwart evildoers using their individual powers, including freezing time and the ability to levitate objects.

Secret Ingredient: In Season 4, Phoebe was given a hexed engagement ring that would turn her into a 1950s housewife, which she feared would force her to suppress her magic skills, like Samantha on *Bewitched*.

6 Tabitha Lennox

(Juliet Mills), *Passions*

Her sweet, kindly persona hides the fact that most of her time is actually spent torturing the citizens of Harmony because their witch-hunting ancestors burned her at the stake centuries ago.

Spell Check: Among the 300-year-old witch's many evil misdeeds: keeping apart lovers Louis and Sheridan, and Miguel and Charity; and trying to send Eve to jail.

Secret Ingredient: Juliet also played a nanny with psychic powers on the short-lived 1970s sitcom *Nanny and the Professor*.

7 Witch Hazel

(voiced by June Foray), *Looney Tunes*

With pale green skin, a shock of frightful black hair, twig-like legs and a cackling laugh, Hazel was the creepy witch who was always outwitted by Bugs Bunny.

Spell Check: Dressed as a witch, Bugs raised Hazel's ire because she was afraid he was uglier than she was. She finally realized he was really a rabbit, but her delight turned to horror when Bugs tricked her into drinking the "pretty potion" that caused her to lose her cherished bad looks.

Secret Ingredient: June is a legendary voice artist who's the sound behind Tweety's owner Granny, Bullwinkle's pal Rocky, and, in an episode of *Bewitched*, Baby Darrin.

8 Sabrina Spellman

(Melissa Joan Hart), *Sabrina, the Teenage Witch*

Sabrina's magical powers didn't prevent her from experiencing the normal trials and tribulations of school, friendship and dating.

Spell Check: She used truth sprinkles on her enemy, Libby, who not only confessed her catty misdeeds but also revealed that the object of her affection was Sabrina's crush, Harvey.

Secret Ingredient: The Sabrina character was a spin-off from the wholesome *Archie* comic-book series. When Melissa Joan posed for some racy magazine photos in 1999, the Archie Comics CEO demanded that she apologize for the pics or the company would fire her from the show. She didn't and they didn't.

9   Tabitha Stephens
(Lisa Hartman), *Tabitha*

The grown-up witch daughter of *Bewitched*'s Samantha and Darrin moved to Los Angeles, where she and mortal brother Adam worked at TV station KLXA.

Spell Check: Adam, like his father, was against Tabitha's witchcraft, but that didn't stop her from using it to save her boss/love interest Paul (Robert Urich) from a coven of angry witches, or to cast a little truth spell to find out Paul's true feelings for her.

Secret Ingredient: Unfortunately, Tabitha's magic didn't extend to the Nielsen ratings, and the show lasted less than a season.

10   Grandmama Addams
(Marie Blake), *The Addams Family*

Grandmama was the well-intended, but meddlesome mama of Gomez—though in the animated spin-off series and the Addams Family movies, she was Morticia's mom.

Spell Check: The only thing Grandmama loved more than resting on her bed on nails: cooking up love spells, like Love Potion 666; and, ahem, tasty treats for the family, like the infamous yak stew that turned Gomez into a sleepwalking cat burglar.

Secret Ingredient: During the run of the series, Marie was actually credited under her other (much more colorful) stage name, Blossom Rock.

Scene Stealers

Whether it's a double-take, a smarmy comeback or a cute kid's precociousness, we can't take our eyes off of these characters each time they enter stage right.

Ed Norton, played by Art Carney on *The Honeymooners*

Barney Fife on *The Andy Griffith Show* AND Mr. Furley on *Three's Company*, played by Don Knotts

Ted Baxter, played by Ted Knight on *The Mary Tyler Moore Show*

Col. Flagg, played by Edward Winter on *M*A*S*H*

Lenny & Squiggy, played by Michael McKean and David L. Lander on *Laverne & Shirley*

Florence Jean 'Flo' Castleberry, played by Polly Holliday on *Alice*

Reverend Jim Ignatowski and Latka Gravas, played by Christopher Lloyd and Andy Kaufman on *Taxi*

Rudy Huxtable and Olivia Kendall, played Keshia Knight Pulliam and Raven-Symone on *The Cosby Show*

Mona Robinson, played by Katherine Helmond on *Who's the Boss?*

Dan Fielding, played by John Larroquette on *Night Court*

Sophia Petrillo, played by Estelle Getty on *Golden Girls*

Michelle Tanner, played by Mary-Kate and Ashley Olsen on *Full House*

Charley Dietz, played by David Leisure on *Empty Nest*

Kirk Morris, played by Jere Burns on *Dear John*

Steve Urkel, played by Jaleel White on *Family Matters*

Cosmo Kramer, played by Michael Richards on *Seinfeld*

The Lone Gunmen, played by Tom Braidwood, Bruce Harwood and Dean Haglun on *The X-Files*

Bill McNeal, played by Phil Hartman on *NewsRadio*

Frank Barone and Peter MacDougall, played by Peter Boyle and Chris Elliott on *Everybody Loves Raymond*

Nina Van Horn, played by Wendie Malick on *Just Shoot Me!*

Faith and Angelus, played by Eliza Dushku and David Boreanaz on *Buffy the Vampire Slayer* and *Angel*

Frank Costanza on *Seinfeld* and Arthur Spooner on *The King of Queens*, both played by Jerry Stiller

Jack McFarland and Karen Walker, played by Sean Hayes and Megan Mullally on *Will & Grace*

Samantha Jones, played by Kim Cattrall on *Sex and the City*

Janice Soprano, played by Aida Turturro on *The Sopranos*

Emily Gilmore and Paris Geller, played by Kelly Bishop and Liza Weil on *Gilmore Girls*

Christopher Turk and Perry Cox, played by Donald Faison and John C. McGinley on *Scrubs*

Denny Crane, played by William Shatner on *Boston Legal*

Hugo 'Hurley' Reyes, played by Jorge Garcia on *Lost*

Barney Stinson, played by Neil Patrick Harris on *How I Met Your Mother*

Matthew, played by Hamish Linklater on *The New Adventures of Old Christine*

Jack Donaghy, played by Alec Baldwin on *30 Rock*

Single Dads

Throughout the years, whether alone or with a little help from friends and family, these guys have tried their hardest to raise a family the best they know how.

Ben Cartwright (played by Lorne Greene), *Bonanza*

Steve Douglas (played by Fred MacMurray), *My Three Sons*

Sheriff Andy Taylor (played by Andy Griffith), *The Andy Griffith Show*

"Uncle Bill" Davis (played by Brian Keith), *Family Affair*

Tom Corbett (played by Bill Bixby), *The Courtship of Eddie's Father*

Fred Sanford (played by Redd Foxx), *Sanford and Son*

Rick Marshall (played by Spencer Milligan), *Land of the Lost*

Capt. Merrill Stubing (played by Gavin MacLeod), *Love Boat*

Gov. Eugene Gatling (played by James Noble), *Benson*

Philip Drummond (played by Conrad Bain), *Diff'rent Strokes*

Chief Carl Kanisky (played by Dolph Sweet), *Gimme a Break!*

Edward Stratton III (played by Joel Higgins), *Silver Spoons*

Tony Micelli (played by Tony Danza), *Who's the Boss?*

Henry Warnimont (played by George Gaynes), *Punky Brewster*

Michael Hogan (played by Josh Taylor), *The Hogan Family*

Deacon Ernest Frye (played by Sherman Hemsley), *Amen*

Michael Taylor and Joey Harris (played by Paul Reiser and Greg Evigan), *My Two Dads*

Danny Tanner (played by Bob Saget), *Full House*

Dr. Harry Weston (played by Richard Mulligan), *Empty Nest*

Mitch Buchannon (played by David Hasselhoff), *Baywatch*

Nick Russo (played by Ted Wass), *Blossom*

Maxwell Sheffield (played by Charles Shaughnessy), *The Nanny*

Det. Andy Sipowitz (played by Dennis Franz), *NYPD Blue*

Ross Geller (played by David Schwimmer), *Friends*

Dr. Peter Benton (played by Eriq La Salle), *ER*

Ray Campbell (played by Tim Reid), *Sister, Sister*

Mel Horowitz (played by Michael Lerner and Doug Sheehan), *Clueless*

Luke Danes (played by Scott Patterson), *Gilmore Girls*

Mark "Flex" Washington (played by Flex Alexander), *One on One*

Dr. Andrew Brown (played by Treat Williams), *Everwood*

Robert James Sr. (played by Duane Martin), *All of Us*

Alan Harper (played by Jon Cryer), *Two and a Half Men*

Michael Bluth (played by Jason Bateman), *Arrested Development*

Kevin Hill (played by Taye Diggs), *Kevin Hill*

Michael Dawson (played by Harold Perrineau), *Lost*

Keith Mars (played by Enrico Colantoni), *Veronica Mars*

Robby Stewart (played by Billy Ray Cyrus), *Hannah Montana*

Ignacio Suarez (played by Tony Plana), *Ugly Betty*

Single Moms

M is for the memories that they gave us.
O is for opinions that they shared.
T is for their trials and tribulations.
H is for the hearts that always cared.
E is for the endless nights of worry.
R is for the rebellion they endured.

Put them all together they spell MOTHER, the actresses
and roles that we adore.

Kate Bradley (played by Bea Benaderet), *Petticoat Junction*

Victoria Barkley (played by Barbara Stanwyck), *The Big Valley*

Julia Baker (played by Diahann Carroll), *Julia*

Lucille Carter (played by Lucille Ball), *Here's Lucy*

Shirley Partridge (played by Shirley Jones), *The Partridge Family*

Carol Traynor (played by Adrienne Barbeau), *Maude*

Florida Evans (played by Esther Rolle), *Good Times*

Ann Romano (played by Bonnie Franklin), *One Day at a Time*

Alice Hyatt (played by Linda Lavin), *Alice*

Elaine Nardo (played by Marilu Henner), *Taxi*

Abby Cunningham Ewing Sumner (played by Donna Mills), *Knots Landing*

Laurie Morgan (played by Swoosie Kurtz), *Love, Sidney*

Gloria Bunker Stivic (played by Sally Struthers), *Gloria*

Allie Lowell and Kate McArdle (played by Jane Curtin and Susan Saint James), *Kate & Allie*

Angela Bower (played by Judith Light), *Who's the Boss?*

Mary Jo Shively (played by Annie Potts), *Designing Women*

Dr. Beverly Crusher (played by Gates McFadden), *Star Trek: The Next Generation*

Murphy Brown (played by Candice Bergen), *Murphy Brown*

Grace Kelly (played by Brett Butler), *Grace Under Fire*

Ellenor Frutt and Lindsay Dole (played by Camryn Manheim and Kelli Williams), *The Practice*

Miranda Hobbes (played by Cynthia Nixon), *Sex and the City*

Lily Manning (played by Sela Ward), *Once and Again*

Amy Madison Gray (played by Amy Brenneman), *Judging Amy*

Lorelai Gilmore (played by Lauren Graham), *Gilmore Girls*

Karen Roe (played by Moira Kelly), *One Tree Hill*

Neesee James (played by LisaRaye McCoy), *All of Us*

Susan Mayer (played by Teri Hatcher), *Desperate Housewives*

Murphy Brown

The exterior shots of the house shown as Murphy Brown's home is the same one used for the home of Diana Prince on *Wonder Woman*.

13 Unbearable Mothers-in-law

Whether nasty, overbearing or flighty, these women are the best of the worst. Woe to those unlucky enough to marry into their families.

 1 Livia Soprano
The Sopranos

 2 Gloria Hodge
Desperate Housewives

3 Marie Barone
Everybody Loves Raymond

 4 Endora
Bewitched

 5 Mother Jefferson
The Jeffersons

6 Mrs. Slaghoople
Fred Flintstone's mother-in-law
The Flintstones

 7 Deb Scott
One Tree Hill

 8 Bunny McDougal
Sex and the City

 9 Bev Harris and Roseanne Conner
Roseanne

 10 Benita "Benny" Lopez
The George Lopez Show

11 Kay Buell and Kay Hubbard
The Mothers-in-Law

Popular Pets

Whether animated or real-life animal actors, these pets have educated us, made us laugh, saved the day and won our hearts.

Mr. Ed
(*Mister Ed*) Syndicated/CBS

Trigger
(*Roy Rogers*) NBC

Lassie
(*Lassie*) CBS/Syndicated

Ben
(*Gentle Ben*) CBS

Flipper
(*Flipper*) NBC/Syndicated/PAX

Rin Tin Tin
(*Rin Tin Tin*) ABC

Dino the Dinosaur
(*The Flintstones*) ABC

Snoopy
(*Charlie Brown*) CBS

Arnold the Pig
(*Green Acres*) CBS

Scooby-Doo
(*Scooby-Doo*) CBS/ABC

Fred the Cockatoo
(*Baretta*) ABC

Morris the Cat
(Nine Lives commercials)

Spuds McKenzie
(Bud Light spokesdog)

Wishbone
(*Wishbone*) PBS

Dreyfuss the dog
(*Empty Nest*) NBC

Marcel
(*Friends*) NBC

Salem
(*Sabrina the Teenage Witch*) ABC/WB

Eddie
(*Frasier*) NBC

Santa's Little Helper
(*The Simpsons*) Fox

TV's Most Shocking Deaths

Lt. Col. Henry Blake (McLean Stevenson), *M*A*S*H*
Died: March 18, 1975

Cause of death: The bumbling Col. Blake finally got his papers in the Season 3 finale—but Radar (Gary Burghoff) broke the news to the shocked staff that Henry's plane was shot down before he made it home.

The aftermath: Blake was replaced the next season by the no-nonsense, but still beloved Col. Sherman T. Potter (Harry Morgan).

Rosalind Shays (Diana Muldaur), *L.A. Law*
Died: March 21, 1991

Cause of death: After McKenzie (Richard Dysart) turned down her marriage proposal, Roz hit the elevator button and stepped into...an empty elevator shaft!

The aftermath: The frosty, hard-nosed lawyer hadn't made a lot of friends at the firm. Said her own attorney of her demise: "If anything, death probably warmed her up a few degrees."

Bobby Ewing (Patrick Duffy), *Dallas*
Died: May 17, 1985

Cause of death: In the Season 8 finale, Pam's jealous sister Katherine (Morgan Brittany) tried to run over Pam (Victoria Principal) with her car, but when Bobby pushed Pam out of the way, Katherine mowed him down.

The aftermath: Patrick returned in the infamous shower scene at the end of the next season, revealing that his death—and the whole ninth season—had been a bad dream.

Teri Bauer (Leslie Hope), *24*
Died: May 21, 2002

Cause of death: In the shocking final minutes of Day 1, Jack goes looking for wife Teri, who was recently released from her kidnappers. When he enters the transformer room, he sees her lying lifeless, having been shot by the duplicitous Nina Myers (Sarah Clarke).

The aftermath: That first endless day took its toll: just as Jack and his daughter believed their nightmare has ended, they lost Teri. Jack and daughter Kim become estranged, and though Jack leaves CTU, he comes back to fight another day (several, actually) when the nation needs him in their fight against terrorism.

Boone Carlye (Ian Somerhalder), *Lost*
Died: April 5, 2005

Cause of death: Boone was investigating a wrecked plane that was hanging high in a tree. When the plane fell, he suffered severe internal injuries that even heroic doc Jack (Matthew Fox couldn't treat.

The aftermath: Boone's stepsister/ex-lover Shannon (Maggie Grace) tried to kill Locke (Terry O'Quinn), who led Boone to the plane.

Dolores Landingham (Kathyrn Joosten), *The West Wing*
Died: November 9, 2001

Cause of death: President Bartlet's sassy secretary finally got a new car, the first one she'd ever bought. She was driving it to the White House to show Bartlet (Martin Sheen) when she was hit by a drunken driver.

The aftermath: An angry Bartlet—who, at the funeral, stubbed out a cigarette on the church floor—suffered a crisis of faith at the unfairness of the tragedy. Although he considered not running for reelection, memories of her faith in him pushed him to seek another term.

Dr. Robert Romano (Paul McCrane), *ER*
Died: November 20, 2003

Cause of death: Not only did the crabby doc lose his arm in a Season 9 helicopter accident, but he was also crushed when a copter fell on top of him in Season 10.

The aftermath: Romano had alienated so many ER coworkers that only Dr. Elizabeth Corday (Alex Kingston) attended his memorial service.

Gary Shepherd (Peter Horton), *thirtysomething*
Died: February 12, 1991

Cause of death: An emotional roller coaster of an episode revealed that long-suffering Nancy (Patricia Wettig) survived her battle with ovarian cancer, but laid-back English professor Gary was killed in a traffic accident.

The aftermath: "Ghost" Gary continued to pop in on pal Michael (Ken Olin), and Peter Horton went on to become the executive producer of the hit medical drama *Grey's Anatomy*.

Rex Van de Kamp (Steven Culp), *Desperate Housewives*
Died: May 22, 2005

Cause of death: Obsessed with winning back Bree (Marcia Cross), creepy pharmacist George (Roger Bart) swapped Rex's heart meds with potassium pills, which caused fatal heart damage.

The aftermath: Bree found herself in desperate legal straits when Rex's doctor suspected she gave her husband the potassium.

James Evans (John Amos), *Good Times*
Died: September 22, 1976

Cause of death: James had gotten a promising new job and the Evanses were leaving Chicago to move to Mississippi. But the celebration was short-lived when they found out James had been killed in a car accident.

The aftermath: Amos left because he felt the show, and especially Jimmie Walker's character, J.J., perpetuated racial stereotypes. A year later, Esther Rolle, as mom Florida, left the show for the same reasons, although she returned for the final season.

Colin Hart (Mike Erin), *Everwood*
Died: May 2003

Cause of death: A car accident left teen Colin in a coma until surgery by world famous neurosurgeon Andy Brown (Treat Williams) brought him out of it. But seizures made another surgery necessary, and we learned in the Season 2 opener that Colin didn't survive the follow-up operation.

The aftermath: His girlfriend Amy (Emily VanCamp) sank into a depression and a bad relationship with druggie Tommy (Paul Wasilewski).

Hail to the Chief:

TV's Top 10 Presidents

 Josiah "Jed" Bartlet (Martin Sheen), *The West Wing*

Politically speaking: A Nobel Prize winner and former New Hampshire governor, Bartlet served two terms in the White House.

Leader of the free world: He was shot, his daughter was kidnapped and he had to deal with the ongoing effects of his multiple sclerosis, but Bartlet remained an effective leader and even won a second term in office after revealing his illness to the public.

Presidential trivia: Sheen portrayed legendary leader John F. Kennedy in NBC's 1983 miniseries *Kennedy*.

 Mackenzie Allen (Geena Davis), *Commander in Chief*

Politically speaking: The first female president was the elected VP, who took office when her boss died.

Leader of the free world: A working mom, she dealt with a husband (Kyle Secor) who was her Chief of Staff and was stuck playing Mr. Mom. Also battled sexist politicians who wanted her to resign instead of taking office.

Presidential trivia: Why Geena says she took the role: To balance out the fact that "boys take up much more space on TV than in real life." You go, girl!

 Lisa Simpson (Yeardley Smith), *The Simpsons*

Politically speaking: In a 2000 episode, a mystic told Bart that, 30 years into the future, Lisa would become the first "straight female President."

Leader of the free world: Bart showed up to mooch off his successful sis, and Homer destroyed the property with a pickax as he searched for gold he thought was hidden by Abraham Lincoln.

Presidential trivia: Lisa names Bart the Secretary of Keeping It Real.

David Palmer (Dennis Haysbert), *24*

Politically speaking: The charming, principled president faced public scandals and several assassination attempts, and was killed by terrorists after he left office.

Leader of the free world: He was a smart, decisive leader who made difficult decisions, but his personal life, which included a divorce from scheming wife Sherry (Penny Johnson Jerald), a son accused of murder and a girlfriend accused of corporate crimes, eventually led him to drop out of the race for a second term.

Presidential trivia: David Palmer's brother, Wayne, kept the family honor alive by also becoming President, during the 2007 season.

Henry Hayes (William Devane), *Stargate SG-1*

Politically speaking: A brave, no-nonsense commander who was shocked to learn of the existence of the top-secret Stargate program, the government's attempt to control an ancient alien device used for intergalactic travel.

Leader of the free world: Hayes' first days in office included finding out that his VP, Kinsey (Ronny Cox), was corrupt, and refusing to bow down—literally—to Anubis, the leader of Earth's alien enemies.

Presidential trivia: Devane portrayed real-life prez John F. Kennedy in the classic 1974 Emmy-nominated TV-movie "The Missiles of October."

Glenallen Walken (John Goodman), *The West Wing*

Politically speaking: When VP Hoynes (Tim Matheson) resigned and President Barlet temporarily yielded power because of his daughter's kidnapping, Speaker of the House Walken became acting President.

Leader of the free world: His efforts failed to win him the Republican Party nomination when he made a bid against Sen. Arnold Vinick (Alan Alda).

Presidential trivia: Goodman also tasted power as the King of England (in 1991's "King Ralph").

Laura Roslin (Mary McDonnell), *Battlestar Galactica*

Politically speaking: Became president of 12 human colonies by default after her home planet was destroyed, and just after she was diagnosed with breast cancer.

Leader of the free world(s): Cdr. Adama (Edward James Olmos) had her imprisoned but she escaped, and he saw that they made better cohorts than adversaries.

Presidential trivia: In 1996's "Independence Day," McDonnell played First Lady Marilyn Whitmore.

Mike Brady (Gary Cole), "The Brady Bunch in the White House"

Politically speaking: Mike's philanthropy prompted the Brady pop to become the new U.S. honcho in this 2002 made-for-TV movie.

Leader of the free world: It was retro business as usual for Mike Brady and his clan, except that Carol (Shelley Long) was the Vice President.

Presidential trivia: Cole played Vice President Bob Russell on *The West Wing*.

Samuel Arthur Tresch (George C. Scott), *Mr. President*

Politically speaking: Tresch was a grumpy commander, surrounded by a squabbling staff and a family unprepared for public scrutiny in this short-lived 1987 Fox comedy.

Leader of the free world: He was forceful in office, but with his family it was another matter: Wife Meg takes off, leaving Sam as a single dad whose kooky sister-in-law (Madeline Kahn) put the moves on him.

Presidential trivia: When his 1963 CBS drama *East Side/West Side* was canceled George swore off TV. He created a stir by returning as prez, stating that he was only doing it for the money.

10   Julia Mansfield (Patty Duke), *Hail to the Chief*

Politically speaking: On this wacky 1985 ABC sitcom, first female President Mansfield averted World War III.

Leader of the free world: She also dealt with a cheating hubby and a son who got the daughter of one of her cabinet members pregnant.

Presidential trivia: In 1984, Patty became the first female president of the Screen Actors Guild.

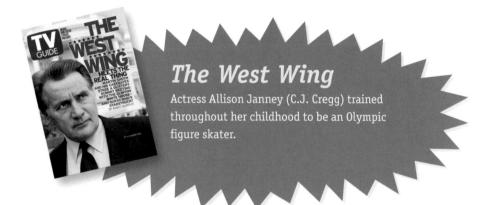

The West Wing

Actress Allison Janney (C.J. Cregg) trained throughout her childhood to be an Olympic figure skater.

12 **Memorable** TV Characters

Whose Faces We've Never Seen

How can characters who were nearly invisible leave such an indelible impression?

1 **Carlton the doorman** from *Rhoda*; voiced by Lorenzo Music

2 **Charlie Townsend** from *Charlie's Angels*; voiced by John Forsythe

3 **Consuela**, Suzanne Sugarbaker's maid from *Designing Women*

4 **Lars Lindstrom**, Phyliss's husband from *The Mary Tyler Moore Show*

5 **Maris Crane**, Niles' wife from *Frasier*

6 **Robin Masters**, Thomas Magnum's employer from *Magnum, P.I.*; voiced by Orson Welles

7 **Orson**, Mork's boss from *Mork & Mindy*; voiced by Ralph James

8 **George Steinbrenner**, New York Yankees owner and George Costanza's boss from *Seinfeld*; voiced by Larry David

9 **Ugly Naked Guy**, the neighbor from *Friends*

10 **Vera Peterson**, Norm's wife from *Cheers*; played by Bernadette Birkett (George Wendt's real-life wife) *Viewer's one real shot at seeing Vera was dashed when she walked into a room and was hit in the face with a pie.

11 **Wilson Wilson**, the over-the-fence neighbor from *Home Improvement*; played by Earl Hindman

Honorable Mention

Columbo's wife, from *Columbo*
Throughout the entire run of the series, Lt. Columbo referred to 'the missus,' but viewers never saw her...until she got a show of her own in 1979 (title *Mrs. Columbo*, then *Kate Loves a Mystery*). Incidentally, the lieutenant must have had quite the caseload, because he never appeared on his wife's show either.

Successful Spinoffs

1 *Angel*, spun off from *Buffy the Vampire Slayer*

2 *Benson*, spun off from *Soap*

3 *The Bionic Woman*, spun off from *The Six Million Dollar Man*

4 *Boston Legal*, spun off from *The Practice*

5 *The Colbert Report*, spun off from *The Daily Show*

6 *The Colbys*, spun off from *Dynasty*

7 *CSI: Miami* and *CSI: New York*, spun off from *CSI: Crime Scene Investigations*

8 *Daria*, spun off from *Beavis and Butt-head*

9 *Degrassi: The Next Generation*, spun off from *Degrassi Junior High*

10 *Diagnosis Murder*, spun off from *Jake and the Fatman*

11 *A Different World*, spun off from *The Cosby Show*

12 *Empty Nest*, spun off from *The Golden Girls*

13 *The Facts of Life*, spun off from *Diff'rent Strokes*

14 *Family Matters*, spun off from *Perfect Strangers*

15 *Frasier*, spun off from *Cheers*

16 *Go, Diego Go!* spun off from *Dora the Explorer*

17 *Good Times*, spun off from *Maude*

18 *Gomer Pyle, USMC*, spun off from *The Andy Griffith Show*

19 *Green Acres*, spun off from *Petticoat Junction*

20 *Knots Landing*, spun off from *Dallas*

21 *Laverne & Shirley* and *Mork & Mindy*, spun off from *Happy Days*

22 *Law & Order: Criminal Intent* and *Law & Order: Special Victims Unit*, spun off from *Law & Order*

23 *Lou Grant, Phyllis and Rhoda*, spun off from *The Mary Tyler Moore Show*

24 *Mama's Family*, spun off from *The Carol Burnett Show*

25 *Maude and The Jeffersons*, spun off from *All in the Family*

26 *Melrose Place*, spun off from *Beverly Hills, 90210*

27 *NCIS*, spun off from *JAG*

28 *Port Charles*, spun off from *General Hospital*

29 *Promised Land*, spun off from *Touched by an Angel*

30 *The Simpsons*, spun off from *The Tracey Ullman Show*

31 *Star Trek: The Next Generation*, *Star Trek: Deep Space Nine*, *Star Trek: Voyager* and *Star Trek: Enterprise*, spun off from *Star Trek*

32 *Trapper John, M.D.*, spun off from *M*A*S*H*

33 *Xena: Warrior Princess*, spun off from *Hercules: The Legendary Journey*

From Silver Screen

to Small Screen

Plenty of TV series have been based on films, with mixed results.

My Big Fat Greek Life

Series: 2003   **Movie:** 2002 (as "My Big Fat Greek Wedding")

Nia Vardalos's sleeper hit (one of 2002's top-grossing films) did not fare well as well on the small screen. Even though much of the movie's original cast appeared in the series, after just two months audiences claimed this a Big Fat Greek Flop.

Buffy the Vampire Slayer

Series: 1997-2003   **Movie:** 1992

The rarest of cases: a show that actually improved upon, and overshadowed the feature as Sarah Michelle Gellar stepped in for Kristy Swanson in a vampire soap opera that resonated with teens.

Parenthood

Series: 1990   **Movie:** 1989

Ed Begley Jr. got the Steve Martin role, but even with the young Leonardo DiCaprio and David Arquette in the cast, the series couldn't live up to the original comedy.

Alice

Series: 1976-85   **Movie:** 1974 (as "Alice Doesn't Live Here Anymore")

A durable hit for CBS with Linda Lavin taking over the part of a waitress from Oscar winner Ellen Burstyn, but the sitcom's only similarity to Martin Scorsese's realistic look at single motherhood was Vic Tayback as diner owner Mel Sharples.

Shaft

Series: 1973-74   **Movie:** 1971

Richard Roundtree was one of the few stars to re-create a film role for TV, but many found the new *Shaft* so watered-down that it lost its punch. What else would you expect? It alternated with the Jimmy Stewart mystery *Hawkins*.

M*A*S*H

Series: 1972-83   **Movie:** 1970

The Holy Grail of movie-to-TV translations, even with two very different Hawkeyes. While the film featured a dark Donald Sutherland, the series' Alan Alda lent a more whimsical touch.

Mr. Smith Goes to Washington

Series: 1962-63   **Movie:** 1939

Jimmy Stewart made way for Fess Parker, but even guest stars like Harpo Marx couldn't help this show.

Casablanca

Series: 1955-56, 1983   **Movie:** 1942

Not one but two unsuccessful efforts to succeed Bogie: first, with Charles McGraw ("The Birds") and then with David Soul—yes, the guy who played Hutch.

The Odd Couple

In one episode, characters from the show walk down the street in New York City and encounter playwright Neil Simon. Simon wrote the play on which this show was based.

The Unlucky 13:

Unsuccessful Spin-offs

1. **AfterMASH**, spun off from *M*A*S*H*
Was shot down in just 15 months

2. **Beverly Hills Buntz**, spun off from *Hill Street Blues*
Dennis Franz made up for this five-month spin-off with his exceptional turn as another cop, Det. Andy Sipowicz

3. **Checking In**, spun off from *The Jeffersons*
Checked out after one month

4. **Flo**, spun off from *Alice*
Couldn't cook up much of an audience; lasted only 17 months

5. **Gloria**, spun off from *All in the Family*
Lasted one year

6. **Grady, Sanford** and **The Sanford Arms**, spun off from *Sanford and Son*
Grady's life span was 3 months; *Sanford* lasted a little over a year, but *The Sanford Arms* closed after less than a month

7. **Joanie Loves Chachi** and **Out of the Blue**, spun off from *Happy Days*
Joanie and Chachi returned to Milwaukee after 18 months away; while *Out of the Blue* was out of there in three months

8. **Law & Order: Trial by Jury** from *Law & Order*
Four months, case closed

9. **The Lone Gunmen**, spun off from *The X-Files*
The truth might be out there, but after three months, these guys never found it

10. **Richie Brockelman, Private Eye**, spun-off from *The Rockford Files*
Brockelman closed up shop in five months

11. **The Ropers** and **Three's a Crowd**, spun off from *Three's Company*
Both spin-offs lasted only one season

12. **Tabitha**, spun off from *Bewitched*
Nine months is all it took for this show to disappear

13. **The Tortellis**, spun off from *Cheers*
We gave them the brush off after just 13 episodes

Stars' Former Professions

That Turned Out to Be Dead Ends

Luckily, they decided to quit their day jobs.

1 **Aerobics instructor:**
Calista Flockhart

2 **Bartender:**
Bruce Willis and Sandra Bullock

3 **Bellboy:**
Tom Hanks

4 **Bouncer:**
John Goodman

5 **Cemetery-plot salesman:**
Ken Kercheval

6 **Chicken-farm worker:**
Josh Holloway

7 **Cincinnati mayor:**
Jerry Springer

8 **Coal miner:**
Charles Bronson

9 **Coffin polisher:**
Denzel Washington

10 **Fireman:**
Steve Buscemi

11 **Fry cook:**
Lorenzo Lamas

12 **Funeral-parlor makeup artist:**
Whoopi Goldberg

13 **Garbage collector:**
Norm Macdonald

14 **Gym teacher:**
Mr. T

15 **Hairdresser:**
Danny DeVito

16 **Hatcheck girl:**
Carol Burnett

17 **Janitor:**
Jim Carrey

18 **Mechanic:**
Jay Leno

19 **Oyster shucker:**
Ellen DeGeneres

20 **Pajama-factory worker:**
Lucy Liu

21 **Phone sales (light bulbs):**
Jerry Seinfeld

22 **Postman:**
Dennis Franz

23 **Restaurant mascot (chicken):**
Brad Pitt

24 **Street mime:**
Robin Williams

25 **Substitute teacher:**
Carroll O'Connor

26 **Toy-store employee:**
Jack Nicholson

27 **Video-store clerk:**
Quentin Tarantino

28 **Weatherman:**
David Letterman

29 **Wig cleaner:**
Groucho Marx

30 **Wig-company receptionist:**
Kathy Kinney

The Real Names

of 40 Celebrities

It's not unusual for actors to change their names when they arrive in Hollywood. Looking at some of the real names below, who can blame them??

Alan Alda = Alphonso D'Abruzzo

Woody Allen = Allen Stewart Konigsberg

Eve Arden = Eunice Quedens

Beatrice Arthur = Bernice Frankel

Lauren Bacall = Betty Joan Perske

Anne Bancroft = Anna Maria Louisa Italiano

Taurean Blacque = Herbert Middleton Jr.

Robert Blake = Michael James Vijencio Gubitosi

Morgan Brittany = Suzanne Cupito

Red Buttons = Aaron Chwatt

Charo = Maria Rosario Pilar Martinez

Cher = Cherilyn LaPiere Sarkisian

Alice Cooper = Vincent Damon Furnier

Elvis Costello = Declan Patrick MacManus

Joan Crawford = Lucille Fay LeSueur

Tony Curtis = Bernard Schwartz

Kirk Douglas = Issur Danielovitch

Bob Dylan = Robert Allen Zimmerman

The Edge = David Howell Evans

Carmen Electra = Tara Patrick

Redd Foxx = John Elroy Sanford

Judy Garland = Frances Ethel Gumm

Whoopi Goldberg = Caryn Johnson

Cary Grant = Archibald Leach

Pee-wee Herman = Paul Reubens/Rubenfeld

Terry "Hulk" Hogan = Terry Bollea

Elton John = Reginald Dwight

Ted Knight = Tedeusz Wladyslaw Konopka

Michael Landon = Eugene Maurice Orowitz

Liberace = Wladziu Valentino Liberace

Walter Matthau = Walter Matuschanskayasky

Minnie Pearl = Sarah Ophelia Cannon

Stefanie Powers = Stefania Zofja Federkievicz

Dirk and Dack Rambo = Orman and Norman Rambo

Charlie Sheen = Carlos Estevez

Martin Sheen = Ramon Estevez

Jon Stewart = Jon Liebowitz

Sting = Gordon Matthew Sumner

Mr. T = Lawrence Tureaud

Danny Thomas = Muzyad Yakhoob

The Sonny & Cher Comedy Hour

The show was a Top 20 hit in the ratings for its entire run (1971-74).

The Biggest Role

They Didn't Get

1 Katie Holmes

Part: Buffy Summers on *Buffy the Vampire Slayer*

Lost to: Sarah Michelle Gellar

Year: 1997. Tom Cruise's beloved was a big contender to play Buffy, but had to be eliminated when the casting director realized she was under 18 and therefore could not legally work the hours the role required.

Postscript: The same casting director snapped her up for *Dawson's Creek* a year later.

2 Whitney Houston

Part: Sondra Huxtable on *The Cosby Show*

Lost to: Sabrina Le Beauf

Year: 1984. Then a 20-year-old model, Whitney auditioned to play Bill Cosby's daughter Sondra on what became America's No. 1 show.

Postscript: Whitney went on to great success in music and acting ("The Bodyguard"; "The Preacher's Wife") before drugs stalled her career.

3 Lisa Kudrow

Part: Roz Doyle on *Frasier*

Lost to: Peri Gilpin

Year: 1993. Lisa Kudrow won the role of Roz Doyle but during rehearsals for the pilot, producers decided Lisa wasn't right for the part, and she was replaced with Peri Gilpin.

Postscript: A few months later, Lisa was cast as wacky Ursula on *Mad About You*, a part that led to her being hired as Ursula's twin sister, Phoebe, on *Friends*.

4 Jason Bateman

Part: Alex P. Keaton on *Family Ties*

Lost to: Michael J. Fox

Year: 1982. Jason Bateman lost the role to Michael—who himself was the second choice for the role. Producers wanted Matthew Broderick, but he didn't want to do TV.

Postscript: Justine Bateman accompanied her brother to the audition and won the role of Mallory, with no acting experience.

5 Patricia Heaton

Part: Elaine on *Seinfeld*

Lost to: Julia Louis-Dreyfus

Year: 1990. It's hard to imagine anyone but Julia Louis-Dreyfus playing Elaine (or anyone else but Patricia playing Debra on *Everybody Loves Raymond*). But TV history could have been quite different had Patricia bettered Julia in the auditions.

Postscript: Megan Mullally (Karen Walker on *Will & Grace*) and Rosie O'Donnell also tried out for the part of Elaine.

6 Matthew Perry

Part: Billy Campbell on *Melrose Place*

Lost to: Andrew Shue

Year: 1992. Future Friend Matthew tried out for the role of sweet Billy Campbell on *Melrose Place*, but lost the role to Stephen Fanning.

Postscript: Days before shooting began, Fanning was fired and Shue was hurriedly cast in the role.

7 Lara Flynn Boyle

Part: Ally McBeal

Lost to: Calista Flockhart

Year: 1997. Lara tried out for the title role on *Ally McBeal*, but lost to a little-known stage actress named Calista Flockhart, who was every bit as skinny as Lara.

Postscript: She went on to play Assistant District Attorney Helen Gamble on *The Practice*.

8 Teri Hatcher

Part: Jamie Buchman on *Mad About You*

Lost to: Helen Hunt

Year: 1992. Long before she became a desperate housewife, Teri Hatcher screen-tested to be the woman Paul Reiser was mad about. She made it to the final two, but lost the part to Helen Hunt, who won four Emmys for the role.

Postscript: A year later, Teri chopped off her hair to snare the lead role in *Lois & Clark*.

9 Michael Richards

Part: Al Bundy on *Married...With Children*

Lost to: Ed O'Neill

Year: 1987. Three years before he burst into Jerry Seinfeld's apartment as neighbor Kramer, Michael Richards was auditioning to play Al Bundy. "I was very, very close to getting that part," recalls Michael. "But it wasn't meant to be. That was Ed's role, and he was wonderful."

Postscript: In *Seinfeld*'s last season, Michael earned $600,000 per episode.

10 Raquel Welch

Part: Mary Ann on *Gilligan's Island*

Lost to: Dawn Wells

Year: 1964. The '60s sexpot tried out for the part of the wholesome Mary Ann rather than the obvious character, Ginger. Legend has it that she had the part—until *Gilligan* creator Sherwood Schwartz met Dawn Wells.

Postscript: Jayne Mansfield was the first choice for Ginger, but turned it down.

I Quit!

> Below are 10 stars who walked away from plum roles...for better or worse!

1 David Caruso

Year: 1994 **Show:** *NYPD Blue*

The then 38-year-old actor infuriated producers, fans and castmates alike when he quit the acclaimed police drama after just one season to pursue a film career. It didn't help that he arrogantly predicted during the bitter contract dispute that followed that "*NYPD Blue* will not be successful when I leave."

Postscript: His movie career a flop ("Kiss of Death," "Jade"), Caruso returned to TV in the short-lived 1997 series *Michael Hayes* before once again hitting the television jackpot by landing the coveted lead role on *CSI: Miami*.

2 Mario Vazquez

Year: 2005 **Show:** *American Idol*

Just days after being named one of the 12 finalists in Season 4, Vazquez announced that he was dropping out of the competition for "personal reasons." When none surfaced, it was assumed that the singer—confident he would win—decided to take his chances on landing a recording contract on his own rather than be beholden to *Idol* execs.

Postscript: The strategy appears to have paid off. Vazquez landed a deal with music mogul Clive Davis's J Records; his debut album was released in September 2006.

3 Shelley Long

Year: 1987 **Show:** *Cheers*

Long hung up her barmaid apron after five seasons, in the hopes of becoming a movie star. Though she would never recapture her sitcom success, she insists she has no regrets. "People ask why I don't beat myself up for having left *Cheers* too early," Shelley says. "How can I when, if presented with the same scenario, I'd do the same thing?"

Postscript: After a string of forgettable flicks, she was back on the tube, doing made-for-television movies, a sitcom with Treat Williams and, most recently, a guest-starring role on *Boston Legal*.

4 David Cassidy

Year: 1974 **Show:** *The Partridge Family*

One of the biggest teen idols ever (the David Cassidy Fan Club was larger than both Elvis's and the Beatles'), Cassidy nonetheless chose to walk away from the show that made him famous. Already tired of being hounded by fans and the press, he made his decision after a 14-year-old British girl with a weak heart died after being crushed by a mob of fans who got carried away at one of his concerts.

Postscript: David spends most of his time breeding and racing Thoroughbreds, though he still performs in concert.

5 Farrah Fawcett
Year: 1977 **Show:** *Charlie's Angels*

Farrah became an industry pariah when she walked away from the sexy detective series after its first season. The ensuing lawsuit ended when she agreed to return in a series of guest spots. Those appearances turned out to comprise most of her work for the next several years, until her performance in the TV-movie "The Burning Bed" won her critical acclaim and more job offers.

Postscript: The actress's most recent stints include her own reality series, *Chasing Farrah*, and a notoriously ditsy appearance on the *Comedy Central Roast of William Shatner*.

6 Sasha Alexander
Year: 2005 **Show:** *NCIS*

When Agent Kate Todd was assassinated in the Season 2 finale, distraught fans demanded to know why CBS would kill off such a popular character. The answer? Sasha wanted off the show, finding the shooting schedule for the one-hour drama too grueling.

Postscript: So, far, the decision hasn't hurt Sasha's career: the actress starred opposite Tom Cruise in "Mission Impossible III" in 2006.

7 Rob Lowe
Year: 2003 **Show:** *The West Wing*

Lowe's beef with the presidential drama was reportedly over money: NBC sources said the star—furious that castmates Allison Janney, Richard Schiff, Bradley Whitford and John Spencer had their $30,000-per-episode salaries boosted in the neighborhood of his own $75,000 wage—demanded that his pay be raised to something on par with main man Martin Sheen. The producers balked, and Lowe walked.

Postscript: He starred in two failed series—*The Lyon's Den* and *Dr. Vegas*—but continues to find work in movies and, in 2006-07, in the drama *Brothers & Sisters*, playing a Republican senator.

8 Wayne Rogers
Year: 1975 **Show:** *M*A*S*H*

After three years of playing Trapper John, Rogers quit, reportedly because he felt his character had become nothing more than a sidekick to Alan Alda's Hawkeye. He was sued for breach of contract, but the case was thrown out when it was discovered he'd never signed his contract—in protest of a morality clause he felt the studio bigwigs should be compelled to sign as well!

Postscript: Four year after leaving *M*A*S*H*, Rogers turned down the lead in the spin-off *Trapper John, M.D.*, another show that turned out to be a hit (the part went to Pernell Roberts). But the actor's pickiness hasn't hurt his pockets: Having amassed a small fortune with his investment firm Wayne Rogers & Company, he is a business contributor on the Fox News Channel.

9 Rory Cochrane
Year: 2004 **Show:** *CSI: Miami*

Two years on the hit spin-off were enough for the actor, who asked producers to release him from his contract. They complied by killing him off in the third-season opener. Cochrane, who played Agent Tim Speedle, was simply tired of the grind. "It wasn't a money thing," he said. "You get up, go to work, come home, get up, go to work, come home—it takes a toll on your soul, kind of."

Postscript: Cochrane had two movies released in 2006: the thriller "Right at Your Door "and the sci-fi drama "A Scanner Darkly."

10 Chevy Chase

Year: 1975   **Show:** *Saturday Night Live*

The comic disappointed many fans when he abandoned the groundbreaking sketch show after its first season for a career in movies. But unlike others who walked away from a sure thing only to fail in their quest for big-screen stardom, Chase had a number of hits ("Caddyshack," the "National Lampoon" and "Fletch" franchises) to balance his many turkeys (the biggest being his disastrous 1993 late-night talk show, which was canceled after five weeks).

Postscript: Chase went through a lean period in the '90s when film offers dried up. Now older, wiser, and humbled ("I was more than a little arrogant; I've burned a few bridges"), he's now being rediscovered by young moviemakers.

Cheers

The hospital Carla delivered her babies in was Boston's St. Eligius, the hospital from *St. Elsewhere*.

Backstage Feuds

Laverne & Shirley (Cindy Williams vs. Penny Marshall)

Charlie's Angels (Farrah Fawcett vs. the producers)

Three's Company (Suzanne Somers vs. the producers and cast)

Moonlighting (Bruce Willis vs. Cybill Shepherd)

Designing Women (Delta Burke vs. the producers)

Beverly Hills, 90210 (Shannen Doherty vs. Jennie Garth)

All My Children (Susan Lucci vs. Sarah Michelle Gellar)

Grace Under Fire (Brett Butler vs. the producers)

Cybill (Cybill Shepherd vs. Christine Baranski)

7th Heaven (Jessica Biel vs. the producers)

Charmed (Shannen Doherty vs. Alyssa Milano)

Sex and the City (Kim Cattrall vs. Sarah Jessica Parker)

CSI (Jorja Fox and George Eads vs. the producers)

American Idol (Paula Abdul vs. Ryan Seacrest)

The Simple Life (Paris Hilton vs. Nicole Richie)

Desperate Housewives (Teri Hatcher vs. the Housewives)

Grey's Anatomy (Isaiah Washington vs. T.R. Knight)

Charlie's Angels

Actresses who auditioned over the years for various *Angels* roles included Kim Basinger, Kathie Lee Gifford and Michelle Pfeiffer.

Celebrities Who Died
While Their Series Were Still on the Air

Bea Benaderet Kate Bradley on *PetticoatJunction*, 1968

Dan Blocker Hoss Cartwright on *Bonanza*, 1972

George Cleveland Gramps Miller on *Lassie*, 1957

Nicholas Colasanto Ernie "Coach" Pantusso on *Cheers*, 1985

Ray Collins Lt. Arthur Tragg on *Perry Mason*, 1965

Darlene Conley Sally Spectra on *The Bold and the Beautiful*, 2006

Michael Conrad Sgt. Phil Esterhaus on *Hill Street Blues*, 1983

Richard Crenna Jared Duff on *Judging Amy*, 2003

Jim Davis Jock Ewing on *Dallas*, 1981

Richard DeAngelis Col. Raymond Foerster on *The Wire*, 2005

Colleen Dewhurst Avery Brown Sr. on *Murphy Brown* and Marilla Cuthbert on *Avonlea*, 1991

Selma Diamond Selma Hacker on *Night Court*, 1985

Peter Duel Hannibal Heyes/Joshua Smith on *Alias Smith and Jones*, 1971

Redd Foxx Alfonso Royal on *The Royal Family*, 1991

Will Geer Grandpa Zebulon Walton on *The Waltons*, 1978

Florence Halop Florence Kleiner on *Night Court*, 1986

John Hancock Ike Johnson on *Love & War*, 1992

Richard Hart Ellery Queen on *The Adventures of Ellery Queen*, 1951

Phil Hartman Bill McNeal on *NewsRadio*, 1998

Benjamin Hendrickson Hal Munson on *As the World Turns*, 2006

Jon-Erik Hexum Mac Harper on *Cover Up*, 1984

Diana Hyland Joan Bradford on *Eight Is Enough*, 1977

Steve Irwin *The Crocodile Hunter*, 2006

Joseph Kearns George Wilson on *Dennis the Menace*, 1962

Dorothy Kilgallen Panelist on *What's My Line?* 1965

Ted Knight Henry Rush on *Too Close for Comfort*, 1986

Michael Landon Jeff Hayes on *Us* (a pilot for CBS), 1991

Anna Lee Lila Quartermaine on *Port Charles*, 2004

Robert Lansing Paul Blaisdell on *Kung Fu: The Legend Continues*, 1994

Nancy Marchand Livia Soprano on *The Sopranos*, 2000

Jerry Orbach Det. Lenny Briscoe on *Law & Order: Trial by Jury*, 2004

Alice Pearce Gladys Kravitz on *Bewitched*, 1972

Freddie Prinze Chico Rodriguez on *Chico and the Man*, 1977

Larry Riley Frank Williams on *Knots Landing*, 1992

John Ritter Paul Hennessy on *8 Simple Rules for Dating My Teenage Daughter*, 2003

Will See Mr. Harold Hooper on *Sesame Street*, 1983

Gene Siskel Film critic on *Siskel & Ebert*, 1999

John Spencer Leo McGarry on *The West Wing*, 2005

David Strickland Todd Stites on *Suddenly Susan*, 1999

Dolph Sweet Chief Carl Kanisky on *Gimme a Break!* 1985

Lynne Thigpen Ella Farmer on *The District*, 2003

Michelle Thomas Myra Monkhouse on *Family Matters*, 1998

Robert Trow Bob Dog on *Mister Rogers' Neighborhood*, 1998

Celebrity Couples
Who Met on the Set

Jennifer Garner and Scott Foley: Met when she guest-starred on *Felicity*, married and later divorced when she took up with Michael Vartan.

Jennifer Garner and Michael Vartan: Dated while on *Alias*; later split.

Jennifer Garner and Ben Affleck: Filmed "Daredevil" together; later married.

Jennifer Morrison and Jesse Spencer: Met on the set of *House*; got engaged in 2007.

Evangeline Lilly and Dominic Monaghan: Dating; met on the set of *Lost*.

Sophia Bush and Chad Michael Murray: Met on the set of *One Tree Hill*; married and split after four months; he then became engaged to an extra on *One Tree Hill*.

Keri Russell and Scott Speedman: Costars on *Felicity*; dated and split.

Nikki Cox and Jay Mohr: Met on *Las Vegas*; later married.

Rachel Bilson and Adam Brody: *The O.C.* couple dated but later split.

Katie Holmes and Joshua Jackson: *Dawson's Creek* castmates dated but later broke up.

Kelly Ripa and Mark Consuelos: Married after meeting on *All My Children*.

Deborra-Lee Furness and Hugh Jackman: Wed after meeting on the Australian series *Correlli*.

Mariska Hargitay and Peter Hermann: *Law and Order: Special Victims Unit* brought together this married couple.

Tracy Pollan and Michael J. Fox: Playing a couple on *Family Ties* led to their being a real married couple.

Laura Leighton and Doug Savant: Met on the set of *Melrose Place*; later married.

Josie Bissett and Rob Estes: Also met on *Melrose Place* and married, but later divorced.

Alex Borstein and Jackson Douglas: Became engaged when Douglas proposed during the taping of a *Mad TV* skit.

Alyson Hannigan and Alexis Denisof: This husband and wife costarred on *Buffy the Vampire Slayer*.

Juliette Lewis and Brad Pitt: Dated after meeting on the set of the 1990 TV-movie "Too Young to Die."

Tori Spelling and Dean McDermott: Met on the set of the 2005 TV-movie "Mind Over Murder"; later wed.

Kyra Sedgwick and Kevin Bacon: This long-time couple met on the set of the TV-movie "Lemon Sky" (1988).

Adrianne Curry and Christopher Knight: Married after a stint on *The Surreal Life*.

Alexis Bledel and Milo Ventimiglia: *The Gilmore Girls* costars dated then split.

Susan Seaforth Hayes and Bill Hayes: This longtime *Days of Our Lives* couple have been married for more than 30 years.

Kristina and Jack Wagner: The *General Hospital* costars married, filed for divorce and then reconciled.

Vanessa Marcil and Tyler Christopher: After meeting on the *General Hospital* set, they became engaged but later split.

Vanessa Marcil and Brian Austin Green: The *Beverly Hills, 90210* costars dated and share a son, but later split.

Jada Pinkett-Smith and Will Smith: *The Fresh Prince of Bel-Air* set was where their love bloomed.

Helen Hunt and Hank Azaria: The *Mad About You* costars were mad about each other—for a while; they married but later divorced.

Britney Spears and Justin Timberlake: The pop stars dated after costarring on *The Mickey Mouse Club*.

Pamela Bach and David Hasselhoff: This *Knight Rider* couple's marriage ended in divorce.

Rita Wilson and Tom Hanks: First met on the set of Hanks's sitcom *Bosom Buddies* in 1981, then reunited for the 1985 movie "Volunteers," when their romance took off; they wed In 1988.

12 Wildest Celebrity Meltdowns Ever!

Think Tom Cruise was the first star to flip out on national TV? Don't be crazy!

1 — TOM CRUISE loses control.

Declaring his love for Katie Holmes, Cruise jumped on Oprah's couch. He pumped his fists and squatted like a scary version of The Thinker. He made weird faces. In short, he acted nuts. Then he went on *Today* and loonily challenged Matt Lauer's knowledge of psychiatric history. Of course, Cruise's 2005 publicity-grabbing antics didn't hurt the box office for "War of the Worlds" (or for Holmes' "Batman Begins"), so who's crazy?

2 — MICHAEL JACKSON dangles a baby.

Jacko had pulled plenty of wacko stunts before, but this one seemed dangerous: holding his son (nicknamed "Blanket") over the railing of a Berlin hotel balcony in 2002. "I got caught up in the excitement of the moment," Jackson explained. Perhaps most shockingly, no charges were filed.

3 — FARRAH FAWCETT spaces out.

The *Charlie's Angels* goddess denied allegations that she was flying high on *The Late Show With David Letterman* in 1997. Sure, she was distracted by the faux skyline backdrop (which she thought was real), but she later claimed she was just "pretending." We had no idea Fawcett was such a talented actress.

4 — MARIAH CAREY breaks down.

Her rambling 2001 MTV striptease was attributed to "exhaustion." This was before "Glitter" came out.

5 — WHITNEY HOUSTON just says "no."

Houston, we have a problem: In a 2002 chat with Diane Sawyer, the diva admitted to doing drugs but insisted, "I make too much money to ever smoke crack. Crack is whack." Judging from her bizarre behavior on *Being Bobby Brown*, so is Houston.

HOWARD DEAN screams.

He may have finished third among Iowa voters in 2004, but the Democratic presidential contender shot to the top of late-night comics' hit lists when he let loose an earsplitting, bloodcurdling wail at a post-caucus rally. What a howler!

ANNA NICOLE SMITH slurs her speech.

It wasn't the TrimSpa talking when the reality-TV train wreck woozily introduced Kanye West at the 2004 American Music Awards. In a barely coherent falsetto, Smith squealed, "Like my body?" and dubbed the rapper "a freakin' genius." As opposed to just being a freak.

JACK PAAR walks off.

The weepy host quit *The Tonight Show* for a month in 1960 after NBC's censors nixed a joke about a "water closet" (that means a toilet, kids). In an era when Mini-Me pees on TV, a "WC" gag seems downright quaint.

VERNE TROYER relieves himself.

The Surreal Life was never more surreal than in 2005, when a blotto Mini-Me rode his scooter into a corner and went number one. This is why pixilation was invented.

COURTNEY LOVE goes wild.

OK, it was cute when Drew Barrymore flashed David Letterman in 1995. But when the wobbly warbler repeated the stunt in 2004, it was just plain creepy. Not that Letterman was complaining.

JOE NAMATH makes a pass.

"I want to kiss you," the ex-Jets quarterback leeringly burbled to ESPN sideline reporter Suzy Kolber in 2003. Alas, Namath didn't score, but he did rush into alcohol rehab.

TYRA BANKS blows up.

It wasn't pretty when, in 2005, Banks chewed out *America's Next Top Model* wannabe Tiffany for—no kidding—not taking the show seriously. "I have never in my life yelled at a girl like this!" she bellowed. Here's one model who's not afraid to show her bad side.

A Baker's Dozen of TV Chefs

Who Know How to Spice Things Up

Whether they're making crème brulée or simply boiling water, these TV chefs make everyday cooking fun and exciting.

1
Julia Child
The French Chef,
In Julia's Kitchen with
Master Chefs

2
Graham Kerr
The Galloping Gourmet,
Graham Kerr's Kitchen

3
Jacques Pepin
Everyday Cooking
with Jacques Pepin,
Today's Gourmet

4
Emeril Lagasse
The Essence of Emeril,
Emeril Live

5
Martin Yan
Yan Can Cook

6
Wolfgang Puck
Wolfgang Puck's
Cooking Class

7
Rachael Ray
30-Minute Meals,
$40 a Day

8
Mario Batali
Molto Mario,
Mario Eats Italy

9
Bobby Flay
Hot off the Grill with
Bobby Flay,
Boy Meets Grill

10
Alton Brown
Good Eats

11
Sara Moulton
Cooking Live
with Sara Moulton,
Sara's Secrets

12
Jennifer Paterson &
Clarissa Dickson Wright
Two Fat Ladies

20 Stars Who Shouldn't Have

Become Talk-Show Hosts

It seems every celebrity tries out their own gabfests these days, some with more success than others. Those below didn't fare very well.

1
ALF

2
Tempestt
Bledsoe

3
Danny
Bonaduce

4
Gabrielle
Carteris

5
Chevy
Chase

6
Whoopi
Goldberg

7
George
Hamilton

8
Lauren
Hutton

9
Vicki
Lawrence

10
Megan
Mullaly

11
Magic
Johnson

12
Howie
Mandel

13
John
McEnroe

14
Sharon
Osbourne

15
Roseanne

16
Pat
Sajak

17
Martin
Short

18
Alana
Stewart

19
Alan
Thicke

20
Carnie
Wilson

Stand-Up Comics
Who Have Headlined Sitcoms

1 Sid Caesar
(*The Sid Caesar Show*)

2 Bob Newhart
(*The Bob Newhart Show, Newhart*)

3 Redd Foxx
(*Sanford and Son*)

4 Freddie Prinze
(*Chico and the Man*)

5 Robin Williams
(*Mork & Mindy*)

6 Paul Rodriguez
(*aka Pablo*)

7 Bill Cosby
(*The Cosby Show, Cosby*)

8 Bob Saget
(*Full House*)

9 Roseanne Barr
(*Roseanne*)

10 Richard Lewis
(*Anything but Love*)

11 Jerry Seinfeld
(*Seinfeld*)

12 Rodney Dangerfield
(*Where's Rodney?*)

13 Tim Allen
(*Home Improvement*)

14 Jonathan Winters
(*Davis Rules*)

15 Garry Shandling
(*The Larry Sanders Show*)

16 Martin Lawrence
(*Martin*)

17 Paul Reiser
(*Mad About You*)

18 Billy Connolly
(*Billy*)

19 Brett Butler
(*Grace Under Fire*)

20 Sinbad
(*The Sinbad Show*)

21 Margaret Cho
(*All-American Girl*)

22 John Caponera
(*The Good Life*)

23 Jeff Foxworthy
(*The Jeff Foxworthy Show*)

24 Drew Carey
(*The Drew Carey Show*)

25 Andrew Dice Clay
(*Bless This House*)

26 Phil Hartman
(*NewsRadio*)

27 Bonnie Hunt
(*The Building, Bonnie, Life With Bonnie*)

28 Ray Romano
(*Everybody Loves Raymond*)

29 Jamie Foxx
(*The Jamie Foxx Show*)

30 Anthony Clark
(*Boston Common*)

31 Eddie Griffin
(*Malcolm & Eddie*)

32 Louie Anderson
(*The Louie Show*)

33 Robert Wuhl
(*Arli$$*)

34 Steve Harvey
(*The Steve Harvey Show*)

35 Kevin James
(*King of Queens*)

36 D.L. Hughley
(*The Hughleys*)

37 Norm Macdonald
(*A Minute With Stan Hooper, The Norm Show*)

38 Ellen DeGeneres
(*Ellen, The Ellen Show*)

39 Jay Mohr
(*Action*)

40 Larry David
(*Curb Your Enthusiasm*)

41 David Alan Grier
(*DAG*)

42 Bernie Mac
(*The Bernie Mac Show*)

43 Jim Belushi
(*According to Jim*)

44 George Lopez
(*The George Lopez Show*)

45 Damon Wayans
(*My Wife and Kids*)

46 Tracy Morgan
(*The Tracy Morgan Show, 30 Rock*)

47 Wanda Sykes
(*Wanda Does It; Wanda at Large*)

48 Rodney Carrington
(*Rodney*)

49 Louis CK
(*Lucky Louie*)

50 Sarah Silverman
(*The Sarah Silverman Program*)

You're Fired!

TV's Top 10 Pink Slips

We look back at 10 stars who know what it's like to be booted from a TV show...

1 — Shannen Doherty

Year: 2005   **Show:** *Love, Inc.*

In May 2005, just one week after Shannen told TV advertisers how excited she was to be starring in the new UPN sitcom *Love, Inc.*, a terse press release announced that she was no longer with the show. Shannen, of course, has had her ups and downs: She left both *Beverly Hills, 90210* and *Charmed* amid rumors of jumping before being pushed.

Postscript: The actress moved to the reality-show genre with two series: *Scare Tactics* (in which terrifying practical jokes are staged on unsuspecting victims) and *Breaking Up With Shannen Doherty* (where she helps people stuck in bad relationships to dump their significant other).

2 — Suzanne Somers

Year: 1990   **Show:** *Three's Company*

After four seasons of playing Chrissy Snow on the popular sitcom, Suzanne Somers asked producers to increase her pay from $30,000 a show to $150,000—plus give her a piece of the profits. "I was fired the day that I asked," says Suzanne. "There was no negotiating. They just said, 'Get out'."

Postscript: After being, in her words, "unofficially blackballed" by the TV industry for more than a decade, Suzanne returned to the small screen in 1991 in the sitcom *Step by Step*. The best-selling author, Vegas entertainer and Thighmaster pitchwoman has now amassed a small fortune as a one-woman fitness and fashion industry.

3 — Hilary Swank

Year: 1997   **Show:** *Beverly Hills, 90210*

When the struggling actress was hired to play Carly Reynolds on the Fox hit, she was thrilled. But after less than a year on the show, she was summoned by the producer. "Aaron Spelling called me into his office and told me, 'Hilary, this is not working'," she recalls. "I was like, 'Huh?' So I go home, flopped on my bed and started crying. And I said, 'Oh my gosh, I just got fired from *90210*! If I'm not a good enough actor to be on *90210*, I think I need to quit!' I was totally devastated."

Postscript: Three weeks later, she won the lead in "Boys Don't Cry," a role that led to her first Best Actress Oscar. She won her second in 2004 for "Million Dollar Baby."

4 — Jerry Seinfeld
Year: 1980   **Show:** *Benson*

In 1980, the 26-year-old New York comic moved to Los Angeles when he won a recurring role on the sitcom *Benson* playing Frankie, the governor's speechwriter. It was Jerry's acting debut, but rather than defer to the producers, he soon clashed with them over the direction of his character. After just four episodes, they fired him.

Postscript: Seinfeld swore he'd never do another sitcom unless he had creative control. Nine years later, *The Seinfeld Chronicles* debuted, which evolved into the now-legendary *Seinfeld*.

5 — George Eads and Jorja Fox
Year: 2004   **Show:** *CSI*

The stars, who play Agents Nick Stokes and Sara Sidle on *CSI*, were fired in July 2004 when CBS felt they were pulling stunts for money (George hadn't shown up for taping; Jorja reportedly had not delivered on a promise letter stating she'd be at work). George apologized and claimed he'd overslept; Jorja supposedly said the letter was in the mail.

Postscript: The duo were rehired after reportedly agreeing to come back for their pre-firing pay: $100,000 per episode. Talk about an expensive lesson: Both are said to have been offered a $20,000-per-show raise before being axed.

6 — Delta Burke
Year: 1991   **Show:** *Designing Women*

When Delta was fired from the popular sitcom, many people presumed it was because the producers were unhappy that her weight had ballooned to 200 pounds: Suzanne Sugarbaker, after all, was the vain beauty queen of the show. At the time, Delta blamed the rift on abusive behavior from the shows creators, Linda Bloodworth-Thomason and Harry Thomason. But Delta later revealed that she'd been suffering from panic attacks that made work difficult for her and everyone else.

Postscript: After leaving the show, Delta got treatment for her anxiety and ironically, got her weight down to 150 with the diet she adopted when she was diagnosed with diabetes in 1997.

7 — John Amos
Year: 1976   **Show:** *Good Times*

The talented actor, who played poor but proud patriarch James Evans in the hit sitcom about a family living in a Chicago housing project, was fired after the second season, supposedly for complaining too much about the way African-Americans were portrayed on the show. It probably didn't help that he had caused a week's delay in taping Season 2 because of a salary dispute.

Postscript: A year later, John appeared in the groundbreaking and critically acclaimed miniseries *Roots*, playing Toby (Kunta Kinte as an adult).

8 — Valerie Harper
Year: 1997   **Show:** *Valerie*

After two seasons, star Valerie Harper—who helped create the sitcom—asked that her salary be increased from $56,750 per episode to $100,000. When the producers refused, Valerie stayed home.

Postscript: After an acrimonious trial, during which Valerie was described as combative and paranoid, a jury ruled that she had been wrongfully dismissed and awarded her $1.4 million and a cut of the profits of the show, renamed *The Hogan Family*.

(9) Debbie Matenopoulos

Year: 1999   **Show:** *The View*

The then-24-year-old was totally humiliated when Barbara Walters announced in January 1999 that Debbie was leaving by "mutual decision." Of course, there was nothing mutual about it. "I felt like they were showing my beheading on pay-per-view," Debbie said.

Postscript: Debbie looks on the bright side: "If I hadn't been fired, I wouldn't be a household name!" She's parlayed her *View* gig into numerous other hosting forays, including those for the TV GUIDE Channel, VH-1 and E!

(10) Norm Macdonald

Year: 1997   **Show:** *Saturday Night Live*

Though he won critical raves for his cutting jokes and deadpan delivery as host of *SNL*'s "Weekend Update," the actor/comedian was fired by former NBC West Coast president Don Ohlmeyer, reportedly for not being funny. But insiders said the real reason Norm got the ax was because he was making too many jokes about Ohlmeyer pal O.J. Simpson.

Postscript: Norm "retired from show business" for a year before making the big-screen comedy "Dirty Work" in 1998. The following year, he returned to *SNL* to host the show and to publicize his short-lived TV series *The Norm Show*. He starred in another failed TV comedy in 2003 (*A Minute With Stan Hooper*) and now concentrates on film roles.

Good Times

Good Times was a spin-off of the sitcom *Maude* (itself a spin-off of *All in the Family*).

Romance Bloomed

On the Set of a Music Video

Brad Paisley and Kimberly-Williams Paisley:
Began dating after she appeared in his 2002 video, "I'm Gonna Miss Her (The Fishin' Song)"; later married.

Nick Lachey and Vanessa Minnillo:
This couple's relationship started during the making of his video "What's Left of Me."

Enrique Iglesias and Anna Kournikova:
Met on the set of his 2001 video for "Escape."

Josh Kelley and Katherine Hiegl:
Met when his video for "Only You" was being made.

Sean Combs and Jennifer Lopez:
This former couple fell for each other while filming his music video for "Been Around the World."

John Mellencamp and Elaine Irwin:
"Get a Leg Up" brought the couple together; they married in 1992.

TV's Best Comebacks

In 2005, as we reflected on former Friend Lisa Kudrow's return to TV in the HBO series *The Comeback*, we found 10 other stars enjoying a second turn in the limelight.

1 Ellen DeGeneres

B.C (Before Comeback): Won a 1997 Emmy for *Ellen*, in which her character outed herself just as Ellen confirmed she was gay. The show was canceled the following season, and a 2001 sitcom attempt failed.

The comeback trail: Hosted the Emmy Awards and voiced Dory in "Finding Nemo," but her comeback wasn't complete until 2003, when she launched her Emmy-winning talk-fest *The Ellen DeGeneres Show*.

Says Ellen: "Now I'm able to be myself."

2 David Caruso

B.C: Ditched his Emmy-nominated role on *NYPD Blue* in 1994 for film stardom that never materialized.

The comeback trail: Since 2002, he's been Miami-Dade Crime Lab honcho Horatio Caine on CBS's hit drama *CSI: Miami*.

Says David: "I mishandled the *NYPD Blue* situation, but I've had a number of opportunities to grow up and realize what has been provided for me."

3 Kiefer Sutherland

B.C: In the late '80s and early '90s, starred in "The Lost Boys," "Young Guns" and "Flatliners," but joined the professional rodeo circuit when choice roles started drying up.

The comeback trail: Rodeo made him realize he missed acting, and he signed on to star in *24*, garnering Emmy, Golden Globe and SAG Awards.

Says Kiefer: "Now I really enjoy and appreciate it more."

4 Matthew Fox

B.C: He was best known as eldest Salinger sibling Charlie on Fox's 1994-2000 drama *Party of Five*.

The comeback trail: Leader of a pack of plane-crash survivors as heroic Dr. Jack Shepard on *Lost* where his many shirtless scenes have also won him a place among the sexiest men on TV.

Says Matthew: "If it takes my whole life to gain people's respect as an actor, that's good."

5 Teri Hatcher

B.C: Superman's girlfriend on the 1993 hit *Lois & Clark* became known for Radio Shack ads when the series took a ratings nosedive and flew off the air in 1997.

The comeback trail: At 40, she won a Golden Globe and a Screen Actors Guild Award for her role on *Desperate Housewives*.

Says Teri: "Two years ago I'm crying thinking I'll never be able to pay my mortgage. That's the depths of where I came from."

6 Charlie Sheen

B.C: He starred in some of the biggest movie hits of the '80s, including "Platoon" and "Wall Street," before he became more famous for partying than acting.

The comeback trail: He won a Golden Globe in 2002 after taking over for Michael J. Fox on *Spin City* and sealed the comeback with his role as ladies' man Charlie Harper on *Two and a Half Men*.

Says Charlie: "It's pretty cool."

7 Nicollette Sheridan

B.C: She was the heartbreaker of the late '80s as *Knots Landing*'s Paige, but spent most of the '90s starring in made-for-TV dramas.

The comeback trail: She's a scene stealer as *Desperate Housewives*' neighborhood hussy Edie Brit.

Says Nicollette: "I seemed to be playing stroke victims or somebody's mother. But I wanted to have fun. It's really nice doing this at this point in my life."

8 Jason Bateman

B.C: He was an '80s teen pinup thanks to roles on sitcoms like Ricky Schroder's *Silver Spoons* and *The Hogan Family*, but floundered on four failed series in the '90s.

The comeback trail: He won his first Golden Globe in 2005 for his role as Michael, the (relatively) sane member of the scandal-plagued Bluth family on Fox's Emmy-winning sitcom *Arrested Development*.

Says Jason: "Most people retire after 25 years in this business. I got to start over."

9 Paula Abdul

B.C: The former Laker Girl had six No. 1 hits with 1988's pop classic *Forever Your Girl*. But two follow-up CDs didn't sell as well, and Paula spent most of the next decade working behind the scenes as a choreographer.

The comeback trail: She's rocketed back to stardom as the "nice judge" on *American Idol*.

Says Paula: "I'm a bigger star now than I was (before), all because I'm on this hit TV show."

10 Patrick Dempsey

B.C: An '80s heartthrob ("Can't Buy Me Love"), he had a tough time finding more grown-up fare in the '90s.

The comeback trail: Won an Emmy nomination in 2001 for *Once and Again*, but it's his role as Dr. Derek Shepherd on *Grey's Anatomy* that's put him back on top.

Says Patrick: "In the past, I felt guilty about success. Now I'm just thankful to be here."

Long-Running Series

We tend to overlook TV's most durable programs, some of which have been educating or entertaining audiences for several decades. The series below are 22 of the oldest programs on TV, having aired for 10 years or more, yet few show signs of wear.

Meet the Press (NBC) Began airing in 1947

The Tonight Show (NBC) 1954

The Price Is Right (NBC/ABC/CBS) 1956

60 Minutes (CBS) 1968

Sesame Street (PBS) 1969

Monday Night Football (ABC/ESPN) 1970

Saturday Night Live (NBC) 1975

20/20 (ABC) 1978

Late Show With David Letterman/Late Night With David Letterman (NBC/CBS) 1982

America's Most Wanted (Fox) 1988

Cops (Fox) 1989

PrimeTime Live (ABC) 1989

The Simpsons (Fox) 1989

America's Funniest Home Videos (ABC) 1990

Law & Order (NBC) 1990

Dateline NBC (NBC) 1992

Late Night With Conan O'Brien (NBC) 1993

ER (NBC) 1994

Mad TV (Fox) 1995

7th Heaven (WB/CW) 1996

South Park (Comedy Central) 1997

King of the Hill (Fox) 1997

Daytime soap operas are often ignored when series longevity is assessed, but considering that most have been airing for several decades—on a daily basis—their staying-power is unprecedented.

Guiding Light (CBS) 1952 (began on radio in 1937)

As the World Turns (CBS) 1956

General Hospital (ABC) 1963

Days of Our Lives (NBC) 1965

One Live to Live (ABC) 1968

All My Children (ABC) 1970

The Young and the Restless (CBS) 1973

The Bold and the Beautiful (CBS) 1987

Passions (NBC) 1999

Addresses

of TV Families and Businesses

1 328 Chauncey Street
Brooklyn, New York
Home of Ralph and Alice Kramden,
The Honeymooners

2 623 East 68th Street, Apt. 4A
(later Apt. 3D)
New York, New York
Home of Lucy and Ricky Ricardo,
I Love Lucy

3 1313 Mockingbird Lane
Mockingbird Heights
Home of *The Munsters*

4 342 Gravelpit Terrace
Home of *The Flintstones*

5 704 Hauser Street
Queens, New York
Home of Archie and Edith Bunker,
All in the Family

6 119 North Weatherly Avenue, Apt. D
Minneapolis, Minnesota
Home of Mary Richards,
The Mary Tyler Moore Show

7 1164 Morning Glory Circle
Westport, Connecticut
Home of Darrin and Samantha Stephens,
Bewitched

8 4222 Clinton Way
Los Angeles, California
Home of the Brady family,
The Brady Bunch

9 698 Sycamore Road
San Pueblo, California
Home of *The Partridge Family*

10 1020 Palm Drive
Cocoa Beach, Florida
Home of Capt. Anthony and Jeannie
Nelson, *I Dream of Jeannie*

11 565 North Clinton Drive
Milwaukee, Wisconsin
Home of Howard and Marion Cunningham,
Happy Days

12 Corner of Hudson & Charles Streets
Greenwich Village, New York
Location of The Sunshine Cab Company,
Taxi

13 173 Essex Drive
Denver, Colorado
Home of Blake and Krystal Carrington,
Dynasty

14 714 Delaware Street
Lanford, Illinois
Home of Dan and Roseanne Conner,
Roseanne

15 84 Beacon Street
Boston, Massachusetts
Location of *Cheers* bar

16 Rte. 125
East Middlebury, Vermont
Location of The Stratford Inn, run by Dick
and Joanna Loudon, *Newhart*

17 **933 Hillcrest Drive
Beverly Hills, California 90210**
Home of the Walsh family,
Beverly Hills, 90210

18 **698 Candlewood Lane
Cabot Cove, Maine**
Home of Jessica Fletcher,
Murder, She Wrote

19 **9764 Jeopardy Lane
Chicago, Illinois**
Home of the Bundys,
Married...With Children

20 **10 Stigwood Avenue
Brooklyn Heights, New York**
Home of the Huxtable family,
The Cosby Show

21 **2102 Willow Lane
Evening Shade, Arkansas**
Home of Wood and Ava Newton,
Evening Shade

22 **742 Evergreen Terrace
Springfield**
Home of *The Simpsons*

23 **129 West 81st Street, Apt. 5A
New York, New York**
Home of Jerry Seinfeld, *Seinfeld*

24 **1630 Revello Drive
Sunnydale, California**
Home of Buffy Summers,
Buffy the Vampire Slayer

25 **1329 Prescott Street
San Francisco, California**
Home of the Halliwell sisters, *Charmed*

I Love Lucy

Gale Gordon and Bea Benaderet, costars on
My Favorite Husband, were originally
approached for the roles of Fred and Ethel
Mertz, but both were unavailable.

TV's Bad Boys...

And Why We Love Them

In real life, no one likes a hothead. But on TV, the bigger the scoundrel, the better. In April 2004, TV GUIDE offered up the five biggest and best.

James Gandolfini as Tony Soprano, the overprotective father, unfaithful husband and Prozac-taking, decapitating waste-management consultant and mob boss on HBO's *The Sopranos*.

Crimes: Drinks milk from the carton. Calls his therapist really bad names. Put the financial squeeze on his estranged wife. Kills lots of people.

Saving graces: Helped clean up the mess after his sister shot her fiancé. Protects his family against bears. Seems genuinely conflicted about the horrible things he does.

How dare we love him? On a scale of one to five bullets, Gandolfini steals six. He's the best killer in TV history.

Dennis Franz as Det. Andy Sipowicz, the cantankerous, 12-stepping cop with questionable interrogation habits on ABC's *NYPD Blue*.

Crimes: Serious anger-management issues. History of insensitivity when it comes to gays, minorities, women and pretty much anyone else not himself. Has been known to rough up any skell who gets in the way of cracking a case. Showed a flabby backside in an exceedingly gratuitous shower scene.

Saving graces: Quit drinking and smoking. Has worked on being tolerant, however awkwardly (notably with receptionist Gay John). Has endured numerous trials and tribulations. Adores his growing new family.

How dare we love him? Andy broke ground (and hearts) with his self-destructive ways, even if he settled down, grew up and went a little stale.

James Spader as Alan Shore, the reptilian, cunning and perverse yet surprisingly moral attorney on ABC's *The Practice*. (Note: Spader has since taken this role to his own series, *Boston Legal*.)

Crimes: Embezzles. Conceals and destroys evidence. Not above blackmail to win a case. Disrespects judicial authority. Oozes smugness and snobbery. Creeps out young women ("I touched myself with you in mind last night"). Slept with his best friend's mother.

Saving graces: Honest to a fault (see his quote above). Loyal, too, as he returned to his hometown to defend a childhood friend accused of murder. Paid a settlement with his own money just so a client would think she won. Single-handedly saved the show, making viewers forget all about Dylan McDermott.

How dare we love him? This snakelike charmer hypnotizes and amuses.

Michael Chiklis as Det. Vic Mackey, the brutish, violent, kick-back taking, evidence-tampering rogue cop on FX's *The Shield*.

Crimes: Killed a fellow cop in the very first episode. Smashed a drug dealer's face onto a hot stove. Stole from the Armenian mob. Spends as much time covering up his crimes as he does working the streets. Cheats on his wife. Plants evidence.

Saving graces: Catches lots of criminals (the kind without badges) and actually has scruples—about crimes against kids, especially. Used ill-gotten gains to get guns off the streets. Extremely loyal to his strike team. Loves and worries about his autistic child. Keeps an eye on the orphan of a prostitute snitch he befriended.

How dare we love him? Vic challenges our moral compass every time we root for him. But we keep doing it.

Julian McMahon as Dr. Christian Troy, the womanizing, substance-abusing, superficial and barely competent plastic surgeon on FX's *Nip/Tuck*.

Crimes: Suggests cosmetic enhancements to his sex partners. Takes on questionable but high-paying clients, like drug dealers and child molesters. Traded his girlfriend for a sports car. Installed a butt implant upside down. Feeds body parts to alligators. Calls his yacht the Boatox.

Saving graces: That face, for starters. Charming as all get-out. His genuine affection for his medical partner and best friend extends to the friend's family—although he may be the real father of his buddy's son. Gave moral support to a sexaholic he thought was pregnant with his child (the baby turned out not to be his).

How dare we love him? This doc's seductive bedside manner makes George Clooney look like an intern.

On Second Thought...

TV keeps dishing out those naughty boys...here are a few more we love to loathe.

David Boreanaz as Angel on WB's *Angel*

Eric Dane as Mark Sloane on ABC's *Grey's Anatomy*

Josh Holloway as Sawyer on ABC's *Lost*

Paul Johansson as Dan Scott on WB's *One Tree Hill*

Hugh Laurie as Dr. Greg House on Fox's *House*

James Marsters as Spike on WB/UPN's *Buffy the Vampire Slayer*

Ian McShane as Al Swearengen on HBO's *Deadwood*

Wentworth Miller as Michael Scofield on Fox's *Prison Break*

Michael Rosenbaum as Lex Luthor on WB's *Smallville*

Charlie Sheen as Charlie Harper on CBS's *Two and a Half Men*

Pioneers:
10 Who Got There First

1 **Milton Berle**
Hit the air in 1948. Who else could be called Mr. Television?

2 *Tonight* **before Johnny**
Steve Allen and Jack Paar gave the country something to talk about

3 **Jack Benny**
Mixed prissy vanity with impeccable timing in the '50, decades before *Frasier*

4 **Ernie Kovacs**
The 1950s precursor of Letterman

5 *Dr. Kildare*
Richard Chamberlain's gorgeous intern beat Ben Casey to the E.R. by four days in '61

6 *Perry Mason*
Opened the practice back in '57

7 *The Adventures of Ozzie & Harriet*
Set up house in '52, five years before the Cleavers

8 **The Flintstones**
The original made-for-TV cartoon clan (1960)

9 *I Spy*
Integrated espionage; debuted in '65; the next day, Bill Cosby was a star

10 *American Bandstand*
A good beat, 41 years before MTV's *TRL*. And you could dance to it.

Theme Songs

That Hit Billboard's Top 10

These songs weren't just snappy tunes that stuck in your head...they made it to the big time, charting at the top of the Pop chart.

#1

"S.W.A.T."
by Rhythm Heritage (1975)

"Welcome Back, Kotter"
by John Sebastian (1976)

"Miami Vice"
by Jan Hammer (1985)

"How Do You Talk to an Angel"
from *The Heights* (1992)

#2

"Believe It or Not"
by Joey Scarbury from
The Greatest American Hero (1981)

#3

"Dragnet"
by the Ray Anthony Orchestra (1953)

"Secret Agent Man"
by Johnny Rivers (1966)

#4

"Hawaii Five-0"
by the Ventures (1969)

#5

"Happy Days"
by Pratt and McClain (1976)

"Makin' It"
by David Naughton (1979)

#7

"Addams Groove"
by Hammer from
The Addams Family (1991)

#8

"Peter Gunn"
by the Ray Anthony Orchestra (1959)

"Bad Boys"
by Inner Circle from *Cops* (1993)

#10

"Three Stars Will Shine Tonight"
by Richard Chamberlain from
Dr. Kildare (1962)

"The Rockford Files"
by Mike Post (1975)

"Hill Street Blues"
by Mike Post (1981)

Then & Now

Just like yesteryear, television is still populated by doctors, castaways and ditsy socialites, but with some, er, mind-boggling twists.

Housewives

THEN: **Donna Reed** Cooks hot meals for her family.

NOW: **Susan Mayer** (*Desperate Housewives*) Always looks like a hot dish.

Therapists

THEN: **Bob Newhart** Has patients with punch lines that can make you die laughing.

NOW: **Dr. Melfi** (*The Sopranos*) Has a patient who can kill you with a punch.

Castaways

THEN: **Gilligan** (*Gilligan's Island*) Stranded with a millionaire, a movie star and a large skipper.

NOW: **Jack** (*Lost*) Stranded with a millionaire, a rock star and a large monster.

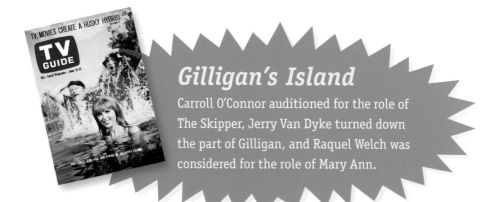

Gilligan's Island

Carroll O'Connor auditioned for the role of The Skipper, Jerry Van Dyke turned down the part of Gilligan, and Raquel Welch was considered for the role of Mary Ann.

Game-Show Challenges

THEN: *What's My Line?* The panel wonders if the contestant actually trains spiders to dance.

NOW: *Fear Factor* Leaves you wondering which contestant will eat the spiders.

Blonde Socialites

THEN: **Lisa Douglas** (*Green Acres*) Learns to love living in Hooterville.

NOW: **Paris Hilton** (*The Simple Life*) Loves to flaunt her hooters.

Doctors

THEN: **Marcus Welby** Great bedside manner with his patients.

NOW: **Christian Troy** (*Nip/Tuck*) Great at bedding his patients.

Tycoons

THEN: **J.R. Ewing** (*Dallas*) Covers head with a Stetson; fires family members.

NOW: **Donald Trump** (*The Apprentice*) Covers head with aerodynamic comb-over; fires almost everyone.

Grannies

THEN: **Granny** (*The Beverly Hillbillies*) Cooks up gourmet "vittles" like possum she bagged herself.

NOW: **Emily Gilmore** (*Gilmore Girls*) Has her maid serve gourmet food prepared by her staff.

Wacky Families

THEN: **The Munsters** Act normal but look like monsters.

NOW: **The Bluths** (*Arrested Development*) Look normal but act like monsters.

Wild West Men

THEN: **Marshal Dillon** (*Gunsmoke*) Swore to uphold the law.

NOW: **Al Swearengen** (*Deadwood*) Swears a blue streak.

TV Loves

a Man (or Woman) in Uniform

Here's our 21-gun salute to the greatest military shows ever.

1 — *M*A*S*H* (CBS, 1972-83)

A great comedy and a great drama, it used the unlikely setting of a remote surgical outpost during the Korean War to comment on conflict of all kinds, most notably the Vietnam War. Its randy but dedicated doctors and nurses used laughter as a tonic against the atrocities of combat. Striking the perfect balance between antibureaucratic rage and idealism, Larry Gelbart's brilliant refashioning of Robert Altman's hit film, with a dream cast led by Alan Alda, was good medicine for TV. Our tour of duty with these wonderful characters lasted 11 years on CBS—seven years longer than the Korean conflict itself. We never tire of a show, still airing in reruns, that seems as necessary and topical now as ever.

2 — *China Beach* (ABC, 1988-91)

War on television had never been seen through women's eyes until this series, set in a hospital, hit the airwaves. The personal, even soapish dramas of its doctors and nurses, juxtaposed against the darker story of Vietnam, proved to be a riveting combination. Besides offering breakout roles for Dana Delany and Marg Helgenberger, *China Beach* gave viewers a humanized view of a controversial war by taking us into the lives of the people who were there.

3 — *The Civil War* (PBS, 1990)

Ken Burns' 11-hour masterpiece used period music and the photos and written sentiments of the soldiers and their loved ones to perfectly capture the violence, grief and passions—the haunting humanity—of this most devastating of American wars. In doing so, it also redefined TV documentaries and established Burns as a master storyteller.

4 — *The Phil Silvers Show* (CBS, 1955-59)

Anyone who's served a day in the Army knew a schemer like Sgt. Ernie Bilko (Phil Silvers), the scam artist who operated out of the Fort Baxter motor pool. And every military comedy after this classic has had Bilko DNA in it. But the pace, the scripts and Silvers' perfectly pitched imperfect con man have never been equaled.

5 — *Victory at Sea* (NBC, 1952-53)

This vivid 26-part compilation of footage from World War II's most famous battleship encounters in the Atlantic and Pacific won a Peabody and an Emmy. Years later, Richard Rogers' score remains transcendent.

Band of Brothers (HBO, 2001)
Hope mixed with disillusion and despair set the tone for this landmark WWII miniseries, based on Stephen Ambrose's book and produced by the dream team of Tom Hanks and Steven Spielberg.

 The Winds of War/War and Remembrance (ABC, 1983 and 1988)
Herman Wouk's epic novels revolving around the Henrys, a WWII-era Navy family, were brought to living-room screens via two massive, majestic miniseries. Unflinching death-camp scenes paved the way for "Schindler's List."

 Combat! (ABC, 1962-67)
Starring Vic Morrow as the flinty-cool Sgt. Saunders, this tough WWII drama followed troops as they battled through Europe. It gave Americans their first taste of a living-room war, ending as Vietnam was heating up.

 JAG (NBC, 1995-96; CBS, 1997-2005)
What at first looked like just another derivative show—"Top Gun" meets _Law & Order_—became one of TV's most enduring uniform dramas, with topical military-legal issues smartly mixed with personal tales.

 F Troop (ABC, 1965-67)
Hysterically dumb yet cult-classically brilliant. The men, woman and very strange Indians (Don Rickles was one) in and around the misnamed Fort Courage brought goofiness to the Old West nearly a decade before "Blazing Saddles."

 The Adventures of Rin Tin Tin (ABC, 1954-59)
For baby boomers, this _was_ the Army: a brilliant German shepherd living with his boy Rusty (who wore a mini infantry uniform) in the Wild West's Fort Apache. Yo-ho, Rinty!

 McHale's Navy (ABC, 1962-66)
Ernest Borgnine's comic turn aboard a PT boat stationed in the Pacific, and the masterful timing of then-newcomer Tim Conway, made this bit of bombast and bilgewater a pure pleasure.

 Tour of Duty (CBS, 1987-90)
As it followed Bravo Company from first tour of duty to last, this series unflinchingly presented all the issues and contradictions that made Vietnam Vietnam.

Hogan's Heroes (CBS, 1965-71)
Anyone back in '65 who thought a weekly sitcom about a happy-go-lucky band of POWs in a Nazi prison camp would be humorless and tasteless obviously knew _nussing_!

Gomer Pyle, USMC (CBS, 1964-70)
"Gaw-aw-aw-leee!" Mayberry's Gomer (Jim Nabors) joined the Marines and offered a wholesome twist on the old vaudeville routine of the hick outsmarting the city slicker.

16 — *The Rat Patrol* (ABC, 1966-68)
A commando unit consisting of three Americans and one Brit almost single-handedly undid Rommel's Sahara forces in this rollicking WWII action-adventure.

17 — *Call to Glory* (ABC, 1984-85)
An überpatriotic Air Force colonel (Craig T. Nelson) tried to keep both his country and his family safe in this sweeping series set in the early years of the Cold War. Future star Elisabeth Shue played the colonel's daughter.

18 — *The Rebel* (ABC, 1959-61)
Johnny Yuma (Nick Adams) was the Confederate-capped title character, a Johnny-come-marching-not-quite-home. Changed and chastened by the Civil War, Yuma wandered the West, writing in his diary about his untethered life. Adams was James Dean cool.

19 — *Hennesey* (CBS, 1959-62)
Like the pre-Vietnam Navy in which it was set, this comedy was upbeat. It depicted the life and love of ship's doctor Chick Hennesey (Jackie Cooper) as he ministered to the needs of a wacky crew based in San Diego.

20 — *Twelve O'Clock High* (ABC, 1964-67)
This no-nonsense Air Force action-adventure, based on the classic 1949 Gregory Peck film, depicted dangerous WWII bombing runs. Robert Lansing starred and Quinn Martin produced.

21 — *Ensign O'Toole* (NBC, 1962-63)
The likeable O'Toole (Dean Jones) enjoyed Navy life aboard the battleship Appleby just fine, so long as he could steer clear of any superior officer who might order him to do something horrible—like work.

Babies Who Caused Their Shows

to Jump the Shark

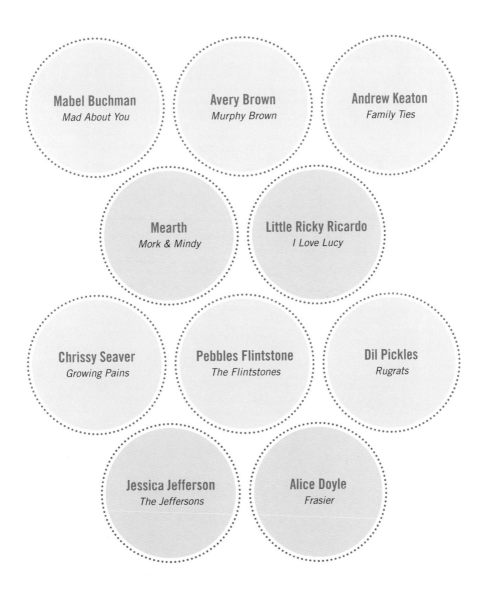

Mabel Buchman
Mad About You

Avery Brown
Murphy Brown

Andrew Keaton
Family Ties

Mearth
Mork & Mindy

Little Ricky Ricardo
I Love Lucy

Chrissy Seaver
Growing Pains

Pebbles Flintstone
The Flintstones

Dil Pickles
Rugrats

Jessica Jefferson
The Jeffersons

Alice Doyle
Frasier

Reasons Series
Jump the Shark

jumptheshark.com

Each of the categories that follows illuminates why some good series go bad, from births to puberty, the consummation of a relationship to, well, Ted McGinley being cast in the show. TV execs, take heed...

Making the Move to The Big Screen

"The X-Files"

"South Park: Bigger, Longer & Uncut"

"Private Parts"

"Transformers"

"Mission: Impossible"

"Rugrats in Paris: The Movie" and *"Rugrats Go Wild"*

"Mr. Bean"

"Beavis and Butt-head Do America"

"G.I. Joe—The Movie"

"Absolutely Fabulous: The Last Shout"

A Very Special Episode...

JUMP THE SHARK

Ellen
Ellen comes out

Mad About You
Paul and Jamie almost break up

The West Wing
Isaac and Ishmael

Frasier
Nile's heart hurts

Diff'rent Strokes
Dudley gets molested

Will & Grace
Grace chooses Leo over Will

Moonlighting
Maddie has a miscarriage

Blossom
On a very (frequent) special episode of *Blossom*...

Quincy, M.E.
Quincy rallies against punk rock

Nip/Tuck
Christian's fatherly sexual abuse

A Very Special Episode...

JUMP THE SHARK

Scooby-Doo, Where Are You?
Scrappy-Doo

Howard Stern
Artie

Buffy the Vampire Slayer
Dawn

The Brady Bunch
Cousin Oliver

Married...With Children
Seven

Ally McBeal
Maddie (Ally is a mom)

The Cosby Show
Olivia (Denise is a stepmom)

The Cosby Show
Cousin Pam

Diff'rent Strokes
Sam

Little House on the Prairie
Albert

Hitting the Sheets

JUMP THE
SH🦈RK

Moonlighting
Maddie and David

Ed
Ed and Carol

Northern Exposure
Maggie and Joel

Alias
Sydney and Vaughn

The Drew Carey Show
Drew and Kate

Angel
Connor and Cordelia

Buffy the Vampire Slayer
Spike and Buffy

CSI: Crime Scene Investigation
Sara and Grissom

Frasier
Niles and Daphne

Gilmore Girls
Lorelei and Christopher

Moonlighting

During the episode "Take a Left at the Altar" there is a chase between a car and a biplane, and part of the theme from "North by Northwest" (1959) can be heard. Eva Marie Saint, who costarred in the film, guest-stars in the episode as Maddie's mother.

Exit...Stage Left

The Andy Griffith Show
Barney Fife (Don Knotts)

Howard Stern
Jackie "The Jokeman" Martling

Beverly Hills, 90210
Brenda Walsh (Shannen Doherty)

ER
Dr. Doug Ross (George Clooney)

The West Wing
Aaron Sorkin and Tommy Schlamme

Northern Exposure
Joel Fleishman (Rob Morrow)

The X-Files
Agent Fox Mulder (David Ducovney)

Designing Women
Suzanne Sugarbaker (Delta Burke)

Stargate SG-1
Daniel Jackson (Michael Shanks)

Monk
Sharonna (Bitty Schramm)

Hair Care

M*A*S*H
B.J. grows a mustache

Seinfeld
Elaine

Felicity
Felicity cuts off her hair

Buffy the Vampire Slayer
Buffy crops it

M*A*S*H
Hot Lips

Cold Case
Lily glams it up

Xena: Warrior Princess
Gabrielle

The Brady Bunch
Mike Brady gets a perm

CSI: Crime Scene Investigation
Grissom's beard

The Apprentice
Ring around the Donald's head

Same Character, Different Actor

Bewitched
Darrin (Dick Sargent replaces Dick York)

Mystery Science Theater 3000
Mike replaces **Joel**

Roseanne
Becky (Sarah Chalke replaces Lecy Goranson, and vice versa)

The Fresh Prince of Bel-Air
Vivian (Daphne Maxwell-Reid replaces Janet Hubert-Whitten)

All That
The cast

Due South
Ray Vecchio

My Wife and Kids
Claire Kyle (Jennifer Nicole Freeman replaces Jazz Raycole)

The Waltons
John Boy Walton (Richard Wightman replaces Richard Thomas)

Red Dwarf
Kochanski

Doctor Who
The Doctor (Peter Davison replaces Tom Baker...Colin Baker replaces Peter Davison)

A "Very Special" Musical Episode

Buffy the Vampire Slayer

The Drew Carey Show

Oz

Boston Public

Star Trek

Xena: Warrior Princess

Alice

The Osbournes

The Simpsons

Northern Exposure

Puberty

The Wonder Years
Kevin Arnold (Fred Savage)

Leave It to Beaver
Beaver Cleaver (Jerry Mathers)

Home Improvement
The Taylor kids

The Cosby Show
Rudy Huxtable (Keshia Knight Pulliam)

Malcolm in the Middle
Malcolm Wilkerson (Frankie Muniz)

Family Ties
Jennifer Keaton (Tina Yothers)

Boy Meets World
Cory Matthews (Ben Savage)

The Facts of Life
The Girls of Eastland

Full House
Stephanie Tanner (Jodi Sweetin)

Blossom
Blossom Russo (Mayim Bialik)

The Wonder Years

The movie "A Christmas Story" (1983) was the inspiration for this show.

I Do

Will & Grace
Grace and Leo

Everybody Loves Raymond
Robert and Amy

The Nanny
Fran and Maxwell

Get Smart
Max and Agent 99

Boy Meets World
Corey and Topanga

Wings
Helen and Joe

Lois & Clark
Lois and Clark

Buffy the Vampire Slayer
Xander and Anya

I Dream of Jeannie
Tony Nelson and Jeannie

Ed
Ed and Carol

Special Guest Stars

Howard Stern
Cabbie

Scrubs
Heather Locklear

Sex and the City
Sonia Braga

ER
Sally Field

Will & Grace
Cher, Madonna, etc., etc.

The Simpsons
Too many to mention

That '70s Show
Roger Daltrey and the Rock Opera

Boston Public
Vern Troyer

Dharma & Greg
Kevin Sorbo

The Oprah Winfrey Show
Dr. Phil McGraw

Deaths

Buffy the Vampire Slayer
Tara

M*A*S*H
Henry Blake

The Simpsons
Maude Flanders

8 Simple Rules for Dating My Teenage Daughter
Paul Hennessy

NewsRadio
Bill McNeal

Charmed
Prue Halliwell

Seinfeld
Susan Biddle Ross

Ally McBeal
Billy Thomas

Good Times
James Evans Sr.

Angel
Doyle

A Change of Venue

All in the Family
Meathead, Gloria and Joey move

The X-Files
Vancouver to L.A.

Laverne & Shirley
Milwaukee to L.A.

I Love Lucy
New York City to Connecticut

Coach
Minnesota to Florida

The Facts of Life
Eastland School to Edna's Edibles

Perfect Strangers
Chicago apartment to a Victorian house

The Mary Tyler Moore Show
New apartment

Pinky and the Brain
To Elmyra's House

Crime Story
Chicago to Las Vegas to Mexico

Ted McGinley: Jump the Shark's Patron Saint

Chances are that if Ted is anywhere near your cast, consider the show on the downward spiral. That's not to take away from Ted's fine acting skills. Consensus here enjoys Ted more on the big screen ("Revenge of the Nerds") than on our TV screens.

Happy Days
as Roger Phillips

The Love Boat
as Ashley `Ace' Covington Evans

Married...With Children
as Jefferson D'Arcy

Sports Night
as Gordon

Work With Me
as Murray Epstein

The Practice
as Michael Hale

The West Wing
as Mark Gottfried

Charlie Lawrence
as Graydon Cord

Hope & Faith
as Charley

From Black and White to Color

The Andy Griffith Show

The Beverly Hillbillies

The Adventures of Superman

Bewitched

Lost in Space

Dragnet

The Avengers

F Troop

Gomer Pyle, USMC

I Dream of Jeannie